The United States Federal Air Marshal Service: A Historical Perspective, 1962 – 2012

"Fifty Years of Service"

By

Clay W. Biles

ISBN 978-0-615-826523

PRINTED IN THE UNITED STATES OF AMERICA

10 9 8 7 6 5 4 3 2 1

First Edition

This Historical Perspective
is dedicated to the men and women,
past and present,
of the United States Federal Air Marshal Service.

*"Anytime a U.S. airliner is flying in the world, FAMs can be aboard;
that woman up in first class can be a FAM;
that student in economy can be a FAM;
and every person in between."*

**Vice Admiral (Ret.) Cathal "Irish" Flynn
(Former FAA Associate Administrator
for Civil Aviation Security)**

Contents

Foreword

Building a strong, motivated, vibrant organization, involves establishing a culture retaining traditions, along with utilizing the latest developments in training and equipment. They are prerequisites for molding a modern team. Yet, there is a lack of understanding, even amongst current FAMs, of the history from which they come. Pride and esprit are not possible without a thorough appreciation for the path travelled and the people that have gone before.

This is the heritage of the Federal Air Marshals covering a period of fifty years, from the early days of the "FAA Peace Officers" to the present day FAM. It is a work of non-fiction that reveals an immensely changing world of Federal Air Marshals through experience and perception; it tells of transformation, expansion and contraction, of conflict and complications, and of endurance and dedication.

The current FAMs should see no heroes or villains in the pages that follow, but rather momentary views of behavior of unexpected virtue, as well as of a more disturbing nature. In a sense, this work does not belong to the author: It belongs to the men and women of the past. Try to understand and embrace the challenges, fears, and experiences of those that travelled your path before.

G.M. McLaughlin
Director, Federal Air Marshal (Ret.)

Dramatis Personae

The Agitators

Dawa 17
Fulgencio Batista
Fidel Castro
Osama bin-Laden

The Administrators, Program Managers, and Upper Echelon

Andrew Card
Benjamin O. Davis Jr.
Donald D. Engen
Eugene T. Rossides
John S. Pistole
John M. Poindexter
Jane Garvey
Kevin Houlihan
Martin J. McDonnell
Michael Jackson
Monte R. Berger
Najeeb Halaby
Oliver North
Robert A. Clarke
Robert F. Kennedy

The Associate Administrators

Major General (Ret.) Orlo K. Steele
Lieutenant General (Ret.) Michael A. Canavan
Lynne Osmus
Vice Admiral (Ret.) Cathal "Irish" Flynn

The Civil Aviation Security Professionals

John Marsh
Joseph K. Blank
Richard Noble
Ted Brient
Moses A. Aleman
David Hubbard

The Criminals

Albert Truitt
Albert Charles Cadon
Antulio Ramirez Ortiz
Arthur Barkley
Cody Bearden
D.B. Cooper
Francisco Paulo Gonzalez
Garrett B. Trapnell
George Wright
Henry D. Jackson
Jack Graham
Julian A. Frank
John J. Divivio
Leon Bearden
Louis Cale
Louis G. Babler
Melvin C. Cale
Peruvian Revolutionaries
Rafael Minichiello
Robin Oswald
Samuel Byck
Yuji Nishizawa

The Directors

Billie H. Vincent
Dana Brown
Gregory M. McLaughlin
James T. Murphy
John Brophy
Richard F. Lally

Raymond A. Salazar
Robert S. Bray
Thomas Quinn

The Presidents of the United States

Dwight D. Eisenhower
George W. Bush
John F. Kennedy
Richard M. Nixon
Ronald W. Reagan

The Terrorists and Terrorist Organizations

Ayatollah Khomeini
Al-Qaeda
Abu Ibrahim
Abu Nidal Organization
Black September Organization
Commando Martyr Halime
Haffez Dalkamoni
Hussein Ali Mohammed Hariri
Imad Mughniyah
Khaled Sheik Mohammed
Leila Khaled
May 15 Organization
Ramsi Yousef
Richard Colvin Reid
Umar Farouk Abdulmutallab
Zohair Youssif Akache

Authors Preface

The history of, what is now, the United States (U.S.) Federal Air Marshal Service (FAMS) is vastly different from other law enforcement organizations. Federal Air Marshals (FAMs) do not have cool artifacts to show off, such as vehicles confiscated, or stories of important figures "collared" over the years. The history of the air marshals is really about people. All of the people that have served and currently serve have a story to tell, and it is their stories that really make up the history.

This historical perspective was for me dreamed up in 2008, while I was attending air marshal training in Atlantic City, NJ; it was during a power point presentation on the history of the air marshals that my interest was sparked. Later, I began to try and expand on the information from that presentation and it quickly became apparent that there was a lot of sparse and conflicting information out there, especially when first researching material on the internet.

Having had some previous research experience writing grant proposals at Stanford University Medical Center helped me form a protocol in attacking this project; however, I had never tackled something on history. The internet contributed greatly to the initial searches, and again there was much conflicting information; any conflicting information was highlighted for further verification.

After internet searches were exhausted, there was a move towards developing sources that were knowledgeable on the subject, either directly or indirectly. When a source was identified they were interviewed, usually on numerous occasions. All information was cross-referenced with those interviews to help improve on determining specific dates for important events. In regards to this, I tried to interview people that were directly involved in major decisions revolving around the development of the air marshals.

Next, the historians of the various law enforcement agencies were contacted, and documents from these invaluable sources were cross-referenced with any interviews and internet information I had acquired.

Finally, open source government documents were consulted to help with the timeline and fact finding process. These documents were also cross-referenced with all internet searches, interview notes, and historic documentation sources, in order to finalize the most complete and factual timeline, for what I consider the most notable moments in Federal Air Marshal history. This historical perspective and timeline consists of information spanning over four-years of research.

To narrow the focus of this historical perspective, I decided to identify and expand only on certain key positions of the air marshals; this is most relevant for the time period prior to, and immediately following, the terrorist attacks of September 11, 2001. Thus, I only considered the positions of Associate Administrator for the Office of Civil Aviation Security, Director of the Federal Air Marshal Program within the Federal Aviation Administration (FAA), and the Director of the Federal Air Marshal Service, under its many guises, for my research and the narrative within.

Also, for references throughout the narrative, the American Psychological Association (APA) 5th addition was used: Footnotes at the bottom of each page were meant to serve as both standard footnote and APA reference. Although multiple sources were used in creating the federal air marshal historical timeline, and narrative within, to conserve space in the body of this perspective only the major source(s) of information are cited: The complete list of referenced documents, interviews, and other publications that contributed to the total product can be found at the end of the book.

There are a number of people that should be thanked for helping with this project. In no particular order I would like to extend my gratitude towards those individuals here:

First and foremost, I would like to thank Dr. Terry Kraus, the Chief Historian of the FAA, for her cooperation and lovely additions to this perspective. Dr. Kraus helped me with initial contacts and guided my gathering of information on the early years of the FAA Peace Officers. Her help in obtaining these contacts will hopefully serve in helping preserve the legacies of the original air marshals: May they forever be a role model for future FAMs.

I would like to thank Max T. Ratterman, a former FAM and lawyer who previously instructed with the FAMS, for his invaluable additions. Mr. Ratterman's contributions came from his interest in air marshal history, and his sharing of that knowledge. His information served as an excellent base upon which to expand.

Gregory M. McLaughlin was instrumental as well in helping to plug many gaps in the air marshal timeline. As one of the longest serving air marshal director's, Mr. McLaughlin's records and fact gathering, which was compiled months prior to the 9/11 attacks, and his keen ability to recall dates and other factual information, along with his many archival additions, were essential in broadening this historical perspective's statistical and fact content.

The power point that helped give me inspiration was designed with the tremendous help of Laurie Zaleski, the owner of Art-Z Graphics. Mrs. Zaleski is a government contractor, with an office at the William J. Hughes Technical Center in Atlantic City, NJ. Her help was instrumental in the success of that power point presentation and hinged on her contributions, and I would like to thank her for all she did on that project and for giving me a vision.

I would also like to thank David Turk, the U.S. Marshals Service (USMS) Chief Historian in Washington DC, for his contributions to the content and material on the U.S. Marshals Service's sky marshal program, along with David McKinney, PhD, of the Historical Department for U.S. Customs and Border Protection (USCBP), and his team of historians. These men provided a wealth of information on the sky marshal programs of the USMS and U.S. Customs Service (USCS), and the many pioneering projects they were involved in.

I would very much like to thank Joseph "Joe" A. Pontecorvo, who was instrumental in helping document the beginnings of the air marshals, having been one of the original FAA Peace Officers to fly missions. Mr. Pontecorvo and his wife of 62 years are still active, alive, and well. Mr. Pontecorvo is a living legend, and it is my opinion that he belongs deeply embedded in the culture of the current Federal Air Marshal Service. He should serve as a role model for current and future air marshals. His words, which are a large part of the early history and narrative, should serve to inspire current air marshals to always perform at their highest.

I would like to thank Steve Rustad, a former sky marshal working out of San Francisco from 1971-72, who donated some of his beautiful vintage cartoons, and for taking the time to tell his story.

I must also thank Vice Admiral (Ret.) Cathal Flynn, Lynne Osmus, Major General (Ret.) Orlo Steele, and Billie H. Vincent, for their insight into the position of Associate Administrator for Civil Aviation Security. These professionals, with their dogged pursuit of expertise in their field, and having afforded me a view into the looking glass of the upper echelon and inner workings of civil aviation security throughout the early 1980s' to the attacks of September 11, 2001 and the challenges inherent in their positions, broadened this perspective immensely.

Finally, for the time they took to help tell the story of civil aviation security, and their roles in helping shape the FAA Federal Air Marshal Program and civil aviation security, I would like to thank the following: John E. Marsh, Joseph K. Blank, and Moses A. Aleman. These gentleman, and the men and women for whom they speak, exemplified true professionalism. Their actions, in the roles they served during long careers, forever changed civil aviation security. The many events affecting commercial aviation over the many decades were witnessed by these men, and letting me have access to their memories will leave me forever indebted.

The research in this historical perspective draws on the help of these and numerous other sources. It includes interviews with a number of prior FAMs, as well as persons whom served in historically significant positions. Prior Customs Security Officers (sky marshals) and countless others, were interviewed for this project as well, and *all* should be thanked for helping to piece together the history and for the time they gave to tell their stories.

In addition to thanking the above, I would like to thank all of those that helped to make this book possible of whom cannot be mentioned by name. You all do your jobs daily as quiet professionals to help protect others; the words in this book cannot begin to express my admiration for all of you.

This historical perspective is not meant to highlight all the negatives, or positives, nor is it meant to record every aspect of the Federal Air Marshal Service. This is due to the fact that a majority of the information is Sensitive Security Information (SSI) or classified. It also takes into account that one cannot possibly list every detail, no matter how exhaustive the research, on any subject. I hope this historical perspective will be sufficient to appease those in the organization.

Since bombings and hijackings targeting civil aviation have had a direct impact on the FAMS, this story must also be told. The sheer number of violent and criminal acts targeting aviation over the past eight decades would fill volumes, and thus many events were excluded.

None of this historical perspective reflects the views of the U.S. Department of Homeland Security (DHS), Transportation Security Administration (TSA), or

Federal Air Marshal Service. The information gathered for this historical perspective was, and is, open source, and only contains information gathered from
interviews with former federal air marshals, internet searches, FAA archival
information, periodical articles, book references, and other publicly available
government archives and documents.

I started this project as a hobby, and it eventually blossomed into something
else. I wanted to put together the pieces of FAM history, but as the project pro-
gressed I wanted to tell that story through the personal accounts of some of the
men and women that had served as air marshals. This is their story. It is my
hope that all who read this will find it interesting and of historical significance,
and that the information contained within will be preserved for the enjoyment of
those in the future.

Fly Safe

Introduction

The United States (U.S.) government has a duty to protect its people *"against all enemies, foreign and domestic."* It has roots in the very constitution upon which this great nation was founded.

The men and women that protect the citizens of the U.S., along with the millions of tourists that visit this beautiful country each year, are usually an afterthought. Those behind the lines in the national security arena are vitally important. The current U.S. Federal Air Marshal Service (FAMS) is one such entity that operates covertly, across the U.S. and around the world to protect the general public.

Air marshals have been called many things over the years, such as FAA Peace Officers, Special Deputy U.S. Marshals, Sky Marshals, Customs Security Officers (CSOs), Civil Aviation Security Specialists, Civil Aviation Security Liaison Officers (CASLOs) and more recently, Federal Air Marshals (FAMs). Whatever their name, all of the men and women that served have helped keep the skies safe for citizens of all nations for over fifty years.

These air marshals have all selflessly served. Every day FAMs go out into the shadows to blend in with the general public in a multitude of operational environments, domestically and internationally, to help protect the approximately two million people who fly on U.S. air carriers on any given day.

Although air marshals in one shape or another have been operating for over five decades, there has never been any history written on them. Their story has never been told. There have been prior attempts within the FAMS in the past, however, through time those attempts have either faded or been squashed. Those men and women of the past deserve to have their stories told and their service recognized.

The history of the air marshals is also closely rooted with the history of hijackings and bombings targeting commercial aircraft. Some of the bombings and hijackings throughout history had more of an impact than others on FAM tactics, manpower, and security procedures. These events and the responses of those in civil aviation and the U.S. government are essential to understand the need for air marshals as a last line of defense.

The history of the Federal Air Marshal Service tells the story of emerging threats to civil aviation security and the response of the U.S. government to address those threats. In fact, the history of air marshals demonstrates the ability of the U.S. to adapt to an ever changing world and the rising tide of terrorism.

Presidents' of the past and present have understood the need for an organization that safeguards our civil aviation interests. They have fulfilled their duty in protecting the men and women of this great nation against all enemies "*foreign and domestic*" by utilizing air marshals to protect its skies for the last five decades. Presidents' of the future will likely do the same.

Chapter I

The Beginning

In the early days of aviation there was not a lot of emphasis put on aviation security. The first hijacking of an aircraft ever recorded* did not even occur in the United States. Instead, this hijacking was far away in Peru, in May 1930, and involved Peruvian Revolutionaries trying to use a hijacked Pan American World Airways (Pan Am) mail plane for dropping leaflets to support their cause. Later rewarded with $100 dollars for his actions, 22-year old Captain Byron Richards, intent on delivering the mail, convinced hijackers to let him deliver his mail first, thereafter caving into their demands of dropping the leaflets. This incident must have felt a world away and detached from anything that could happen in America, besides, although labeled a hijacking, it was not violent. At the time passenger air travel was rare, leaving people feeling secure on the ground. [1]

Although this hijacking occurred outside the U.S., and contrary to other reports, it *was* the first recorded hijacking carried out against a U.S. air carrier.

---

[1] (Administration D. o., "Summary of background and current status of the Federal Civil Aviation Security Program", July 31, 1972), (Company, February 1998)
*In many articles and publications it has been suggested that the first hijacking of a U.S. aircraft was not until 1961 however, this May 1930 hijacking was the first *recorded* hijacking and it was a U.S. flagged aircraft.

On December 7, 1944, fifty-two countries signed a document in Chicago, IL, that would become known as the *Chicago Convention*, or the *Convention on International Civil Aviation*. The Chicago Convention established rules on airspace management, aircraft registration and safety, and specific details regarding the rights of those signatories for commercial air travel.

Following the May 1930 hijacking, there were no other acts of air piracy until 17-years later when, in 1947 three Romanian's killed an aircrew member. The hijackings numbered 23 from 1947-58, and involved mostly European's seeking political asylum.[2]

On March 5, 1947, the legal framework of the Chicago Convention took effect. Also, on this date, the International Civil Aviation Organization (ICAO) was established. ICAO had grown out of the International Commission for Air Navigation (ICAN), which had held several conventions prior to the establishment of ICAO. ICAN had worked hard convincing the international aviation community for the establishment of radio call signs and other air navigation protocols. As a specialized agency under the United Nations (UN), ICAO would work to further build on ICANs accomplishments, to enhance safety and regulation for commercial air travel.

Although most acts of air piracy were happening overseas, the U.S. was not immune to violence targeting civil aviation. On November 1, 1955, the first act of violence occurred on United Airlines Flight 629, from Denver to Seattle. Before Flight 629 had taken off, Jack Graham placed a bomb in his mother's luggage, hoping to cash in on her life insurance. His mother's luggage was ultimately loaded onto her flight, Flight 629, and the bomb detonated en route to Seattle. At a time when air travelers could purchase a one-day insurance policy before their flight, Jack Graham had purchased several on his mother, and had named himself as the beneficiary. He never had a chance to cash in those policies however, and was instead sentenced to death for the murder of all 44 people onboard.[3]

Only two years later, on July 25, 1957, dynamite exploded on a Western Airlines Convair 240 aircraft, blowing the man who had detonated it out of the bathroom somewhere over California. A flight attendant sitting near the blast said *"I heard a horrible blast, [felt] a terrific gush of wind, and the cabin filled with a thick fog and an eerie light."* Fortunately, the plane landed with no other

---

[2] (Centennial of Flight)
[3] (Grado, 2009)

casualties. This event, however, in combination with the many preceding it, showed a trend in aircraft hijackings and bombings. [4]

Only three years later, the first suspected suicide-bombing of a U.S. aircraft occurred. In January 1960, on Nation il Airlines Flight 2511, from New York International Airport (Idlewild)* to Miami, FL, a Douglas DC-6B aircraft exploded over Bolivia, North Carolina.

Inspectors determined that Julian A. Frank, a lawyer from New York, had wounds consistent with those caused by dynamite. This, among other factors, pointed towards the theory by investigators that Mr. Frank had willingly taken dynamite onboard the aircraft and placed it under his seat, which eventually detonated killing all passengers and crew. Although it was suspected that the explosion was caused by a murder-suicide, the investigation remains open to this day. [5]

On May 1, 1961, an event took place on American soil that would foreshadow events to come, and would change the way the U.S. would approach aviation security in the future. This was the day that the first U.S. airliner was successfully hijacked out of the continental United States.

The flight for National Airlines was prepared for departure from Miami International Airport (MIA) to Key West, FL, when it was hijacked. The hijacker, or *"skyjacker"* as it was referred to at the time, demanded he be flown to Cuba. The hijacker had used the alias *"Cofresi El Pirata,"* or *"Cofresi the Pirate,"* after the 19th century pirate Roberto Cofresi; he was later identified as Antulio Ramirez Ortiz. Upon landing in Cuba, the hijacker was released. Fidel Castro, the Cuban dictator, allowed the plane to return to the U.S. the next day. [6]

Prior to the May 1, 1961 hijacking, there had been numerous issues between the U.S. and Cuba. The regime in Cuba had been under the dictator Fulgencio Batista, and his regime was unpopular with the United States. The Batista regime ruled Cuba from 1933-44, and 1952-59, and was overthrown as a result of the Cuban Revolution under Fidel Castro on January 1, 1959. However, there had never been any hijackings of U.S. aircraft to Cuba before the May 1, 1961 incident. [7]

---

[4] (Board C. A., January 9, 1958)
[5] (Wikipedia, National Airlines Flight 2511), (Grado, 2009)
[6] (Wikipedia, List of Cuba - United States Aircraft Hijackings), (Centennial of Flight)
[7] (Marsh, 2011)
*The predecessor of John F. Kennedy International Airport.

The government under Fidel Castro eventually became the Communist Party of Cuba. The U.S. government had placed an arms embargo on the country as far back as 1958, during Batista's rein. Shortly after the embargo, the Federal Aviation Agency (FAA) helped put in place special regulations that prohibited flights to and from the U.S. and Cuba.

The FAA had an interest in figuring out how *"no fly rules"* and special aviation regulations levied against Cuba could affect commercial aviation, and on addressing the hijacking issues then coming to light. A committee of eight people within the FAA was thus established and led by FAA Administrator Najeeb Halaby, to study the hijacking problem and other issues. Mr. Halaby had been appointed Administrator only two months prior, and was about to play an important role in the establishment of what would later become the United States Federal Air Marshal Service. [8]

The FAA committee found that the special *"no fly rules"* had helped lead to the rash of skyjackings, and the first U.S. hijacking of a commercial aircraft. They found that the hijackings were being perpetrated mostly by Cubans wanting to return to their country, but could not fly there legally. These people were referred to as *"homesick Cubans,"* and they resorted to these hijacking activities in order to return home. They found that hijackings involving Cuban leftists wanting to join the Castro regime occurred, but were rare.

One of the members serving on the FAA committee included a man named John E. Marsh, who acted as legal counsel. Other members came from various departments within the FAA, with each bringing their own perspective towards solving the Cuban hijacking problem. As attorney John Marsh and the others strategized with Administrator Halaby, it was determined that there was a need for drafting regulation in order to prosecute individuals that engaged in this type of activity; at the time, no laws existed for prosecuting hijackers. Mr. Halaby agreed with the committees view: They had to do something soon.

John Marsh had started with the FAA just six weeks after it switched over from the Civil Aeronautics Administration (CAA), on August 3, 1958, and already had ample legal experience within the government. The handover of CAA's duties to the FAA in 1958 was due to the signing of the Federal Aviation Act, by President Dwight D. Eisenhower. One of the many major responsibilities of the FAA Administrator, as outlined by this act, was *"the regulation of air commerce in such manner as to best promote its development and safety and fulfill the requirements of national defense."* [9]

---

[8] (Marsh, 2011)
[9] (Congress)

Prior to his employment at the CAA and FAA, Mr. Marsh had worked for the Office of Price Stabilization, an organization which was tasked with controlling prices during the Korean War. He had also been a B-24 bomber pilot, and understood aviation safety and security issues. He had been selected for the committee given this experience, coupled with his legal expertise.

While the FAA committee worked on the various issues revolving around Cuban air travel, three more hijackings occurred within three-months of the March 1, 1961 hijacking. One, occurring on August 9, involved a mental patient, Albert Charles Cadon. The situation intensified after Cadon hijacked a DC-8 aircraft, Pan Am Flight 501, and it was discovered that a Columbian diplomat was onboard. This hijacking sparked more concerns over Cuba, since the diplomat had just come off a tour in which he had spoken openly of opposing the dictator Fidel Castro. The diplomat had ended his tour in Mexico City, and the outrage of the Columbian government put pressure on the U.S. to end the hijacking. [10]

In a deranged message, en-route to Havana, the hijacker said *"I estimate my arrival at Havana will be 12:35 Mexico time."* [8] The man may have been suffering from severe combat stress, contributing to his mental condition; Cadon had served in the French Army in Algeria. During the hijacking he stated *"I do not like the way Washington interfered in the Algerian situation. I am taking this means to show my protest."* The Columbian government became further concerned for the diplomat and protested, saying the hijacking was *"an official act of hostility."* In no short terms, the U.S. government realized that something had to be done about the rash of *"skyjackings."*

Finally, on August 10, 1961, President John F. Kennedy held a press conference and announced his plan towards protecting U.S. air carriers and national security interests:

"Now, let me say that we ordered today on a number of our planes Border Patrol men who will ride on a number of our flights. We are also going to insist that every airplane lock its door, and that the door be strong enough to prevent entrance by force, and that possession of the key be held by those inside the cabin so that pressure cannot be put on the members of the crew outside to have the door opened. [W]e should, I think, concern ourselves with procedures which will prevent a repetition, and which will make sure that our own responsibilities are fully met in this regard." [11]

---

[10] (Magazine, "Aviation: The Skyjack Habit", August 18, 1961)
[11] (S. 2268 - Public Law 87-197, 2010), (August 1, 1962 Speech)

Immediately following President Kennedy's speech, the federal government began employing armed in-flight security personnel on U.S. commercial aircraft. The first of these were border patrolmen recruited from the U.S. Immigration and Naturalization Service (INS).

The trend of using sworn Federal Law Enforcement Officers (FLEOs) for in-flight security duties was something that would be repeated later, on numerous occasions. These armed agents would fly some of the first missions, until a permanent force could be trained and deployed.

Since there were now border patrolmen flying missions in response to President John F. Kennedy's speech, there was a need to have laws enacted that would enable a hijacker to be prosecuted. Thus, the first recommendation the FAA committee made after President Kennedy's speech was to draft regulation that would make air piracy a crime.

Air piracy had already been addressed in the Federal Aviation Act of 1958, but it was further refined and spotlighted by Public Law 87-197 in 1961, which was defined as *"any seizure or exercise of control, by force or violence or threat of force or violence and with wrongful intent, of an aircraft in flight in air commerce."*

The new law prescribed death and/or imprisonment for no less than 20 years, for interfering with aircrew members in the performance of their duties. This law was put into effect and signed by President John F. Kennedy on September 5, 1961, and outlined as follows: [12]

> This bill is designed to combat recent aircraft hijackings, by applying Federal criminal law to crimes committed on aircraft in air commerce. These incidents have focused attention on the need for additional laws covering such crimes. There are Federal laws as well as State laws which are now applicable in many instances; however, few specifically meet the unique problems including the venue problems which arise while aircraft are in flight. This measure fills the gap by making criminal certain acts of violence which, if committed within the special maritime and territorial jurisdiction of the United States, would be crimes as defined by sections 113, 114, 111-13, 1363, or 2111 of title 18, United States Code, if committed on board an aircraft *in flight in air commerce*. Included are varying degrees of murder, manslaughter, attempt to commit murder or manslaughter, malicious destruction of property, and robbery. (S. 2268 - Public Law 87-197, 2010)

It is an urban legend, told through air marshal lore, that during the height of Cuban hijackings in 1961, when John F. Kennedy asked who might be able to

---

[12] (S. 2268 - Public Law 87-197, 2010)

stand up a permanent team of peace officers to fly on planes for in-flight securi-ty duties, he first went to the U.S. Border Patrol.

The Border Patrol responded that they would look into it and get back to him. Apparently their answer did not satisfy the president and he turned to the mili-tary, who also said they would get back to him.

He was not satisfied with their answer either, and lastly he turned to the FAA. The FAA, through Administrator Najeeb Halaby, told President Kennedy that they could, without a doubt, stand up a force.

The FAA had people that knew planes inside and out. Halaby elaborated, telling the president that the men he had in mind knew aircrew procedures, and had the proper identification to gain access immediately; with proper law en-forcement training and authority, the FAA could be ready in rapid order. This satisfied the president, and thus the stage was set to bring into existence the world's first air marshals.

What the president had in mind was to stand up a *permanent force* of person-nel, to provide security for a limited number of flights, as directed by either the airlines or the Federal Bureau of Investigation (FBI). The border patrolmen that would initially be used for in-flight security were to be sent back to their respec-tive offices after the FAA's permanent force had been trained. [13]

Administrator Najeeb Halaby and his committee now had authorization to stand up a permanent force of *'anti-skyjack'* personnel. They had already been instrumental in drafting legislation and regulations that would allow crimes of air piracy to be prosecuted. This new role would mark the beginning of a dedi-cated team of security professionals that would form over the next several years, in an attempt to study and develop countermeasures for bombings and diver-sions* of commercial aircraft.

It was now up to the committee, and the new security program beginning to form within the FAA, to have persons selected to serve as armed guards on ci-vilian aircraft. They would also have to determine which offices these security personnel would work out of. The name *"FAA Peace Officers"* seemed to fit, and it was in late 1961 that the committee began referring to the future force as such. [14]

---

[13] (Marsh, 2011)
[14] (Marsh, 2011) (Blank, 2010)
*Diversions, i.e., hijackings.

Chapter II

The Living Legend

When the call went out for a permanent force of in-flight security personnel, an ordinary man named Joseph "Joe" A. Pontecorvo had been working as a member of the Flight Standards Division of the FAA. Mr. Pontecorvo was assigned to the Flight Standards District Office (FSDO), at Washington National Airport* in Washington DC. He was more than aware of the hijackings that were occurring at the time. [15]

Joe was born on June 1, 1926, in City Island, NY, outside of Manhattan. When his mother gave birth to him, her best friend was also pregnant and gave birth to a baby girl named Viola around the same time.

Joe met Viola across the baby carriage, and they later came to know each other as friends. They socialized with the same friends, went to the same ice cream parlor, and generally enjoyed each other's company. Viola later moved with her mother to the Bronx, but they would routinely visit City Island to spend

---

[15] (Pontecorvo J. A., Interviews of Joseph A. Pontecorvo; former FAA Peace Officer (1962 - 1969), 2009 - 2010)
*Now Reagan International Airport – DCA.

time with the Pontecorvo's, with whom they remained friends throughout the years.

As Joe approached adulthood, he delivered newspapers like most young men of the time, and later began working at an outboard motor repair shop, where he helped to repair and maintain Johnson Motors engines in City Island. Joe had always been mechanically inclined and had been fascinated by airplanes. He had dreamt of being a pilot someday, or working as an aviation mechanic.

After working as a mechanic, Mr. Pontecorvo decided to join the U.S. Army Air Corps* in November 1945, with plans to become a pilot. As an enlisted aviation cadet, Joe went to boot camp and studied as an aviation mechanic, where he became engine mechanic certified.

Later, as the war started to wind down, Joe was told that the Air Corps no longer needed pilots, and since this is what he and many others had signed up to do, they would be eligible for an early release. Mr. Pontecorvo decided it was time to move on and was discharged honorably after one year of service, in 1946. [16]

After leaving the military, Joe had no problem finding work at Newark International Airport (EWR) as an aviation mechanic. Much of the work in the industry at the time involved working for non-scheduled** airlines; however, shortly after he started, the CAA passed regulations requiring all airlines to be scheduled.

The scheduling of all commercial aircraft led to a large exodus of non-scheduled airlines, and Joe found himself moving back to City Island to work for his friend Viola's relative's seaplane business.

In 1948, Joe had obtained his pilot's license and purchased his first of several airplanes. Joe would name each of these planes after his girlfriends. One plane in particular became known as *"Viola,"* after his childhood and lifelong friend. Their friendship and love grew, and led to their marriage on October 1, 1949, in City Island, NY.

---

[16] (Pontecorvo J. A., Interviews of Joseph A. Pontecorvo; former FAA Peace Officer (1962 - 1969), 2009 - 2010)
*Predecessor of the U.S. Air Force.
**Non-scheduled airlines were not on regular scheduled routes, as was established by the CAA in the mid-1940s'.

Marriage brought with it certain notions and responsibilities for Joe, and he began to think he needed a *"real job."* During a visit with military friends in Florida, Joe was told that there may be a job for him. His friends had all been working for National Airlines and said that he should talk with the company about a position. Joe went along with this; however, at his interview he told National Airlines that he had no desire to move to Florida. The managers admired his honesty and told Joe they could probably find something for him at Idlewild, in New York.

When Mr. Pontecorvo arrived at Idlewild and spoke with representatives from National Airlines, he was told that the only position was for an electrician. Joe was not an electrician, so they asked him if he had a radio operator's certification: He did not have this either. Joe was told that if he could obtain this certification within 90-days, the airline would have a position for him as a radio operator. Joe became certified, and soon after got himself a *"real job"* to support his new family.

Joe Pontecorvo would rise quickly through the ranks at National Airlines and eventually became a supervisor. After a union strike in 1958, Joe began thinking it might be best for him to start looking elsewhere for a career. Since Joe was a supervisor, he was not part of the union, and his position demanded that he keep operations running within National Airlines even during times of a strike. In light of these events, Mr. Pontecorvo began his search anew, and shortly after was told that the new FAA was hiring.

When Joe received this news, he went down to the FAA and completed an application for a position with the Flight Standards Division. Within six months he was given an offer and left National Airlines for good.

Joe had accepted the job with the FAA Flight Standards Division, and was assigned to Washington National Airport. Here, he worked out of the Public Roads Building - so named due to the Bureau of Public Roads* for the Washington DC area having a nearby facility - where his duties included *promoting safe air transportation, by setting the standards for certification and oversight of airmen, air operators, air agencies, and designees.* [17]

Mr. Pontecorvo had been working in this position for nearly two years when the rash of hijackings started to occur. He and others within the FAA were more than aware of the threat that hijackings posed to civil aviation and the general

---

[17] (Flight Standards Service)
* The Bureau of Public Roads was the predecessor of the Federal Highway Administration.

public. It was in the latter half of 1961, that Mr. Pontecorvo was called in by his supervisor and told he was one of 300 people within the Flight Standards Division across the United States to be selected for a collateral position as an FAA Peace Officer. His supervisor asked him if he would be interested in going through a thorough selection process. [18]

At the time Joe had two small children, and like any rational person he had some concerns with the danger involved if he accepted this assignment. However, Mr. Pontecorvo also understood that he was qualified for the job, since he knew airline operations inside and out, and that someone had to do it.

With these thoughts in mind, Joe decided that he would be willing to selflessly sacrifice these things in order to do a job that he thought needed to be done. His wife Viola was used to Joe travelling, since this was part of his full-time work with Flight Standards, and by Joe's own account she was also somewhat ignorant of the danger involved and Joe did not elaborate on that danger.

Once Joe had accepted the offer and had volunteered to begin the selection process, he started to undergo a battery of tests, both psychological and investigatory. Some questions Mr. Pontecorvo recalled were: Are you willing to kill another human being? Do people talk about you when you are not around? Do you feel the need to hurt yourself or others? There were a number of questions like these that were aimed at gauging an accurate psychological profile of Mr. Pontecorvo and the other candidates, and as the process went along the numbers of candidates quickly dwindled.

There were additional questions regarding his prior jobs, residences, acquaintances, and other investigative questions similar to the current SF-86 National Security Questionnaire*. The FBI would be looking at each candidate carefully, and carrying out a Single Scope Background Investigation (SSBI) on everyone that had been referred to proceed in the selection process.

---

[18] (Pontecorvo J. A., Interviews of Joseph A. Pontecorvo; former FAA Peace Officer (1962 - 1969), 2009 - 2010)

*The SF-86 is the modern National Security Questionnaire form, used by U.S. Government employees and contractors for obtaining a security clearance, for personnel required to work with classified information or material. The information on this questionnaire is filled out by the applicant, and is then used by background investigators for investigation. All information gathered during the investigation, is then presented to the respective agency/department for adjudication.

Mr. Pontecorvo recalled old friends and neighbors asking him what kind of trouble he had gotten himself into. They had all been contacted in person by "*G-men*" (FBI) who had asked them exhausting questions related to Mr. Pontecorvo's character, demeanor, loyalty, and ability to be blackmailed. None of the respondents had been told what the questions were in regards to, and their assumptions ran wild.

Mr. Pontecorvo had been involved with several classified projects* while working in Flight Standards, however, this did not matter to the background investigators, and they carried on with their questioning of any and all people Mr. Pontecorvo had ever been associated with. [19]

Finally, in early 1962, Mr. Pontecorvo was contacted by his supervisor and told that he had been selected for training at Port Isabel, Texas, at the U.S. Border Patrol training facility, to receive training for collateral duty as an FAA Peace Officer. He was one of 18 men that had been selected out of the 300 initial selectees. The men were all to report February 19, 1962. Their average age was 40, and all were married. [20]

---

[19] (Pontecorvo J. A., Interviews of Joseph A. Pontecorvo; former FAA Peace Officer (1962 - 1969), 2009 - 2010)

[20] (Agency F. A., Sky Jack Unit Ready to Grapple Emergencies in the Skies, 1963), (Agency F. A., FAA Peace Officers Course - General Information, 1962)
*Some of the projects Mr. Pontecorvo was involved in are still classified.

Chapter III

The First Air Marshals

FAA Peace Officers

FAA Peace Officer Training

Joseph Pontecorvo and the other 17 trainees arrived at Port Isabel, TX, on February 19, 1962. The men had prepared themselves for training as the first air marshals in history. Only two or three of the men had prior law enforcement experience, and all but one was a veteran of the armed forces. All had been picked due to their specialized training and work within the FAA's Flight Standards Division, and their expert knowledge of flight operations and ability to gain access to air carriers. They had also been chosen strategically based on their office locations around the United States. [21]

The training was scheduled to last until March 2, and was thus only two-and-a-half weeks in length. There was a lot of material to be covered. The subjects included FAA policy, unarmed self-defense, legal, search and seizure, airline operations (of which they were already intimately familiar), firearms safety and marksmanship, physical fitness training, and terrorist/ criminal mindset.

---

[21] (Agency F. A., FAA Peace Officers Course Training Manual, 1962),

All trainees were encouraged to exceed the standards and all complied. Expert marksmanship was especially stressed in the course, due to the tight confines of the aircraft environment in which they would work.

Among the lecturers at the U.S. Border Patrol Academy in Port Isabel, TX, was a man named Leonard W. Gilman*, a law enforcement officer with the Immigration and Naturalization Service (INS). Mr. Gilman helped to disarm and capture two hijackers on a Continental Airlines jet** in El Paso, Texas, on August 3, 1961. [22]

Mr. Gilman spoke to the new FAA Peace Officers about his role in capturing the two hijackers, and recalled the events that played out that day, giving the candidates an up close look at a real-life skyjacking attempt.

On August 3, 1961, INS agent Leonard W. Gilman had boarded a Continental Airlines Boeing 707 in El Paso, Texas. Mr. Gilman recalled that this particular Boeing 707 aircraft cost $5.4 million and had been formerly purchased by Cuba: When Cuba failed to pay the bill, the aircraft was returned to Continental. [23]

The plane had been on a *"routine flight"*** from Albuquerque, NM, to El Paso, TX, when twenty minutes before landing, a man named Leon Bearden, 38, and his son Cody, 16, hijacked the aircraft and demanded they be flown to Cuba. Without regards to his own safety, Mr. Gilman volunteered to be a hostage, without giving up his identity as an INS agent. He did this in order to be close to the hijackers. The hijackers were both armed with firearms.

Mr. Gilman told the men that the hijackers gained access to the cockpit, but the plane had to refuel in El Paso. This led to a standoff from 2 a.m. to 6 a.m., local time, by which time the pilot had sent a secure transmission to flight control that his aircraft had been hijacked. Shortly after landing in El Paso, the aircraft had been surrounded by law enforcement.

---

[22] (Pontecorvo J. A., Interviews of Joseph A. Pontecorvo; former FAA Peace Officer (1962 - 1969), 2009 - 2010)

[23] (Geary, 2008), (Press, One Punch Ends Siege: Pair Awaits Hearing; Kennedy says No Swap, August 4, 1961)

*Leonard W. Gilman would later retire as a GS-18, as the Commissioner of the Southwest region, appointed by the U.S. Attorney General in 1970.

**Flight number unknown.

***It is as dangerous a mindset for in-flight security personnel to call a flight *"routine,"* as a street officer calling any vehicle stop *"routine."*

At 6:00 a.m., the plane was given clearance to take-off. When the plane began its taxi, it was blocked by baggage carts and an ambulance. The armed officers on the tarmac also shot out the airplanes tires. It was at this time that INS agent Gilman hit the elder hijacker Leon Bearden. Gilman punched the hijacker so hard that he was later hospitalized for a broken hand. This brought the hijacking to an end, and both hijackers were later charged under federal law with kidnapping and interstate transportation of a stolen aircraft.

President John F. Kennedy gave a presidential commendation to Mr. Leonard Gilman and FBI Special Agent Francis Crosby, for their *"level headed"* roles in capturing the hijackers of the Continental jet in El Paso, Texas; Special Agent Crosby was the negotiator handling the case on the ground that day.

Although it has often been sited that the May 1, 1961, hijacking from Miami to Cuba was the catalyst for the inception of the FAA Peace Officers, this actually occurred due to the attempted hijacking on August 3, 1961, in El Paso, in combination with the August 9, 1961 hijacking with a Columbian diplomat onboard. These incidents led to President John F. Kennedy issuing his August 10, 1961 speech, ordering armed men to guard U.S. air carriers.

Mr. Gilman had also lectured the candidates on previous *"skyjacking"* incidents. The perspective that Gilman gave the students was a real-world view of hijackings. They learned that if they were aggressive and didn't hesitate, they could successfully deter a hijacking in progress.

After this and many other lectures, on March 1, 1962, Joe Pontecorvo and the other 17 FAA Peace Officer trainees were released from training to fly to Washington DC. They were to be sworn-in* by Attorney General Robert Kennedy the next day. [24]

Mr. Pontecorvo was going home, and after arriving in Washington DC he spent the evening with his family. The next day would be a historic one, and wondered what lay ahead of him: He was ready for any job that his country asked of him.

---

[24] (Pontecorvo J. A., Interviews of Joseph A. Pontecorvo; former FAA Peace Officer (1962 - 1969), 2009 - 2010), (Pontecorvo J. , Information taken from Swearing-in Photograph of Kenneth Hunt signing Oath of Office, 1962) *Swearing-in, or sworn-in, refers to the signing of the Oath of Office. For the FAA Peace Officers, they took the same Oath of Office administered to U.S. Marshal deputies.

The training the men finished had been in response to the threat to civil aviation, due to the heightened number of hijackings occurring within the United States and abroad. When President John F. Kennedy had posed the question, *"Who will heed the call to ensure security of flights within, to, and from the United States?"* the FAA Administrator Najeeb Halaby, with his new *"anti-hijack"* team answered, *"We can."*

Administrator Halaby answered the president's call by initiating the FAA Peace Officers Program, which had been signed into effect by the president on September 5, 1961. Those FAA Peace Officers were now fully trained and ready to detect, deter, and defeat hostile threats to U.S. air carriers.

Since all of the FAA Peace Officers worked out of offices from around the country, the men would not see each other until the following year for recurring training. Only in the rare circumstances that they had missions together, would they see each other during the next year. This day would serve as a chance for all of the men to enjoy the company of one another, and to take in the sites around the Washington DC area before being deputized.

On March 1st, each man retired to their hotel rooms or homes and waited for their meeting with the Attorney General. Mr. Pontecorvo was anxious for this momentous occasion, and spent a sleepless night wondering what the future held.

FAA Peace Officers Appointment (March 2, 1962)

On March 2, 1962, U.S. Attorney General Robert F. Kennedy held a ceremony for the 18 FAA Peace Officer selectees. As the men were greeted, and filed into the room, a large Marlin that hung on the office wall looked them over. They were greeted by the young Attorney General, who asked each man their name and where they were from. He spoke of the important task each of them was beset to undertake, and the demands upon which the nation expected. The Attorney General told them that by accepting this position they were undertaking a selfless service to their country. [25]

---

[25] (Pontecorvo J. A., Interviews of Joseph A. Pontecorvo; former FAA Peace Officer (1962 - 1969), 2009 - 2010)

After speaking of the service to which they were about to be commissioned, he asked if they were willing to perform the duties as FAA Peace Officers; all 18 men assured him they were. It was at this time that the men were asked to raise their right hands and repeat the following:

"I, state your name, do solemnly swear, or affirm, that I will faithfully execute all lawful precepts directed by the U.S. Marshal of any district under the authority of the United States, make true returns, take only lawful fees, and in all things well and truly, without malice or partiality, perform the duties of the office of Special Deputy United States Marshal, during my continuous service. So help me God." [26]

The 18 newly appointed Special Deputy U.S. Marshals, and their respective *"field offices"* included the following: [27]

Florida (Miami)	George E. Bale, Kenneth S. Hunt
Georgia (Atlanta)	Leonard W. Estep
Illinois (Ohare)	Robert T. Barnes
Iowa (Desmoines)	Lee F. Watson, Harold H. Phillips
Massachusetts (Boston)	Arvid L. Hansen
Michigan (Ypsilanti)	Joseph W. Ziskovsky
Missouri (Lambert Field)	Lawrence J. Powers
New Jersey (Teterboro)	Richard C. Clause
New Mexico (Albuquerque)	Charles M. Pomeroy
New York (Idelwild)	Ardo Engleman, John G. Bartell, Robert Cheshire
Oklahoma (Tulsa)	John P. Donnelly
Texas (Dallas/ San Antonio)	James D. Skinner, Floyd T. Kresge
Washington DC (Washington National)	Joseph A. Pontecorvo

These men were now FAA Peace Officers, and had been sworn in as Special Deputy U.S. Marshals* to give them jurisdiction. In attendance was FAA Administrator Najeeb Halaby, among other FAA officials. After the swearing-in ceremony and small talk, refreshments, and back slapping, the newly appointed FAA Peace Officers returned to their homes around the United States, and to their regular jobs in flight standards.

---

[26] (Pontecorvo J. , Information taken from Swearing-in Photograph of Kenneth Hunt signing Oath of Office, 1962)

[27] (Agency F. A., Operation Slingshot Memorandum #1, March 7, 1962), (Agency F. A., Operation Slingshot Memorandum #2, March 20, 1962)
*The men were sworn in as Special Deputy U.S. Marshals because this gave them the jurisdiction necessary to make arrests across state boundaries. This would continue to be the case for future in-flight security personnel as well.

Within two weeks of the ceremony, Mr. Pontecorvo and the other 17 FAA Peace Officers went to procure their issued equipment. The equipment consisted of a .38 caliber Colt revolver, holster, blackjack, handcuffs, and fountain pen teargas gun. [28]

As they resumed their positions within their respective offices, and the FAA Flight Standards Division, they awaited their countries call. Mr. Pontecorvo stayed in Washington DC and went back to the FSDO at Washington National Airport. The FAA and U.S. government had been wise to select people from all across the country, in order to ensure the rapid deployment of the peace officers in response to a threat, or the request of an airline or the FBI. This step would ensure better coverage of gateway airports servicing international destinations. [29]

Operation Slingshot

Weeks later, all of the FAA Peace Officers were called in for a meeting on the 26th and 27th of March, 1962. The meeting was in regards to *"Operation Slingshot,"* which would explain the fact that they would work *"on call"* and would only fly missions* in response to an FBI request, or the specific request of a U.S. airline. The meeting would lay out operational intricacies, and how requests would be fulfilled. In the beginning, and throughout 1962, it was rare that such a request would be made. [30]

These meetings caused a significant change at the FAA. The inception of the FAA Peace Officers, by John F. Kennedy, and the new partnerships being made with law enforcement and intelligence agencies, began a move towards establishing an external security department within the FAA. Empty rooms at FAA headquarters in Washington DC received new white paint. The small team that would staff the new office dusted and swept, typewriters and paper were brought in with chairs, tables, and desks. Soon, by June 1962, the recognizable "click-clack" of typewriters could be heard over the cigarette smoke that would soon turn the newly painted walls yellow. The office of civil aviation security was

---

[28] (Agency F. A., March 12, 1962)

[29] (Marsh, 2011)

[30] (Agency F. A., Operation Slingshot Memorandum #1, March 7, 1962), (Agency F. A., Operation Slingshot Memorandum #2, March 20, 1962)

* *Missions*, and *Missions Covered*, refer to flights that have *'air marshals'* onboard. The number of air marshals *'covering'* a flight, their seating arrangements, tactical response, etc., are all classified.

now in business, although it had no name, and was only beginning to staff and establish its self in its own highly specialized field.

The FAA thus began hiring people from within its ranks, as well as from the civilian sector and other government agencies, in order to staff the new office with the best people possible. This group would begin to study aircraft hijackings and bombings, going back to the May 1930 hijacking in Peru. Old investigations and "cold case files" would be re-opened or re-examined. Every documented hijacking and bombing would be looked at, in order to understand the threat. History had a tendency of repeating itself, and the new team of aviation security experts would seek out every opportunity to become the best in their new field. Eventually these men and women would become *the* experts in civil aviation security, and would be viewed as leaders in the industry by other countries struggling to adapt to the ever evolving threat.

As the first typewriters and desks were being brought into the new civil aviation security offices, and in the first several months after Mr. Pontecorvo had been sworn in, the FAA Peace Officers remained ready to cover mission flights. There were some occasions that he recalled being asked to standby for a mission, only to later have it aborted. Mr. Pontecorvo spoke with other FAA Peace Officers during the first few months of their inception, and it seemed to be a recurring theme.

There were however, two missions that Joe *"covered"* during the first few months which stood out in his mind. The missions he recalled may quite possibly have been the first missions ever manned by personnel from the *"permanent force"* of FAA Peace Officers.

Chapter IV

FAA Peace Officers

FAA Flight Standards Division
(April 1962 – October 1970)

The First Missions

M r. Pontecorvo flew on his first mission within one month of graduation from the FAA Peace Officers course in Port Isabel. As Mr. Pontecorvo recalled, the first mission flight he ever flew on was at the request of the FBI. He was tasked to escort the Minister of Defense of Guatemala, Colonel Alfredo Enrique Peralta Azurdiato, from the U.S. to Guatemala. [31]

Colonel Azurdiato would later become President of Guatemala from 1963 to 1966. There was a coup that had taken place in Guatemala in 1954, sparking a civil war. By 1962, no one in the U.S. government knew who would come out on top as the legitimate government, and the FBI wanted someone to go on the flight with Azurdiato in order to ensure his safety. Given Mr. Pontecorvo's training, and the lectures from Leonard Gilman in regards to the Cuba hijackings,

---

[31] (Pontecorvo J. A., Interviews of Joseph A. Pontecorvo; former FAA Peace Officer (1962 - 1969), 2009 - 2010)

Pontecorvo was the right man for the job and on high alert after his pre-flight briefing.

The flight was originally going to Los Angeles International Airport (LAX), but this particular flight was cancelled due to some names the FBI didn't like on the manifest. They instead flew to San Francisco International Airport (SFO), met the crew, and then proceeded on to Guatemala without incident.

While the plane taxied in Guatemala, the pilot announced on the intercom that they would be pulling to a remote area, due to having too much heat on the brakes during landing; the pilot told everyone that the brakes needed to be inspected. This was pre-arranged by the airline and Azurdiato, so that he could safely disembark away from the airport terminal, with the aid of his security detail. When the aircraft came to a stop, men with Uzis appeared on the tarmac, within full view of the passengers. Someone sitting next to Mr. Pontecorvo asked, *"Since when do they inspect brakes with Uzis?"*

Colonel Azurdiato was escorted off of the flight by armed guards; while Mr. Pontecorvo was escorted off by local national police. Joe was later interviewed at the U.S. embassy by people interested in the details of the flight; however, there was nothing of much relevance to report, and after the short interview Mr. Pontecorvo found himself exploring the city. Due to Pan Am not having consistent routes into Guatemala at the time, Joe spent a couple of days waiting for his return flight. During his stay he was shown around town by local officials and had dinner at some of their homes. [32]

Two or three days after arriving in Guatemala, Mr. Pontecorvo boarded a Pan Am flight bound for the United States. He was met onboard by Customs officials and given back his issued equipment, then traveled on to Washington DC without incident.

One of the only other missions flown by Mr. Pontecorvo in 1962 was in response to another FBI request. There had been a threat against an Easter Seal poster child, and the FBI had information that the child may be attacked on a flight they were scheduled to be on. [33] The Easter Seals is a nonprofit charitable organization that assists children and adults with autism and other disabilities, and Joe could not understand who would want to hurt an Easter Seal poster child. However, Mr. Pontecorvo's main concern was to fulfill the FBI's request, and the security of the aircraft, passengers, and crew.

---

[32] (Pontecorvo J. A., Interviews of Joseph A. Pontecorvo; former FAA Peace Officer (1962 - 1969), 2009 - 2010)
[33] (Easter Seals)

Mr. Pontecorvo was briefed by the FBI prior to the mission, and preceded from Washington DC to LAX with the poster child and without incident. After travelling to LAX, Mr. Pontecorvo caught another flight home.

The Early Years

By late March 1962, after the *"operation slingshot"* briefings, all FAA Peace Officers were considered *"on call,"* and were thereafter mainly involved in their primary responsibilities as flight standards personnel, or aviation safety inspectors. The men and women of the Flight Standards Division were responsible, primarily, for promoting safety and regulation among air carriers; the 18 chosen as FAA Peace Officers worked as Special Deputy U.S. Marshal as collateral duty.

Every year, as part of their assignments as FAA Peace Officers, those that were still active were required to undergo training at the U.S. Border Patrol training facility in Port Isabel, Texas. The recurring training involved all aspects that were covered in the initial course, although this was condensed to three days. The peace officers were also required to complete a physical training assessment and firearms qualification to remain active. [34]

An article in July 1963, in *FAA Horizons*, an internal publication and magazine, talked about the recurrent training of the FAA Peace Officers and their role in helping to thwart aircraft piracy. For the article, FAA Administrator Halaby was interviewed, and it was he who *"pointed out the value of recurrent training in maintaining peace officer proficiency in the techniques of armed and unarmed defense."* [35]

Not long after the article in *FAA Horizons* magazine, people within the FAA began referring to the FAA Peace Officers as *"sky marshals."* The term *"sky marshals"* was derived from the article's *"skyjack"* reference, and was used as a shorthand expression for the FAA Peace Officer. The title of 'Sky Marshal' was *never* an official title of *any* agency, but was instead a condensed term, coupling the *"skyjack"* mention with their having been sworn in as Special Deputy U.S.

---

[34] (Marsh, 2011)

[35] (Agency F. A., Sky Jack Unit Ready to Grapple Emergencies in the Skies, 1963)

Marshals. Although they were referred to as sky marshals within the FAA, the term would not become popular by the media until almost a decade later. [36]

Mr. Pontecorvo firmly believed in the seriousness of the position for which he had volunteered. Joe practiced much of the time while off duty; other than the recurring training, this was a way for him to remain proficient and ready if needed. He knew that, unlike the typical police officer, he had no back-up inside a commercial aircraft while at cruising altitude*. He would have to rely on all his training and preparedness if the situation presented itself. [37]

Joe was an excellent marksman, and he had been interested in reloading handgun cartridges since he was a boy. Joe used his skill to manufacture .38 caliber wax tipped bullets, which he could use in his home for practice. He set up a target in his hallway and would spend hours firing the non-lethal ammunition, which was similar to modern day simmunitions**, as a way to maintain that proficiency. [38]

As of 2012, his oldest daughter, at 61 years of age, still has fond memories of her father Mr. Pontecorvo letting her shoot wax bullets at cardboard targets in the hallway of their home when she was a child.

When it was time for Mr. Pontecorvo to go to Port Isabel, Texas, for his yearly training, his practice at home proved to be time well spent; Joe never had any problems qualifying. Coming together during training meant that all of the FAA Peace Officers had a chance to see each other and time to catch up on the changes in their lives. It also served its purpose, by educating the peace officers on new trends being used by criminals for hijacking commercial airliners. Civil aviation security experts had been busy building an extensive dossier on each major event affecting commercial air travel. The FAA Peace Officer's would also learn of the "Tokyo Convention" of 1963 during their recurrent training.

The Tokyo Convention, also known as the *Convention on Offenses and Certain Other Acts Committed on Board Aircraft*, discussed the legal status of inter-

---

[36] (Marsh, 2011)
[37] (Pontecorvo J. A., Interviews of Joseph A. Pontecorvo; former FAA Peace Officer (1962 - 1969), 2009 - 2010)
[38] (Simmunition)
*Cruising altitude for a commercial aircraft is 30-40,000 feet above sea level.
**Simmunitions ammunition is used by modern day law enforcement agencies for training purposes. Special head gear and other protective equipment are used, as the wax tipped bullets are fired at approximately 300 feet-per-second. They are sometimes referred to as SIMS.

national aircraft, which was a major debate at the time, and commenced on September 14, 1963 in Tokyo, by ICAO. The Tokyo Convention dealt with establishing partnerships on offenses against penal law and any acts jeopardizing the safety of persons or property onboard civilian aircraft. Any of these acts occurring while *in-flight* and engaged in international air navigation, would be subject to prosecution.[39]

For the purpose of the Tokyo Convention, an aircraft was considered to be '*in-flight*', "*...from the moment when power is applied for the purpose of takeoff until the moment when the landing run ends.*" This was the first convention dealing with crimes aboard international civilian airlines, and was signed by several nations. The Tokyo convention and its legal status would go into effect on December 4, 1963.

Also in December 1963, only one month after the assassination of John F. Kennedy, the main international airport in New York, formerly known as Idlewild, with airport designator IDL, was renamed *John F. Kennedy Airport*, or JFK. [40]

On May 7, 1964, Pacific Airlines Flight 773, from Reno* to SFO, was hijacked, and crashed near San Ramon, California, killing all 44 passengers and crew. The crash was said to be the first instance in the U.S. of a pilot being shot as part of a hijacking. Pacific Airlines Flight 773 was a Fokker F-27 aircraft. [41]

The hijacking was defined as a murder-suicide; it was determined that Francisco Paula Gonzales, 27, shot both the pilot and co-pilot before turning the gun on himself. Gonzales, a former member of the Philippine Sailing Team, was going through a series of debt troubles and had planned the suicide in advance.

On August 6, 1964, an FAA emergency rule was put into effect, requiring the closing and locking of compartment doors of scheduled air carriers, to deter persons from intentionally, or unintentionally, entering the flight deck. [42]

By 1965, when the FAA Peace Officers were attending their 2nd year of annual recurring training in Port Isabel, TX, Administrator Halaby suggested to

---

[39] (Convention on Offenses and Certain Other Acts Committed On Board Aircraft (Tokyo Convention), 1963)
[40] (Wikipedia, John F. Kennedy International Airport)
[41] (Wikipedia, Pacific Airlines Flight 773), (Aviation Safety Network)
[42] (Marsh, 2011)
* Reno-Tahoe International Airport (RNO), Nevada.

President Lyndon B. Johnson that transportation be elevated to a cabinet level post, and that the FAA be folded into the Department of Transportation (DOT).

Although the switch from the FAA to the Department of Transportation would not take effect immediately, Halaby's recommendation set the stage for this to happen, later, on April 1, 1967.

On March 27th, 1966, a hijacker attempted to commandeer an aircraft from Santiago de Cuba to Havana, in an attempt to reach the United States. The pilot opposed the hijacking and landed in Havana where he was shot and killed by the Cuban hijacker, Angel Maria Betancourt Cueto. By the end of the hijacking, the pilot Fernando Alvarez Perez and air steward Edor Reyes were both dead, and another crew member injured. Betancourt was later sentenced to death and executed. This event deeply affected Cubans all over the world. [43]

The FAA Peace Officers rarely flew missions during this period, and again, it was only at the request of the FBI or the airlines that they would. There is no FAA archival information available as to how many missions were flown from 1965 to 1967, but research has suggested that they were few.

On April 1, 1967, the FAA was placed within DOT, and it was at this time that the FAA became an *administration*, and was no longer an *agency*; it would thereafter be known as the Federal Aviation Administration. [44]

On November 20, 1967, Louis G. Babler, born in Hungary, successfully hijacked a Crescent Airlines flight from Hollywood, Florida, to Cuba. This was just one more successful hijacking among the many going to Cuba during this time period. By 1967, Cuban hijackings had become routine, however the majority of these did not end in violence; mostly only threats were made. [45]

Over time, some of the FAA Peace Officers had decided to leave the service, and by the April 23-25, 1968 refresher training, the original group of FAA Peace Officers had already lost three members. Fifteen still remained, and the training helped to build the bonds among the men. This training allowed the men to catch up with each other and strengthened their team cohesion; cohesiveness

---

[43] (Centennial of Flight)

[44] (U.S. Department of Transportation), (Aviation Security Chronology - taken from DOT website)

[45] (Wikipedia, List of Cuba - United States Aircraft Hijackings)

was necessary for the men who relied on their partner(s) for their survival, in order to provide proper in-flight security. [46]

The yearly refresher training involved physical fitness training, legal, fire-arms, and aircraft specific tactics. The legal training was usually taught by FAA attorneys. One FAA attorney in particular that helped train the peace officers was John Marsh. Mr. Marsh had already played an important role that had allowed the FAA Peace Officers to come into existence, along with helping to get legislation passed in regards to air piracy; he would later go on to play other critical roles as well.

The remaining 15 FAA Peace Officers took it upon themselves to stay fit and ready if called to duty. Their work was more of a collateral duty at this time; thus, these FAA Peace Officers were mainly in place for use on flights where credible intelligence deemed they were needed. The collateral nature of this position would continue over the next three decades.

The year 1968 turned out to be a busy one for hijackings, and would reach a peak in 1969*. The number and severity of these events caused alarm within the U.S. government. The hijackings of this time period have been attributed to terrorism, extortion, and flight for political asylum, mental illness, and transportation between the United States and Cuba as a result of the ongoing antagonistic Cuba-U.S. relations. Those hijackings occurring within the U.S., however, were all criminal in nature, not terroristic. [47]

On July 19, 1968, the FAA announced that it had begun having its *"sky marshals"* board random flights in Florida, due to the large number of hijackings taking place in Miami. The FAA Peace Officers quickly saw an increase in the number of missions covered. This surge began taking more time away from their aviation safety inspector functions, stripping the FAA of a precious resource, and the FAA began thinking about the possibility of moving the security program to another division within its structure: A battle within the FAA Flight Standards Division had begun.

On October 23, 1968, a Cessna 177 aircraft was hijacked from Key West, FL, to Cuba. By 1968, the hijackings to Cuba had reached somewhat of a *'cult status'*. This was all more apparent with this particular hijacking, as it was perpetrated by the grandson of former U.S. Vice President Alben Barkley, Alben

---

[46] (Pontecorvo J. A., Interviews of Joseph A. Pontecorvo; former FAA Peace Officer (1962 - 1969), 2009 - 2010)
[47] (Killen, January 16, 2005)
*1969 was the busiest year for recorded hijackings in history.

Truitt. Later, Truitt would be arrested by the FBI when trying to return via Canada. He was sentenced to 20 years for aircraft piracy, and another 20 years for kidnapping, with sentences running consecutive. [48]

During this time, the FAA Peace Officers found themselves flying more often as requested by the FBI and air carriers, but there were still an insignificant number of missions being flown. The FAA realized they were ill-equipped to cover all the hijackings that were occurring, and by early 1969 the main focus of aviation security was bolstering ground security, such as baggage and passenger screening. FAA Peace Officer duties were seen as having a minimal impact, and other avenues were explored. Although they were flying slightly more missions, there was significant pushback from the Flight Standards Division due to the amount of time that the FAA's inspectors were being taken away from their regular duties. Flight Standards began lobbying within the FAA to have the program moved to another division.

Amidst these changes, in 1969, the Branch Manager for the FAA's Flight Standards Division at FAA Headquarters, in Washington DC, was Joseph K. Blank. Mr. Blank held several prominent positions with the U.S. government prior to his appointment as Branch Manager. In this position, Mr. Blank would become further involved in shaping the FAA security program that had been formed in 1962. [49]

Mr. Blank had lived an exciting life prior to his work with the FAA. After graduation from high school, and due to the attacks on Pearl Harbor, Mr. Blank decided to join the U.S. Army Air Corps. He went to college after the military and held several different jobs; he worked for the Pennsylvania Railroad Company, the courts of Philadelphia as a Juvenile Probation Officer in Pittsburgh, a background investigator with the Civil Service Commission*, and as the head of security and intelligence with the U.S. Army Corps of Engineers. With his many contacts at the Corps of Engineers, Mr. Blank was put in touch with the U.S. State Department, where he eventually went to work as a Special Agent in 1961.

Joe Blank spent the next year as a Special Agent with the State Department in Washington DC. Mr. Blank worked as part of the Russian Security Group, where he spent much of the time working with the United Nations. After working for one year as a Special Agent, Mr. Blank received a call from the FAA, offering him a position for which he had applied. Mr. Blank always liked the

---

[48] (Press, Plane Hijacker Alben Truitt Said In Canada, Januray 23, 1969)
[49] (Blank, 2010)
* The Civil Service Commission was the predecessor of the modern day Office of Personnel Management (OPM).

civil aviation field, and he felt that this was an opportunity he could not pass up. The State Department offered Mr. Blank a promotion to stay onboard, but he decided his passion was with aviation and accepted the position at the FAA.

Mr. Blank's new responsibility with the FAA was to set up security systems for all air traffic controllers. He worked out of FAA Headquarters in Washington DC and was successful in his new career. After a year in this position, Mr. Blank left for a short time to take care of his brother who had leukemia. He worked for the Internal Revenue Service (IRS) in Pittsburgh, Pennsylvania, while he dealt with his family obligations. In 1964, the FAA called and asked Mr. Blank to come back to headquarters in Washington DC, to conduct internal and external investigations. He accepted, and returned to the FAA. [50]

Shortly after resuming work back at the FAA, Mr. Blank received a call asking him to lead the Office of Operations in all investigations within the FAA, which he gladly accepted as well.

In 1967, Mr. Blank had been brought into the Flight Standards Division as a Branch Manager. As Branch Manager he worked alongside John Marsh, and was tasked with investigating and cataloging all hijackings and acts of air piracy occurring between 1967 and 1968. This statistical data gathering of hijackings and all information gleaned from this study, would be used to establish a profile* of hijackers, to be developed by the FAA over the next several years. [51]

Between 1968 and 1969, the amount of hijackings occurring between the United States and Cuba rose dramatically; these hijackings had reached a level that demanded the use of a much larger in-flight security force.

Due to the escalation in hijackings, the FAA Peace Officers started to boost their mission tempo, however, it was still rare for them to fly missions. This surge in missions commenced in late 1968. Mr. Pontecorvo recalled doing multiple missions in the late 1960s'. Paris, Rome, and other international destinations became priority flights.

---

[50] (Blank, 2010)
[51] (Marsh, 2011)
*The FAA Profile gave certain behavioral indicators of hijackers, and would serve as an ever evolving tool to be used by airport security personnel for attempting to thwart hijackings before hijackers could board an aircraft.

On November 24, 1968, Pan Am Flight 281 was hijacked from JFK to Puerto Rico. The pilot took the three hijackers to Havana, Cuba, where the U.S. State Department later evacuated the passengers on a government aircraft. [52]

Although the hijackings to Cuba were on the rise at the time, the majority ended peacefully; the aircraft was returned, and the crew and passengers were unharmed. The FAA became interested in finding other ways to thwart a hijacking, and to catch a hijacker in the act in order to study them.

By the end of calendar year 1968, there were a total of 22 U.S. aircraft hijackings; more than the first two decades of violence and/or, criminal activity onboard commercial aircraft combined.[53]

In 1969, Mr. Blank, by then the Branch Manager of FAA Flight Standards in Washington DC, was tasked with finding a way to catch a hijacker during a hijacking attempt. This became Mr. Blank's passion, and he spent hundreds of hours over the next year pondering the question. [54]

Mr. Blank was also saddled with the responsibility for setting up a more robust security screening system at U.S. airports, starting with Dulles International Airport (IAD) in Washington DC.* With this being a major priority, Mr. Blank approached the U.S. Customs Service (USCS). It was thought that the USCS would best be able to implement a program, and better understood the legal issues surrounding such an endeavor. Thus, began an air piracy task force that was set up in February 1969, to study and incorporate such changes; the results of this, the aptly named *Task Force on Deterrence of Air Piracy*** would later be revealed in its final report, FAA-AM-78-35. [55]

The establishment of this task force happened in response to the overwhelming amount of hijackings and other criminal activity occurring on U.S. air carriers. In January 1969, alone, there were a total of eight U.S. aircraft hijacked to Cuba. Along with setting up a more robust passenger screening system, the task

---

[52] (Wikipedia, List of Cuba - United States Aircraft Hijackings)
[53] (Aleman, 2012)
[54] (Blank, 2010)
[55] (H.L. Reighard, November 1978)
* Dedicated on November 17, 1962, by President John F. Kennedy, the name was later changed in 1984 to Washington Dulles International Airport.
**Also referred to as the *air piracy task force*, although this was not the official name. The official name was Task Force on Deterrence of Air Piracy.

force began looking at each individual hijacking, and tried to learn how to stop them.

Mr. Blank started setting up new screening procedures, and began using some of the more prominent airlines as test models. The task force quickly realized they needed help at certain key airports in the nation's capital region. Along with the USCS, Mr. Blank approached the U.S. Marshals Service (USMS) to ask for help with law enforcement duties at Dulles. Both the USCS and USMS were quick to respond. In the early half of 1969, both agencies would begin setting up new screening protocols.

By the middle of 1969, the U.S. government was moving to stem the threat of hijackings against U.S. civil aviation. A task force had been set up as a think tank and to implement new security procedures and the FAA's civil aviation security arm was gaining valuable experience. The men and women working on these problems had no idea that the violence of these events were about to reach a new level.

On August 29, 1969, Islamic terrorists diverted TWA Flight 840 from Rome; one of the hijackers was a woman named Leila Khaled. En-route from Rome to Israel, two operatives hijacked the aircraft and diverted it to Syria. During the hijacking, two Israelis' were taken hostage. After landing in Syria, the Israeli's were removed from the aircraft. [56]

The Israeli Ambassador to the U.S., Yitzak Rabin, was supposed to have been on the flight, and the operation was planned long in advance by the Popular Front for the Liberation of Palestine (PFLP)*. They wanted to use the ambassador as a bargaining chip, for the release of Syrian and Egyptian Soldiers being held by Israel. Mr. Rabin was not onboard, and thus the nose of the Boeing 707 aircraft was blown off instead; while on the ground in Syria, passengers watched in fear as the explosive was detonated. Israeli passengers had also been targeted for torture, and in the end, two Israeli hostages were traded for the release of 71 soldiers by Israel. Hijacker Leila Khaled was later arrested and held in Britain.

This new type of hijacking was much more violent in nature, and exhibited a shift in hijackings and hijacker tactics. This new style of hijacking involved a team of hijacker *terrorists*, as opposed to a lone hijacker *criminal*. All of the hijackings prior to TWA 840, with some minor exceptions, were perpetrated by

---

[56] (Aleman, 2012), (Wikipedia, TWA Flight 840 Hijacking (1969))
* The PFLP was founded in 1967 as a Marxist-Leninist and revolutionary leftist organization. The organization would become closely aligned with Syria.

only one hijacker, and none were politically motivated or showed such a propensity for violence.

In light of the new tactics and violent nature of aircraft hijackings, by October 1969, the USMS had started their own anti-air piracy program, specifically out of their southern Florida field office in Miami. This began the USMS's management of their-own sky marshal program. [57]

Having initially been approached by Mr. Blank to help with screening and law enforcement duties at select U.S. airports, the U.S. Marshals Service seized the opportunity, in light of the multiple hijackings, to develop their own program to combat air piracy.

The U.S. Marshals Service was smart in realizing that air piracy was not going away any time soon. It was also understood by the USMS that their wide jurisdiction allowed them to bring the full force of the law, and harsher penalties, to would-be terrorists and hijackers; this would soon be realized by people at the head of the U.S. government as well.

The new violent nature of hijackings was now being seen as a menace, but the U.S. government now had both the FAA Peace Officers program within the FAA *and* the USMS's sky marshal program in Miami, to combat air piracy together.

Although the FAA Peace Officers would continue to be used for future missions, an event loomed on the horizon which would lead to their disbandment and the single largest expansion of armed guards on civilian aircraft in U.S. history.

---

[57] (McKinney, September 30, 2009), (Service U. M.)

Chapter V

Sky Marshal Program

U.S. Marshals Service & U.S. Customs Service Programs
(October 1969 – June 25, 1974)

With new security protocols being implemented in select U.S. airports, Mr. Blank continued to work on his hijacking studies and his attempt to devise a way to capture a hijacker in the act, in order to further study them. It was in the latter half of 1969 that Mr. Blank was convinced he had accomplished this goal. [58]

The method for this project, was presented to the Chief Flight Surgeon for the FAA. He agreed that it would likely work, and it was then taken to an FAA psychologist for approval. After the project was approved, the method was tested on a baboon. The baboon was named Zeke, and the project became known as *"project ZEKE."* Project ZEKE was a success by any measure, and went on hold to be used for an attempted hijacking in the future. [59]

Project ZEKE was a classified project within the FAA's air piracy task force. They had studied aircraft hijackings and found that when a hijacking was in progress, the hijacker usually put a gun to the head of the pilot before telling the

---

[58] (Blank, 2010)
[59] (Marsh, 2011)

pilot where to go. Their study also indicated that on most occasions, after the hijacker told the pilot their new destination, the pilot would get on the radio and relay the information to Air Traffic Control (ATC); the hijacker(s) would get nervous, and thought that the pilot and ATC were talking in code. The hijacker(s) usually wanted to listen to the radio transmission. With all this in mind, it was project ZEKE that came up with a novel way to catch a hijacker. The idea was simple, and when they tested it on the ape, it worked.

For ZEKE* to work, when the hijacker told the pilot where they wanted to go, the pilot would tell the hijacker that they needed to call ATC. The pilot would then hand a *"special headset"* to the hijacker for them to listen to the transmission between the pilot and ATC. When the hijacker had the special headset on, the pilot would activate ZEKE, which was hooked up through the ground. The pilot could push a button which would send an electrical shock into the hijacker's headset. The air piracy task force found that the hijacker would be incapacitated, and would not be able to physically pull a trigger if they were armed with a firearm. Project ZEKE would be ready for deployment by early 1970. [60]

While Mr. Blank and others from the air piracy task force continued studying hijackings, hijackers, perfecting project ZEKE, and developing their profiling tools, the USCS and USMS were busy revising security protocols and airport screening procedures at select U.S. airports. By this point, the U.S. Marshals Service had started flying missions out of their Miami office under the direction of a man named John Brophy.

The U.S. Marshals Service's in-flight security program that began in October 1969 was a shoestring operation. John Brophy led the new sky marshal program out of Miami, Florida, and initially manned the program with five deputies. The USMS fit the bill for helping stand up a force due to their jurisdiction, which enabled them to make arrests under a broad range of powers.

While the FAA's main focus was on Cuban hijackings and the developing of their profiling models, in October 1969 the first hijacking occurred which took an aircraft outside the western hemisphere. This hijacking presented the air piracy task force with a new problem. On October 31, 1969, a 19 year-old U.S. Ma

---

[60] (Blank, 2010), (Marsh, 2011)
*ZEKE was a box which held an electrical charge. After being hooked up through the ground through an electrical terminal it was ready to send a shock to the special headset, designed to be worn by the hijacker, and which would complete the electrical circuit for the desired outcome.

rine, AWOL* from duty, and *"shell shocked** from Vietnam, "* hijacked an aircraft bound for San Francisco. TWA Flight 85 and the passengers onboard would be taken on a 17-hour ride, finally ending in Rome, Italy.[61]

The hijacker, Rafael Minichiello, used strong arm tactics*** and forced the plane to stop and refuel in Denver, where 39 passengers and two flight attendants were released. After leaving Denver, the aircraft continued on to JFK. While in New York, FBI agents spooked Minichiello, who fired his weapon in the aircraft. No one was hurt; however, this would later raise the question of who should be in charge during an aircraft hijacking: The captain****, the FAA, or the FBI?

Minichiello had joined the U.S. Marine Corps after high school, where he had later been injured in Vietnam. Upon his return home, Minichiello was stationed in Camp Pendleton, in southern California. Shortly thereafter, he robbed a store on base, feeling he had been *"cheated out of some pay."* On October 31, 1969, Minichiello bought a $15.50 ticket on a TWA flight (Flight 85) from Los Angeles to San Francisco; his carry-on possessions included an M-1 carbine, ammunition, several dynamite caps, and a large knife. [62]

The pilot of the aircraft, Captain Don Cook, upon landing in Rome, made a statement regarding the FBI's actions at Kennedy airport, stating it was *"damned near a prescription for getting the entire crew killed and the plane destroyed."*

This was just one of many aircraft hijackings in which the FBI mismanaged and endangered lives of the passengers and crew onboard, and this did not go unnoticed in the eyes of the U.S. government or the FAA. Minichiello would become somewhat of a folk hero and the news media treated him kindly. With all the media attention given to the hijacking it was likely to glamorize the event and lead to an increase in others like it.

---

[61] (Axelrod, 1999), (Seattle Marine Hijacks a TWA Airliner to Rome on October 31, 1969)

[62] (Aleman, 2012), (Seattle Marine Hijacks a TWA Airliner to Rome on October 31, 1969)

* AWOL is a military term, meaning Absent without Leave.

** *"Shell-shocked"* was a term which was used to refer to, what is now known as, Post Traumatic Stress Syndrome (PTSD).

*** Strong arm tactics are meant to intimidate by violence, or threat of violence.

**** The captain is referred to as the Pilot in Command (PIC) in legal agreements, and other FAA memorandums; the PIC has ultimate authority over all decisions in regards to the safety of an aircraft *in-flight*.

Ten days after the Minichiello hijacking, a 14 year-old boy attempted to hijack an aircraft in Cincinnati. Fortunately, the boy was persuaded to surrender before the aircraft was forced to take-off. The boy's mother said he had been interested in the Minichiello hijacking the previous week. This was an example of a *"copycat-hijacking,"* which would also become a trend in the future. [63]

On March 17, 1970, Eastern Airlines Flight 1320 was hijacked from Newark to Boston. This hijacking showed the courage of a pilot under pressure, much like that of the now infamous landing in the Hudson by Captain Chesley "Sully" Sullenberger. On that day, Flight 1320 was bound for Boston*, and was hijacked by John J. Divivio, who was armed with a .38 caliber revolver. The flight was piloted by Captain Robert Wilbur Jr., a former U.S. Air Force pilot.

Divivio forced his way into the cockpit and began struggling for control of the aircraft with the captain and co-pilot. Captain Wilbur was shot by the hijacker and bled profusely; his co-pilot had been wounded as well. Captain Wilbur managed to call ATC to relay that his co-pilot had been shot: First Officer James Hartley had been mortally wounded by this time. Captain Wilbur was then able to wrestle the weapon from the hijacker and wounded him with three shots from the revolver, before lapsing into unconsciousness. Despite his grave wounds, Captain Robert Wilbur Jr. was able to regain consciousness and land his aircraft safely, while the hapless hijacker clawed at him, attempting to force a crash. In an emerging time of violent hijackings, the death of James Hartley put the FAA on alert, hardening their resolve, and intensified their focus on preventing weapons and explosives from being brought onboard commercial flights.

In the early half of 1970, with the increasing amount of hijackings, the U.S. government began thinking about enhancing the number of in-flight security personnel manning flights. With the extreme amount of flights to and from the nation's major cities and the increasing threat to civil aviation, it was impossible for the 15 FAA Peace Officers to realistically cover even a minority of these.

By 1970, John Brophy was running the small force of USMS sky marshals with the limited resources he was given. These sky marshals would continue to fly on select flights as their program evolved, and the service continued to support the FAA in their development of new security procedures for carry-on baggage screening and passenger boarding. [64]

---

[63] (Holden)

[64] (Service U. M.)

* Boston Logan International Airport (BOS), named after General Edward Lawrence Logan, a former officer of the Spanish-American War from South Boston; it was dedicated as such in 1943.

While these new programs were operating, one of the first extortion hijackings occurred. On June 4, 1970, a man named Arthur Barkley held a plane at Dulles airport and demanded a ransom of $100 million from the government. He had a former dispute with the IRS over a $400 sum. When he lost a Supreme Court case, he decided to take matters into his own hands. He was recalled having told his wife, *"I am going to handle the tax problem today,"* before heading to the airport in Phoenix, where he ultimately boarded and hijacked TWA Flight 486, bound for Washington DC. John Marsh was working late at FAA Headquarters and received a call from Richard Lally, notifying him of the events. [65, 66]

Mr. Marsh went to the secure area that ZEKE was kept at FAA Headquarters, got the device, and put it into the back of his vehicle for transport to IAD. Mr. Marsh drove fast to the airport and was eventually escorted to the aircraft by a Highway Patrol Officer that was waiting. Upon stepping out of his vehicle, Mr. Marsh saw a man with blood on his hands in the custody of two FBI men. The FBI had stormed the plane prior to Mr. Marsh's arrival and had apprehended the hijacking suspect. Project ZEKE would go back on hold, where it would stay indefinitely, the details or knowledge of which would never be revealed to the public.

The FAA and the U.S. government were fully aware that there was a shift taking place in hijackings in the late 1960's and early 1970's. They had already seen many criminal acts targeting civil aviation: By lone individuals, such as United Airlines Flight 629. By copycats, such as the 14 year-old boy, following the Minichiello hijacking, and by terrorists, who used team-oriented tactics, such as the hijacking targeting TWA Flight 840. As the air piracy task force continued their study, the line between criminal and terroristic acts targeting commercial aircraft became blurred. They would continue to see an increase in these types of hijackings over the next several years, and would struggle to react to these changes, which were occurring at a rapid pace.

A new passenger and baggage screening system was implemented in early 1970. This was was essentially a pilot program with National Airlines that had been drafted earlier in the year; the official program began on July 17, 1970 at Moissant International Airport (MSY) in New Orleans, LA. As this program was evolving, Joseph Blank and John Marsh continued their work with the air piracy task force. At the time, they realized that the next hijacking was just around the corner, however, projects like ZEKE very much revealed the mindset and focus of aviation security for the period. Project ZEKE and the research behind it, was designed to catch a lone hijacker, or criminal. Even after the hi-

---

[65] (Magazine, $100 Million Skyjack, June 15, 1970)
[66] (Blank, 2010), (Marsh, 2011)

jacking of TWA 840, which was viewed as a rare phenomenon, the security procedures and protocols, screening systems, and all focus of the civil aviation security professionals at the FAA was on criminal acts committed on aircraft, by lone individuals. This focus was about to have a major readjustment, following a new and brazen string of hijackings.

On September 6, 1970, five jet aircraft, bound for JFK, were hijacked by members of the PFLP. There was only one fatality and one injury reported on one of the aircraft*, however, this coordinated hijacking, and the violence the hijackers displayed, would set into motion the greatest expansion of in-flight security personnel in history. [67]

Dawson's field, near Zarka, Jordan, was formerly used as a British Royal Air Force Base. This was where TWA Flight 741 (a Boeing 707), coming from Frankfurt, Germany, and Swissair Flight 100, from Zurich Kloten Airport (a Douglas DC-8), were brought after being hijacked. Both flights had a final destination of New York. [68]

These hijackings were accomplished through the use of team oriented tactics meant to dominate and control passengers and crew by use of violence and the threat of violence. Again, like the hijacking of TWA 840 in 1969, the hijackers were Islamic extremists. This new breed of hijacking would lead not only to an expansion of armed guards, but also initiate a rethinking of law enforcement action and training in the area of in-flight security measures.

On September 5, 1970, a Pan Am flight attendant, Sybille Frein Von Fricks, had landed in Brussels; it was her first flight as a new trainee. The flight was originally scheduled from JFK to Amsterdam, however, due to engine failure the flight had landed in Brussels. On the morning of September 6, Sybille and another flight crew went on to Amsterdam. From there, she was joined by a new crew, which would work with her on the return trip home; this final leg of Von Frick's trip departed Amsterdam for JFK. The aircraft was a Boeing 747, Pan Am Flight 93. [69]

Earlier in the morning, on September 6, two hijackers had attempted to board an El Al aircraft, Flight 219, in Amsterdam, but Israeli security blocked the men from boarding for unknown reasons; most likely the men fit an Israeli anti-hijack profile. The two men were escorted from the El Al terminal, at which

---

[67] (Aleman, 2012)
[68] (Aleman, 2012), (Blank, 2010), (Marsh, 2011)
[69] (Fricks, 2011)
*This was on El Al Flight 219.

time they decided to board a different aircraft and ultimately ended up on Pan Am Flight 93. Two other men *had* boarded El Al Flight 219 that day with the intention of hijacking it; the two that were denied boarding would have rounded out their four-man team.

Pan Am had been notified of the two men, and since El Al had rejected them, the pilot for Pan Am Flight 93 decided to frisk them. The pilot found nothing on the two men during his search and they were allowed to board: Both were armed with grenades and pistols.

Flight 93 was hijacked by the terrorists within twenty minutes of take-off. Sybille noticed the plane going in circles and called ahead to the pilots to find out what was going on. She was told that the aircraft had been hijacked and they were going to Beirut. After a tense flight, with the hijackers moving up and down the aisles threatening passengers, the aircraft landed in Beirut. In Beirut, the hijackers picked up two other terrorists, who brought explosives and more weapons onboard. The aircraft then took off for Cairo.

Since the aircraft was large, it was not known by the captain whether it could be safely landed at Dawson's field; the other hijacked aircraft were taken to the air field as part of an elaborate plan. The Boeing 747 needed a longer runway for landing, and for this reason Pan Am Flight 93 ended up in Cairo.

After landing, the hijackers ordered all passengers off of the aircraft. The flight crew quickly ushered passengers young and old out of the hijacked plane. The cool night air greeted all as they tried to distance themselves from the terror inside. As the aircraft sat with engines running on the tarmac, Sybille ran across an open field with the co-pilot and a little girl; the girl had been separated from her parents in the confusion. After being herded into a bus by Egyptian Soldiers, the aircraft was blown up by explosives that had been put next to the planes fuel tanks*. The passengers and crew watched as the jet burned in the desert night. [70]

The hijacking of El Al Flight 219, by the two remaining terrorists, was said to have been stopped by the efforts of the pilot, fellow passengers, and an onboard sky marshal**.

---

[70] (Fricks, 2011)
*The flight attendant Sybille Frein Von Fircks had watched one of the terrorists rig the explosives before landing. In order to maximize the explosives effect the terrorist had ripped apart some of the interior of the aircraft, placing the explosive as close to the fuel tanks (held in the aircraft's wings) as possible.
**The claim that one or possibly multiple Israeli sky marshal(s) were onboard cannot be confirmed. (See Work Cited: Force, Israeli Air)

A sky marshal was reported by the Israeli government to have shot one of the hijackers, and reportedly the other was hit over the head with a bottle of liquor by a passenger; one of the hijackers later died in a hospital.[71]

Due to the Dawson's Field hijackings, President Richard M. Nixon responded by ordering the use of federal armed guards on overseas flights of U.S. airlines, and the immediate build-up of air security personnel.

On September 11, 1970, President Nixon outlined various actions to be taken in response to the hijackings: [72]

"The menace of air piracy must be met – immediately and effectively. I am therefore announcing the following actions to deal with this problem we will place specially trained, armed United States Government personnel on flights of U.S. commercial airliners. A substantial number of personnel are already available and will begin their duties immediately. To the extent necessary they will be supplemented by specially trained members of the Armed Forces who will serve until an adequate force of civilian guards has been assembled and trained. We will also make anti-sabotage training available to airlines personnel."

President Nixon went on to state:

"I have directed the Department of Transportation, Treasury and Defense, the Central Intelligence Agency, the Federal Bureau of Investigation, the Office of Science and Technology, and other agencies to accelerate their present efforts to develop security measures, including new methods for detecting weapons and explosive devices. At the same time, the Department of Defense and Transportation will work with all U.S. airlines in determining whether certain metal detectors and x-ray devices now available to the military could provide immediate improvement in airport surveillance efforts. To facilitate passenger surveillance, appropriate agencies of the Federal Government will intensify their efforts to assemble and evaluate all useful intelligence concerning this matter and to disseminate such information to airlines and law enforcement personnel."

"I am directing the State Department and other appropriate agencies to consult fully with foreign governments and foreign carriers concerning the full range of techniques which they use to foil hijackers. Some foreign airlines – though they are particularly susceptible to hijacking – have been successful in

---

[71] (Aleman, 2012), (Wikipedia, Dawson's Field Hijackings), (Force)
[72] (Nixon, 1970)

deterring hijackers and in coping with piracy attempts. We want to learn all we can from their experience."

"It is imperative that all countries accept the multilateral convention providing for the extradition or punishment of hijackers which will be considered at the International Conference which will be held under the auspices of the International Civil Aviation Organization. I affirm the support of the United States both for this convention and for the Tokyo Convention, which provides for the prompt return of hijacked aircraft, passengers, and crew. I call upon other governments to become parties to these conventions."

"I further call upon the international community to take joint action to suspend airline services with those countries which refuse to punish or extradite hijackers involved in international blackmail. For this purpose and in order to consider other way and means of meeting this new international menace, I have directed the Secretary of State to ask the President of the Council of the International Civil Aviation Organization immediately to convene that council in an emergency meeting."

In closing his speech, President Nixon reiterated the need for combating hijacking attempts: [73]

"Piracy is not a new challenge for the community of nations. Most countries, including the United States, found effective means of dealing with piracy on the high seas of a century and a half ago. We can – and we will – deal effectively with the piracy in the skies today."

It was clear that President Nixon was intent on stemming air piracy and stopping would-be hijackers. His response precipitated the necessary steps for the FAA to increase its efforts in combatting this plague, by enhancing programs that were born with the initial inception of FAA Peace Officers in 1962, and the founding of civil aviation security within the FAA in the early 1960s'.

Shortly after President Nixon's speech, a meeting at FAA Headquarters took place between Administrator Halaby, John Marsh, Joe Blank, and several other FAA aviation security professionals. The meeting was interrupted by a phone call from the White House, and as everyone waited for the Administrator to finish his phone conversation they wondered what could be so important. As the telephone conversation came to a close, Administrator Halaby's expression changed from upbeat, to one of concern. After hanging up the phone, Halaby spoke: *"We have just been told that the U.S. military is going to start being*

---

[73] (Nixon, 1970)

trained for sky marshal duties. Our program, it seems, will no longer be needed. The FAA Peace Officers will continue to fly missions for the next couple of months and will be used to help train the new personnel, but after that it's over." [74]

Administrator Halaby was surprised by the phone call. The Administrator, and the men and women present, having been entrusted with aviation security, would now turn their collective focus on helping the U.S. government stand up a larger force of armed agents for civil aviation security duties.

President Nixon's speech also put in motion the ability of other law enforcement organizations to start their own security programs dedicated to combating air piracy. Almost a year prior to this, however, the U.S. Marshals Service had done just that. With the Nixon administration's response began the process of working out agreements with *other* agencies that would eventually become involved in a joint air-piracy effort. The lawyers at the FAA would have their hands full over the next several months with these changes. [75]

While the various agencies began working on this problem, the original FAA Peace Officers, of which there were then twelve, began a surge of missions in direct response to the Dawson's field hijackings and President Nixon's speech. For the next six weeks they would fly constantly, on mostly international flights. They were free to pick their missions, which were listed on a white board at their headquarters in Washington DC, based on high priority/ high threat flights. They would map out their itinerary for a week or more at a time. [76]

With the heightened amount of travel, the men decided to model their rest breaks and layovers on that of the flight crews. There were, however, times when they could not rest as the crew did, due to their limited manpower and higher priority flights. With the increased mission tempo, the FAA Peace Officers were putting together travel procedures that would be used by future in-flight security personnel.

The remaining FAA Peace Officers found themselves travelling to Paris, London, Frankfurt, Brussels, Cairo, and many other locations. At this time they had begun laying the ground work for a transition from the FAA Peace Officers, to what would become a joint sky marshal program between the Department of Justice, Department of Transportation, and Department of Treasury.

---

[74] (Blank, 2010), (Marsh, 2011)

[75] (Blank, 2010)

[76] (Pontecorvo J. A., Interviews of Joseph A. Pontecorvo; former FAA Peace Officer (1962 - 1969), 2009 - 2010)

The twelve FAA peace officers began logging thousands of miles covering mission flights. It became quickly apparent to the U.S. government that the small FAA program could not possibly manage the undertaking; while new personnel were trained, the many other missions that needed to be covered would have to go unprotected. The FAA did not want to sacrifice any more of their safety inspectors for this duty, and they were happy to find the government moving in a different direction with the sky marshal program.

The transition taking place in the latter half of 1970 was the end of an era for the FAA Peace Officers. Although for the time being they would continue flying missions as directed by the FAA and DOT, their time was limited.

On September 15, 1970, only four days after President Nixon's speech, a Brink's courier, R. E. DeNisco, shot an ex-mental patient as he tried to divert a TWA flight to North Korea. This incident showed the ability of a security agent to successfully thwart a hijacking attempt in progress, and leant credibility to the use of armed, undercover law enforcement personnel, onboard select U.S. flights. [77]

Robert DeNisco would later gain fame from this event, in which he single handedly stopped a hijacking. On the flight, the captain, alerted that a plainclothed DeNisco was sitting in first class, told a flight attendant to relay the following message: *"Tell him I said to go back and shoot that bastard."*

With the U.S. Customs Service starting their own sky marshal program, and after having spoken to President Nixon by phone due to his heroic actions, the FAA, tasked with helping to train the new security personnel, looked to DeNisco as a possible person to lead the new customs program. Mr. DeNisco, however, would not become the leader of the program, but would go on loan for some time to the FAA instead, to help train the new force and relay his experience on the hijacked TWA, Boeing 707 aircraft.

Since the FAA had just been tasked with helping train a new permanent force from other law enforcement agencies, a gap needed to be filled immediately in response to President Nixon's speech. To solve this problem, several law enforcement agencies began flying missions to help combat the rash of air piracy. These included Law Enforcement Officers (LEOs) from various departments, including deputies from the U.S. Marshals Service's sky marshal program, and agents on loan from the U.S. Department of Treasury (TRE), U.S. Secret Service (USSS), Drug Enforcement Agency (DEA), Internal Revenue Service, and the Bureau of Alcohol, Tobacco, Firearms and Explosives (BATFE). The Cen-

---

[77] (Tristani, March 30, 2009)

tral Intelligence Agency (CIA) was also said to have provided people in the surge.

All of this was occurring prior to a more permanent force being implemented by the U.S. Customs Service. The FAA scrambled to ensure all the above surge personnel were aware of certain legalities and procedures regarding air travel. They would all stay on in this capacity until the spring of 1971.

In November 1970, Joseph Pontecorvo and the other eleven* FAA safety inspectors, flying missions in support of Nixon's presidential directive, were brought into FAA Headquarters, and commended for their service. They were all given personalized plaques with their names engraved, that included a picture of the swearing-in ceremony from March 2, 1962. The 12 men were then re- leased back to Flight Standards. [78]

Although most of the men returned to their respective offices, some like Mr. Pontecorvo had been selected to help train the new sky marshals and some of the military personnel at Ft. Belvoir, VA and Ft. Dix, NJ, respectively, on Tempo- rary Duty (TDY) assignment. Due to his work as an aviation security specialist, and his knowledge of aircraft operations, Mr. Pontecorvo would teach the mili- tary men and others how to check-in for ticketing, board the aircraft, and per- form other aviation related duties. He also helped teach aircraft familiarization, showing students where criminals could hide or stow weapons.

Along with Mr. Pontecorvo, the FAA also sent attorneys to teach the men legal issues in regards to jurisdiction and other air piracy statutes. One of the attorneys the FAA sent was John Marsh. In helping train these personnel, the military had their own instructors at Ft. Dix that taught firearms, tactics, and hand to hand combat techniques. The military volunteers, many of which were military police, came from the U.S. Navy, Air Force, and Army, and all were E- 4 or above in rank. [79]

As an FAA Peace Officer, Joe Pontecorvo had served as one of the first air marshals in history. By the time he was notified in October 1970 that his service was no longer needed, he had served on the force for a total of eight years. Mr. Pontecorvo would continue work with the FAA for many more years, with peo- ple close to him never knowing what he had done for his country.

---

[78] (Pontecorvo J. A., Interviews of Joseph A. Pontecorvo; former FAA Peace Officer (1962 - 1969), 2009 - 2010)
[79] (Marsh, 2011)
*By 1970 only 12 FAA Peace Officers remained.

While the training of military in-flight security personnel continued, the U.S. government began ramping up, what would be later referred to as, the *sky marshal program*. There were many meetings at FAA Headquarters on this issue, as they worked to sort out all of the legal paperwork and agreements that would be formed between themselves, the U.S. Marshals Service, U.S. Customs Service, Department of Treasury, Department of Transportation, and the Department of Defense (DOD).

The FAA Flight Standards Division no longer wanted the security program and they were ready to have their safety inspectors back in their traditional roles. Although the FAA Peace Officers were being disbanded, the FAA was still tasked with overseeing the new force, and remained committed to being involved in aviation security duties. It was at this time that the in-flight security program would be moved from the Flight Standards Division to the *Office of Investigations and Security*.

By October 1970, the Office of Investigations and Security created a new division within their office, an *'air marshal division'*, to be housed in the *Office of Air Transportation Security*; this office was responsible for all aviation security duties at the FAA, and was established on August 3, 1970. A man named Ted Brient was assigned to this new division. Mr. Brient had been the Headquarters Administrator of the FAA Peace Officer Program, and his experience would be useful in this transition.

Another man, named Richard "Dick" Noble, was hired on to the Investigations and Security Division in September 1970. Mr. Noble was tasked with writing the agreement between all the various agencies and departments that would be involved in this huge aviation security undertaking. The military contingent had to be taken into account as well, and the FAA had to ensure it had checks and balances throughout the process and with all agencies involved. [80]

The military personnel helping with the effort in combating air piracy were mission capable in a full-time capacity almost immediately. They would remain on loan to the FAA as needed, until the permanent force was ready to assume in-flight security responsibilities.

The training of military personnel at Ft. Dix, which numbered in the hundreds, mostly consisted of military police, and led to the largest ever force, by 1970-71, providing security for flights in and out of the United States. These men would remain on the job for only a few months. By the time they were no

---

[80] (Noble, 2011)

longer needed, there were some 500-600 personnel* flying missions in support of the surge. [81]

The later disbandment of the military personnel, which occurred in December 1970, was mainly due to the initiation of the sky marshal programs of the U.S. Customs and U.S. Marshal Service. However, it was also a byproduct of talk in Washington DC on the use of the U.S. Military for operations within the United States territories. This brought into question the *Posse Comitatus Act*, which limited the powers of local government and law enforcement from using military personnel to enforce the laws of the land. [82]

Benjamin O. Davis Jr., would soon go on to serve as the head of the sky marshal program, under the Department of Transportation (DOT), from 1970-71; he began his assignment as *Assistant Secretary for Safety and Security,* on September 21, 1970. The position of Assistant Secretary for Safety and Security within DOT was new, created after the Dawson's field hijackings.

Mr. Davis was considered a national hero. He had been one of the original Tuskegee airmen, and had earned his wings alongside five other officers in 1942, as one of the first black military pilots. Mr. Davis oversaw the *"sky marshal program"* and helped to coordinate the efforts of the U.S. Customs and U.S. Marshals Service programs under DOT and the FAA.

The program which Mr. Davis inherited was initially referred to as the *"antihijacking program"*, but would later become known as the *"sky marshal program"* by the media; the *'sky marshals program'*, and the term *sky marshal* would never become an official title of any agency.**

On September 25, 1970, the Department of Justice and Department of Transportation wrote a memorandum that helped outline the responsibilities of each department during a hijacking. The memorandum stated that the FBI would have jurisdiction if the aircraft was not airborne, or on taxi to become airborne, and more or less while stationary; the FAA would have jurisdiction and precedence

---

[81] (Noble, 2011)

[82] (Marsh, 2011)

*The total number includes military, law enforcement, and others providing in-flight security.

** Although it was never an official title, since it was such a widely used term, *sky marshal* will be used in this perspective; however for simplicity it will not be italicized. The official title of a sky marshal for the USCS was *"Customs Security Officer,"* or CSO. The two are used interchangeably throughout this historical perspective.

over the pilot at all other times. This memorandum would change over time due to later mismanagements of hijackings by the FBI, and would sway the balance of power even more into FAA hands over time.

On October 28, 1970, the Departments of Transportation and Treasury had reached an agreement to help train a permanent force of sky marshals for work as armed guards onboard U.S. flights, as well as ground assignments for performing baggage checks and other airport security duties.

By late October to early November 1970, the U.S. Customs Service was already actively recruiting for the position of Customs Security Officer (CSO). CSOs would perform 60 day assignments as sky marshals, or in-flight security personnel* and provide airport security and screening duties, as CSOs, when not flying critical missions.

The requirements for CSOs were: [83]

- Be a United States citizen, male, and at least 21 years old.
- Be in excellent physical condition.
- Successfully complete a psychological examination, oral interview, and personal background investigation.
- Successfully complete a four-week training course, which includes instruction in the use of firearms.

Initially, like the FAA Peace Officers before them, the CSOs would not allow women into their ranks. This would change over time; for the first several months that the program was brought into existence, women were not given the opportunity to serve as CSOs.

A November 5, 1970, Bureau of Recruiting and Examining report, listed the duties of *"Security Officer"* as follows:

"The Security Officer detects and prevents criminal acts at airports and in flight on United States flag air carriers. Considerable air travel; possible arduous exertion to protect passengers, crew members, and aircraft against any criminal act; irregular, unscheduled tours: and possible personal risks are part of the job."

---

[83] (Examining, November 5, 1970)
*Customs Security Officers/ Sky Marshals were referred to as *"Security Officer"* in official employment announcements.

It went on, adding, *"In addition, Security Officers, carrying firearms, will also enforce complex Customs and related laws and apprehend any suspected violators. While on uniformed patrol and surveillance, Security Officers apply knowledge and understanding of laws, established procedures, and relevant experience to interrogate people and quickly and accurately evaluate information; then they determine the best, most appropriate action in each situation. Primary objectives are to deter smuggling of narcotics and contraband into the U.S. and to prevent pilferage of merchandise from cargo areas."*

By the end of November 1970, an announcement had been made, naming the Director of the new sky marshal force for the Department of Treasury, and the new Division of Air Security in the Customs Bureau's Office of Investigations, in Washington DC. The person named to this position was Martin J. McDonnell, a former liaison officer in the Office of Investigations and ex-military service member. [84]

Martin McDonnell had flown several missions as a sky marshal, during the surge, shortly after President Nixon's speech on September 11, 1970. He had been with the Customs Bureau since 1958, and had formerly served in the U.S. Army from 1953-55, as an intelligence analyst in psychological warfare with U.S. Army Special Forces at Ft. Bragg, NC. He had also served as a psychologist at the Armed Forces Examining Center, in Philadelphia, PA.

Under the watch of both Assistant Secretary Benjamin O. Davis Jr., and Director Martin J. McDonnell, the U.S. Customs Service's sky marshal program would reach a number of dedicated anti-hijacking personnel even larger than the augmented stand up of military personnel and other interim law enforcement officers. The number of sky marshals would eventually swell to 1,784 dedicated men and women. This was far larger than the U.S. Marshals Service's program would ever become, however both operated independently, reporting to their own respective agencies. [85]

Although the U.S. Marshals Service had their-own program, it was small in comparison with that of the U.S. Customs Service. USMS archives report that there were up to 230 sky marshals being used at the height of the program, between 1969 and 1973. However, the majority of personnel, as was true with the U.S. Customs program, performed mostly ground operations.

Many of the deputies used for the USMS sky marshals program were trained in additional tactics, specific to the aircraft environment, at Quantico, Virginia.

---

[84] (Martin J. McDonnel, 1974)
[85] (Customs T. D., January 1971 - August 1972)

By 1973, the USMS program focused mostly on baggage checking, at which time the FAA had required all carry-on baggage be checked prior to boarding. The USMS program was instrumental in helping airlines adopt the new screening program developed by the FAA.

One of the original USMS deputy marshals who worked as a sky marshal, was former Director Louie McKinney. Mr. McKinney worked out of the U.S. Marshal's Office in Washington DC, and reported *"At first, they would put me on a Pan American flight from Dulles airport to London, and I'd sit in the back of the plane and watch what was going on. We'd get there and then we would turn around and come right back."* He continued flying missions like this for two years, before being assigned to ground duties at Dulles airport. [86]

On December 16, 1970, the U.S. and 49 other countries signed, what would be called *The Hague Convention*, or the *Convention for the Suppression of Unlawful Seizure of Aircraft*. This convention sought to have signatories agree to the extradition of all hijackers, and to impose strict penalties to those engaged in air piracy.

On December 23, 1970, the first class graduated from training under the new U.S. Customs Service (USCS) sky marshal program. The USCS program was to become the major force of in-flight security personnel, of which many other law enforcement officers had been helping to augment.

The Treasury Air Security Officers School (TASOS) was four-weeks in length, and was held at Fort Belvoir, Virginia, a U.S. Army facility. Customs officers were being hired specifically for the position of Customs Security Officer (CSO); along with their regular duties performing security functions at airports, they would also fly missions as sky marshals. [87]

The men and later, women, completing TASOS, would be sworn in as Customs Security Officers for jurisdiction for customs duties, and as Special Deputy U.S. Marshals, like the FAA Peace Officers before them, to give them jurisdiction onboard aircraft when they were serving as sky marshals. One particular gentleman to be offered a position with the customs bureau as a CSO, and selected for training at TASOS, was a man by the name of Dennis Fagan. [88]

Mr. Fagan had served in the military and had wanted to become a New York City police officer after his discharge. Due to a twenty-percent disability in the

---

[86] (McKinney, September 30, 2009)

[87] (Customs B. o., 1971)

[88] (Fagan, 2011)

military, he was not eligible to take the test for the New York Police Department (NYPD). After several years doing odd jobs, Mr. Fagan was able to have his disability downgraded to ten-percent, and he was finally allowed to test for the NYPD.

Having put an application in with U.S. Customs as well, he received a reply from both the NYPD and the USCS on the same day. Due to changes in the city of New York and the treatment of police officers within the NYPD, along with his desire to travel and the lure of an occupation that was unlike many others, he decided to take the position with U.S. Customs.

With this decision, Dennis Fagan started an adventure that would take him places in his career that he never thought were possible. As he put it, *"[The Sky Marshal Position] gave me an adventure I never thought I would have; and it all started on that god damn airplane. And I hate to fly."* Dennis Fagan started his training in TASOS class number 17. This training was the toughest he would encounter in 29 years of federal service.

Training at TASOS included instruction on jurisdiction, the U.S. Secret Service pistol qualification standard, the FAA's profile of hijackers, and baggage screening procedures. Emphasis was put on using any means possible to subdue a hijacker without the use of a firearm. This was an important consideration given the tight confines of an aircraft and risk to passengers. Although it had become a myth portrayed by Hollywood movies, bullets penetrating the skin of an aircraft in-flight would *not* lead to an immediate depressurization of the cabin, or catastrophic failure of a commercial aircraft.

Because of the need for exceptional marksmanship while performing their security functions, the firearms qualification was extremely stringent for CSOs. The qualification was timed, and consisted of a 15-second time limit to fire six-bullets with the right hand, then reload and fire six-bullets with the left hand, into a black bulls-eye target at 15 yards. [89]

Along with firearms training at TASOS, instructors also taught arrest procedures and trade craft. The instructors came from various law enforcement agencies, and were picked for their vast law enforcement experience. Most of the firearms training was conducted by the uniformed division of the U.S. Secret Service, however, there were additional subjects taught by others, such as arrest techniques from U.S. Marshals deputies and legal from FAA attorneys.

---

[89] (Rustad, 2011 - 2012)

The six-shot Smith and Wesson Model 15, .38 caliber, 4" revolver, or *"Combat Masterpiece"*, was being issued and used for all firearms training at TASOS. Aircraft tactics were also stressed along with the mastery of firearms. [90]

Super Vel ammunition, the most powerful cartridges for .38 caliber ammunition at the time, was used for training and was being issued to CSOs for on duty carry when they graduated. The fireball from the immense amount of powder in the cartridge would engulf the hand of the shooter, and many candidates in the sky marshal/CSO program found it difficult to qualify for the tough standards.

The training given at TASOS was well prepared. It included training on how to brief flight attendants on minutiae, such as how to serve them drinks so they would not stand out to passengers. They worked out the following code to be used with flight attendants:

Liquor service (1st Class Only)

- Scotch and Soda - Ginger ale
- Bourbon and coke - Coke
- Vodka - Water
- Martini - Water
- Bloody Mary - Mix Only

Instruction in making a believable cover story for nosy passengers was also given at TASOS and students would get together in groups to practice their stories and try and pick apart others. This would come in handy for the new sky marshals when they took to the skies to prevent hijackings.

During the early 1970s', flying on Pan Am, or any other airline, was a very personal experience; people talked and tried to get to know each other, and conversation would quickly turn to occupation. The new sky marshals would have to think fast on their feet; it was better that they practiced their stories in training, before having to put them into practice on the aircraft during a mission.

Steve Rustad, a CSO flying missions out of San Francisco at the time, recalled establishing and using his cover as an artist. He actually *was* an artist, trained at the University of California at Berkeley, and he found that the easiest way to keep people from asking what he did for a living, was to sit on the flight and sketch pictures.

He recalled the reason for having such a good cover story:

---

[90] (Rustad, 2011 - 2012)

"Walter Cronkite actually told the American people on the six-o'clock news that the sky marshals sat [in seat] 7B on a 747, at the base of the stairway. I flew a whole bunch of flights sitting in 7B. We'd get on the plane first we would go meet the crew, and they get on and they make eye contact with you, and nod, and smile and nudge each other as they are marching on the plane."

"So it was pretty clear to me that, at least the occupant in 7B wasn't anonymous. They also had protocol that stipulated that if anybody was in the lounge on a 747 you would have to be there too; so, if somebody went up the stairs you went up the stairs. Well it didn't take long for the average person to figure out that the second person in the lounge was a sky marshal."

"So people actually used to play games to flush us out."

"So as quickly as I could, I qualified with the chief special (Smith & Wesson, Model 60, snub nose 5-shot revolver) so it would be a little more concealable."

"And when you flew everybody gets real comfortable and loose. Jackets come off, shoes come off; and if you're the only one there with his/ her jacket on - who's the sky marshal?"

"I let my hair grow out, and I dressed down, and I got the 'chief special', and I wore a belly band...basically a girdle with a holster stitched on."

"Everyone on Pan Am wanted to know what you did for a living when you sat down, so I was an artist and cartoonist and I drew, if I had a sketch pad and was drawing people immediately assumed that I was an illustrator."

"So that took care of a lot of questions, and another thing it allowed me to do was I could be looking around all of the time. I had an excuse for being observant, as opposed to some passenger that is always aware and looking around, again you mark yourself as having some kind of a surveillance role, but if you're drawing well of course you are looking around."

The CSOs that were flying missions at the peak of the sky marshal program were travelling quite frequently. Steve Rustad alone flew three-quarters of a million miles out of San Francisco International Airport (SFO) while he was a CSO, and he was only one of almost 2,000 sky marshals at the time. Although not all of the CSOs flew missions, the majority did, and this made for a lot of flight miles. However, even though the government wanted more of a visible deterrent than a covert one, the sky marshals made due with the situation handed

to them. Steve Rustad recalled where he traveled and the conditions at the time:
[91]

> "*I flew from San Francisco to Tokyo, to as far west as Bangkok, and touched down in different times in Saigon and Manila and Hong Kong, and because they hadn't completely phased in 747's I flew a bunch of 707's, and that was pretty interesting because the older ones had a navigator seat, and actually had a portal in the ceiling for the navigator to take sightings with a sextant; those were fairly old aircraft.*"

These were some of the operational issues going on in the field while sky marshals were flying missions. These issues were mostly due to the speed in which the CSOs were hired. Since the USCS sky marshal program had been ramped up so quickly, and the number of people hired, men and women, numbered 2,008 for the entire program, there were many that were sent home during training for not passing their background investigations.

The candidates in training would lose classmates overnight, and called this *"getting the hook."* Many candidates got *"the hook,"* and others would fail either firearms or tactics, both of which were pass/fail evolutions. [92]

On May 14, 1971, *United States vs. Lopez* concluded, which found the FAA's anti-hijacking profile constitutional per the eastern district of New York. The case arose from *"reasonable suspicion"* found through the use of the FAA profiling tool, during which time a man was discovered with narcotics. This was deemed a legitimate use of the anti-hijacking profile and leant credibility to it.

On June 12, 1971, the first death of a passenger from a domestic U.S. hijacking occurred on a flight from Albuquerque to New York. The hijacker demanded to be flown to Vietnam, and when a passenger tried to intervene to help a flight attendant, he was shot and killed.

By the middle of 1971, of the 2,008 hired as CSOs for TASOS training, 1,784 had graduated and were distributed to various offices around the country. Dennis Fagan was one of those graduates in May 1971. He initially went to JFK for a couple of weeks performing ground duties. These ground duties involved searching bags at boarding gates and utilizing the FAA profiling methods to screen passengers. He would then transfer to Atlanta airport for TDY, to begin flying missions throughout the south eastern region of the United States.

---

[91] (Rustad, 2011 - 2012)
[92] (Fagan, 2011)

Also, by May 1971, the first four women had graduated from the CSO program. During the graduation ceremony, of what was the 16th TASOS class, the Assistant Treasury Secretary, Eugene T. Rossides said, [93]

"From now on we double the number of people the skyjacker must fear. Until today they were only concerned that a trained Treasury sky marshal might be among the men accompanying them on flights. Starting today they must add to their fears the knowledge that there may be sky marshals among the women passengers as well."

The women sky marshals were indeed an excellent addition to the force. As the Assistant Treasury Secretary had alluded, the deterrent capability in having women onboard as in-flight security, and to have this known by the public, was very good for security. The four women would go on to help immensely in the program, and some would go on to serve long careers in the federal government.

One such woman, said to be one of the first four women hired as a sky marshal, was the late Bonni G. Tischler. Mrs. Tischler later went on to serve with Dennis Fagan at U.S. Customs in Miami, working money laundering cases in the southern district. Bonni flew many missions as a sky marshal from 1971 to 1974.

Later, during the 1980's, Bonni was called the *"The Women with a Golden Gun"* in a newspaper article. She was one of many people, like Dennis Fagan, that used the sky marshal program within the Bureau of Customs to start their careers. Bonni Tischler would serve at one point as the most senior woman in all federal law enforcement. [94]

By late 1971, there were now men *and* women protecting U.S. civil aviation as sky marshals. The CSOs worked security at airports and performed in-flight security duties on many flights. They were constantly ready and on the alert for a hijacking attempt, and remained vigilant in using the FAA profiling tool to try and thwart attempts prior to boarding.

The signing of the Montreal Convention took place on September 23, 1971. The U.S. and 29 other nation's signed an agreement stemming from this convention, otherwise known as the *Convention for the Suppression of Unlawful Acts Against the Safety of Civil Aviation*. It dealt specifically with prosecution of crimes onboard aircraft, such as people committing violence against others, trying to destroy or endanger an aircraft, and communication of false information.

---

[93] (First Female Sky Marshals Join the Force, Summer 1971)
[94] (Holley, August 10, 2005)

On October 25, 1971, a hijacking took place with three air marshals onboard. The hijacker stood up shortly after take-off and told the crew he had intentions of diverting the plane to Cuba. Sky marshal Dennis Fagan was supposed to have been onboard.

Although Dennis Fagan should have been on this particular flight, his partner, William "Bill" Chilson, a retired New York City Police Officer, had remained, and was joined by two other team mates for this particular mission. [95]

Upon landing in Cuba, the Cuban authorities came onboard and took the hijacker away and released him. They then stood at the front of the aircraft cabin, got on the Public Address (PA) system and asked the people onboard who the FBI agents were. At the time there was a television show called *"FBI,"* that was very popular in the country; they had gotten word that sky marshals were on the aircraft before it had landed in Havana, and assumed they were FBI agents. Bill Chilson told his team mates to remain calm and not to give up their cover.

At this time it was standard procedure to *"go along for a ride,"* if an aircraft was hijacked to Cuba while sky marshals were onboard; this was only if the hijacker did not try and harm the crew or passengers, or try to harm the integrity of the aircraft; if those circumstances did not occur, then the sky marshals were told *not* to intervene. Since hijackings to Cuba during this period were usually peaceful and on most occasions ended in getting the passengers and aircraft back, there was no problem with the sky marshals observing the hijacking and ensuring no one was hurt in the process.

In response to the Cuban authorities' question, a man stood up and announced that *he* was an FBI agent. Cuban officials immediately approached the man and took him away. As this happened, Bill Chilson took all the weapons and handcuffs, identification and other equipment from the men, and put it in his bag. They then deplaned with the rest of the passengers and walked towards customs. [96]

Upon reaching the customs official at the counter, Mr. Chilson started asking the man several questions. The customs official became agitated and told him to get back away from the counter. While Mr. Chilson was talking to the man, he had taken a piece of the chalk used by the authorities to mark inspected bags. He used the chalk to mark their-own bags, without anyone else noticing.

---

[95] (News N. Y., September 30, 2009), (Fagan, 2011)
[96] (Fagan, 2011)

Over the next two nights at the Havana Hilton, Bill Chilson kept all the fire-arms and other equipment locked behind a speaker in the wall of his room. On the 27th of October, they returned to JFK airport to tell their tale.

Mr. Fagan recalled the following about this particular missed flight:

"Just happens to be my story is: I had to go to my in-laws 50th wedding anniversary. But, at that time we had the same partners; I had the same partners on the flights. We were flying the San Juan, New York turn around, which we used to call the 'roach coach', and we did that five days a week."

"I did that for six-months, you go nuts after a while. So, anyways, I'm gone, they replace me, with my two partners, I'm coming up the turnpike going home, and I hear on the radio that the flight I was supposed to be on has been hijacked. They go into SOP (Standard Operating Procedure); they go to Havana."

"They land in Havana, and Cuban authorities come on board, and fortunately for us they watch a lot of television, and FBI was the big series at the time and they asked for the FBI agents. Miami, either radio station or TV station, before the aircraft even landed in Havana, said there were marshals onboard the airplane."

"So, there was an FBI agent on the aircraft. He gets up. He identifies himself. Well, they take him away. Well, my partner, who was a retired New York cop, he takes the other two guys and gets all their weapons, their ID, and puts it all in his bag; and he tells them 'I'll take care of this'."

"So all the people are taken off the airplane, and they're going through customs. And you've probably seen this in a lot of foreign places, they use chalk to mark the bags, that have been inspected."

"So Bill Chilson rushes through the crowd and leans over the counter, talkin' to the Cuban guy, the inspector, askin' him questions and stuff, and their telling him 'get back', and while he's doing that he picks up a piece of chalk; he marks the bags, they get the bags through. Nobody gets their weapons or anything, no one identifies them."

"They go to the Havana Hilton, where they put all the passengers, and in the old hotels you used to have stereo systems in the walls, he takes his handy dandy tool kit, takes the things off the wall, puts all the weapons and everything into the wall, puts the stereo thing back on the wall, and they

stay there for two days. And he just reverses it going back, and they get back to Miami, and no one even knew who they were. "

In 1971, Dr. David Hubbard, a psychologist with the FAA, finished his book *"The Skyjacker; His Flights of Fantasy."* The book illuminated findings from studies being done at the time within the FAA, to form a profile of hijackers for use in passenger screening. In his book, Dr. Hubbard described the FAA model that was being used by the USMS and USCS sky marshal programs. [97]

On November 24, 1971, Thanksgiving Eve, a man using the alias Dan Cooper boarded Northwest Orient Airlines Flight 305, on a Boeing 727 aircraft, in Portland, Oregon. The flight was headed to Seattle, Washington.

Within the first few minutes of flight, a note was passed to a flight attendant stating that there was a bomb onboard; Mr. Cooper stated that he was carrying an explosive in his briefcase. Pilot William Scott was informed by the flight attendants, at which time he notified authorities via ATC.

Cooper did not fit the FAA profile of a hijacker; he acted cool and calm, and the hijacking seemed very well planned; he did not figure into any of the chapters in Dr. Hubbard's book.

In Seattle, Cooper demanded a ransom and got it; he was delivered $200,000 and a civilian parachute upon landing. His plan was so detailed, that he had all cabin lights dimmed in order to deter police snipers. When his demands were met, he released two people and had the pilot take-off at 7:40 p.m. local time. Due to his actions, he appeared to be aware of law enforcement's response and tactics. [98]

At 8:00 p.m., Captain Scott noticed a light indicating the aft *Airstair** had been activated. Later, after landing at Reno airport, it was apparent that "Dan Cooper" had jumped from the aircraft with the aid of one of the civilian parachutes; the man now known as D.B. Cooper has never been apprehended.

This event would go on to spawn a rash of copycat hijackings, all in an attempt to extort money. D.B. Cooper helped cause what would become a fanatic problem, inherited by the new sky marshal force. If one man could extort $200,000 during a hijacking, surely others could as well.

---

[97] (Hubbard, 1971)
[98] (Aleman, 2012)
* An Airstair is a stairway built into the rear of an aircraft, meant to be used for boarding and deplaning.

The CSOs of the USCS were assigned to 33 airports across the United States. At their respective airports, the CSOs would watch passenger boarding and, utilizing the FAA profile of hijackers, clue in on behavioral indicators to try and thwart hijackings before they occurred. [99]

The USMS program had also been using the FAA profile with great success, and had racked up an impressive record. An October 1971 memorandum from former Associate Director William Hall outlined the many achievements of the U.S. Marshals in this arena. Numerous concealed weapons, including firearms, had been seized. One weapon, a .22 caliber firearm, was found during a search by USMS sky marshals, which had been concealed as a ball point pen.

Other illegal items had been found as well, such as narcotics. Inspector Brophy himself had observed a passenger attempting to check in with false identification, and later found the man to be carrying a large amount of heroin. Records indicated that the USMS sky marshal program had foiled 27 hijackings before they could occur. [100]

These achievements, reaped mainly from the new passenger screening program, would highlight the need in enhancing on the existing screening protocols, and over time the baggage and passenger screening continued to be developed. The continued success of this program would lead to more USMS and USCS sky marshals being utilized for ground duties, to help with screening and passenger observation.

By the end of 1971, the FAA had decided to reorganize its security arm. The civil aviation security function was, thus, severed from the Investigations and Security department, which was accomplished by the creation of the *Office of Air Transportation Security*.

The first director of the outfit was James "Jim" Thomas Murphy. At this time the FAA had a handful of personnel trained as in-flight security personnel, and with this small contingent, Jim Murphy could be considered the first *Director* of the *'Federal Air Marshal Program'*, although it was not being referred to by this name at the time. The in-flight security program would be housed within the Office of Air Investigations, as a special division of the air security wing.

The reorganization within the FAA, and the training and retention of a small air marshal contingent, was occurring as the sky marshal program was being run by the U.S. Customs and U.S. Marshals Service's, respectively. The FAA had

---

[99] (Customs T. D., January 1971 - August 1972)
[100] (Service U. M.)

never given up full control of the program, and helped to manage the anti-hijacking/sky marshal program since its inception. Jim Murphy was in a unique position to further enhance this necessary security function and its goals.

James T. Murphy had grown up in Rochelle, NY, and had served in World War II as a bombardier with the U.S. Army Air Corps, flying 25 combat missions during the war. After returning home, he went to College at Fordham University. After graduation he became a sportswriter for a short time, and in 1951 he joined the FBI, where he served as a special agent in the Cleveland and Washington field offices, as well as FBI Headquarters.

In 1963, Mr. Murphy joined the FAA, where he went on to serve as the Director of the Office of Compliance and Security. Finally, in 1971 he was appointed as the *Director of Air Transportation Security* within the new Office of Air Transportation Security. In this position, Mr. Murphy would play a critical role in helping implement the various security procedures at U.S. airports. In this capacity he would ensure a coordinated effort was taken with all airlines, a necessary step, due to the many security changes taking place: He was later awarded the Department of Transportation's Secretary's Award for Outstanding Achievement for his role in this process.

On January 12, 1972, a mentally deranged passenger hijacked Braniff International Airlines Flight 38, a Boeing 727 aircraft. The lone gunman, armed with a .22 caliber handgun, with a history of mental illness, claimed to have dynamite in a hand bag and ordered the pilot to take him to South America. The aircraft landed at Dallas Love Field to satisfy the hijacker's requests for food, cigarettes, $2 million, and a .357 magnum handgun. As the hijacker inspected the package delivered by law enforcement, the crew escaped and the hijacker was apprehended.[101]

Not long after the hijacking of Flight 38, a TWA Boeing 707 was hijacked out of Los Angeles. On January 29, 1972, a man by the name of Garrett B. Trapnell hijacked TWA Flight 2, while over Chicago and bound for New York. This hijacking, like others before it, would lead to further problems with the FAA/FBI relationship.

The hijacking of TWA Flight 2 ended with the FBI storming the aircraft at John F. Kennedy International Airport, where Trapnell was shot and wounded. This hijacking would lead to numerous other hijackings in an attempt to free Trapnell from prison. Trapnell was a con man, and from prison he would rally many people in his defense.

---

[101] (Customs T. D., January 1971 - August 1972)

On February 2, 1972, the FAA issued an emergency rule that required all air carriers to implement a passenger and baggage screening system that was acceptable to the FAA. The Administrator at this time was John Shaffer, who required that all airlines have this system in place no later than February 6, 1972. This was a major undertaking. Although these changes would require the spending of a large amount of money, the airlines had no choice but to comply with the emergency rule. The backlash of this rule led to several lobby groups sprouting up in support of the airlines interests. This would be the beginning of a long battle between the airlines and the FAA over security.

This was a volatile time for civil aviation. The constant threat of hijackings, and the ever changing motives and tactics of hijackers was keeping the FAA and the anti-air piracy task force on its toes. The most recent fad were the extortion hijackings, however there was also an increasing threat to aviation facilities.

On March 4, 1972, TWA received a threat that four of its aircraft would be blown up, unless they paid a ransom of $2 million. Upon news of the threat, the airline grounded all of its aircraft and eventually found an explosive on one of them; the flight was scheduled from New York to Los Angeles. This was an excellent outcome, with the airline having found an explosive, and flight service by TWA quickly resumed. The celebration was short lived however, when one of their aircraft in Las Vegas exploded some 18 hours later while parked at a terminal; the aircraft had originally come from New York. [102]

On May 30, 1972, three Japanese Red Army (JRA) terrorists, posing as tourists, flew to Israel on Air France Flight 132. At baggage claim they picked up their luggage, which contained weapons, ammunition, and hand grenades. They opened fire in the terminal shortly after, killing 24 people and injuring 75 others. Kozo Okamoto was the only terrorist to survive, and from his interrogation the events of the attack were constructed.

To carry out their plan, the JRA had contracted with the Popular Front for the Liberation of Palestine (PFLP) to attack an Israeli target, in return for which the PFLP would attack in Japan. This was an alarming case of terrorist groups working together and using operatives that did not fit the terrorist profile; this particular profile was being used in Israel at the time.

The types of incidents that were occurring at airports were of a major concern to aviation security professionals. The DOT and the FAA agreed that the focus should turn to an increase in security measures at airports, in order to prevent attacks and to try and screen possible hijackers before they boarded flights. With

---

[102] (Aleman, 2012)

the success of their passenger screening program, the FAA, sensing a move towards the targeting of airports and not aircraft, placed more emphasis towards ground security. It was during this time that the FAA, in order to bolster their aviation security efforts, began seeking new employees to work as Aviation Security Specialists.

A man named Moses "Moe" A. Aleman was working with General Dynamics as a contractor in the Dallas/Fort Worth area* at the time, as a lead investigator. Having previously worked as a Special Agent with the FBI in Miami and Tampa for four years, before moving on to General Dynamics, Mr. Aleman had a wealth of investigative experience, and was bi-lingual, having spoken Spanish since he learned to talk.

When General Dynamics began downsizing, Mr. Aleman put his name into the Federal Registry to look into positions with the federal government. He was contacted shortly after by the FAA at Dallas Love Field, and was asked to interview for a position as an Aviation Security Specialist. After a successful interview with Director Jim Murphy, Mr. Aleman accepted the position with the FAA, and soon after began working in the Office of Air Transportation Security. He took this position at a time when aircraft hijackings and other criminal acts targeting aviation were at an all-time high.

Moses Aleman would work in this position for the next 23 years, helping to build the fledgling Office of Air Transportation Security and working to bolster aviation security worldwide. In 1972, as he began a new career in aviation security, Mr. Aleman and the rest of the security professionals at the FAA would concentrate on implementing new screening procedures and other regulations, in an attempt to stem the violence from spilling over to more U.S. air carriers. Although the primary focus was directed at ground security, air piracy would continue to test the task force.

On June 3, 1972, Western Airlines Flight 701, from Los Angeles to Seattle, was hijacked by Black Panthers. The hijackers demanded a ransom, and after they received the money, they let the passengers get off in San Francisco before flying to Algeria. In Algeria, the hijackers were granted political asylum.

With the increasing demand for beefing up airport security in 1972, Steve Rustad was working ground duties as a CSO in San Francisco when the first magnetometers** were introduced at the airport.[103] The magnetometers had

---

[103] (Rustad, 2011 - 2012)
*More commonly referred to as the Dallas/ Ft. Worth Metroplex.
**Metal Detector.

been in use at a limited number of airports, such as in the nation's capital, and those that were considered high-risk. Up until 1972, the USMS had not yet implemented a program at SFO. Initially the magnetometers introduced by Mr. Blank and the USMS were focused on the eastern seaboard, due to the heavier volume of commercial/ international flights in those locations, along with their location in respect to tempting terrorist targets.[104]

Prior to 1972, the men and women working at SFO as CSOs were still performing hand screening of carry-on luggage. This was done on long tables just prior to boarding, while passengers watched as CSOs rummaged through their personal belongings. In 1972, the Magnetron brand magnetometer first appeared at SFO; this coincided with the introduction of that particular model of magnetometer.

The USMS sky marshal program was still in effect at this time, but had started to wind down. They had helped implement the first screening procedures on the east coast, including such high-risk airports as JFK and Dulles. They had also established the first sky marshal program, prior to the Dawson's field event. Their service during this period, in conjunction with the FAA, was instrumental in helping the U.S. establish an effective and viable civil aviation security program.

On May 8, 1972, four terrorists hijacked Belgian National Airlines Flight 571, a Boeing 707 aircraft, shortly after take-off. The hijackers were from the Black September Organization (BSO) and the flight was from Vienna, Switzerland, to Tel Aviv, Israel. The BSO had been founded two years prior, and was a group of Palestinian militants, much like the PFLP. Upon landing at Lod International Airport, in Lod, Israel, the terrorists separated the passengers into two groups: Jewish and non-Jewish. They forced the Jewish passengers to the rear of the aircraft.

Israel had always been well prepared for terrorist acts inside its own country, and the group known as Sayeret Matkal readied for a rescue mission upon the aircrafts arrival in Lod. Sayeret Matkal was a special military group assigned to the military intelligence directorate of the Israeli government. The Special Forces group specialized and trained for such rescue operations, and prepared themselves further by donning aircraft mechanics coveralls when arriving at the airport.

As over 90 passengers onboard watched, the Sayeret Matkal boarded the aircraft, under the guise that the aircraft needed repairs. They killed two of the ter-

---

[104] (Rustad, 2011 - 2012)

rorists and took the other two as prisoners. This terrorist act showed that commercial aircraft continued to be a tool for gaining attention of the world media. Palestinian groups had been trying for many years to gain power and establish a Palestinian state. The BSO, in particular, had tried to gain the release of 315 Palestinian terrorists held in Israel during the hijacking of Flight 571.

Two months later, on July 31, 1972, Delta Airlines Flight 841[105] was hijacked by five members of the Black Liberation Army, including the elusive George Wright*. This particular flight was scheduled to fly from Detroit to Miami. The aircraft, a DC-8, was hijacked by the criminals, whom had boarded the aircraft with three children in tow. The aircraft landed in Miami, where the passengers were exchanged for a $1 million dollar ransom. The plane then headed on to Boston for refueling, before flying on to Algeria**. The aircraft was returned to Delta Airlines after the hijacking, and the hijackers went on to be released by the Algerians, escaping U.S. custody. Incidents like these showed that terroristic and criminal acts targeting aviation were heating up, and international terrorism was on the rise as well.

Two months after the hijacking of Flight 841, the Olympics in Munich were underway. The Black September Organization was sending their-own representatives to Munich, however, they were not athletes. From September 5-6, the world watched as terrorists took Israeli athletes hostage. The terrorists eventually took the hostages to the Munich airport and executed them. The event was deeply disturbing for Israel. For many around the world, it was the first realization of the rising threat of international terrorism.

The threat to airports and airline personnel continued to be high at this time as well, and on October 29, 1972, four convicts killed a ticket agent in Houston, TX. The fugitives went on to hijack an Eastern Airlines Boeing 727 aircraft, taking the plane and passengers from Houston to Cuba.

Only two weeks after the Eastern Airline hijacking and murder of ticket agent Stanley Hubbard, another hijacking event took place. This event would be grossly mismanaged by the FBI, and force a government-wide review of law enforcement protocols for response to a hijacking.

---

[105] (Aleman, 2012)
* George Wright had been convicted of murder in 1962, and later escaped from prison in 1970, just prior to the hijacking of Flight 841.
**This plan was most likely hatched due to the success of the Western Airlines Flight 701 hijacking, during which the hijackers had received asylum in Algeria.

On November 10, 1972, a Southern Airways Douglas DC-9 aircraft, Flight 49, was scheduled to fly from Birmingham to Montgomery, Alabama. Three men onboard were then facing criminal charges for other crimes and shortly after take-off, Melvin C. Cale, Louis Cale, and Henry D. Jackson, brandished firearms and hand grenades and commandeered the aircraft. They demanded a $10 million ransom.

The three hijackers had the aircraft flown to multiple locations throughout the United States, before finally diverting the aircraft to Cuba. Unfortunately for the hijackers, President Fidel Castro refused the hijackers pleas for asylum and the plane was again forced to take-off. The plane was then flown to Orlando, Florida, where the hijackers talked about having the plane flown to Switzerland. Due to the aircrafts limited range, this would not be possible. Instead, they threatened to crash it into the nuclear reactor at Oak Ridge National Laboratory. One of the hijackers was quoted as saying, *"I'm not playing. If you don't get the money together, I'm gonna crash this plane into Oak Ridge."* [106]

The plane took-off again, shortly after a barrage of threats by the hijackers, and then stopped at McCoy Air Force Base, in Orlando, where the FBI was waiting. While in Orlando, the FBI attempted to stop the airplane from taking-off, and shot out two of the DC-9's four main tires. This enraged the hijackers and prompted them to shoot and injure the co-pilot, forcing Captain William Haas to take-off. The plane was subsequently flown back to Cuba, onto a partially foam-covered runway in Havana, where the Cuban authorities met the flight and forcibly removed the hijackers.

This incident caused rage amongst many U.S. congressmen, and led to heated talks about the response of the FBI and their actions in Orlando. Prior to the incident, the main responder to aircraft piracy *was* the FBI, and they were well within their scope of responsibility. This incident, however, brought up the question whether the FBI should retain this control. Congress would also look at procedures and legal issues involving the law enforcement response to aircraft hijackings. [107]

The outcome from this query was that the *FAA* would be in charge during an attempted hijacking, or in the event of air piracy, not the FBI. The FAA would now take the lead in enforcing laws. These laws, governing how the FAA operated - in a quasi-law enforcement capacity- would also change. Again, they

---

[106] (Wikipedia, Southern Airways Flight 49)
[107] (Blank, 2010)

would look into the definition of in-flight, and who's responsibility it was when the aircraft was in-flight.

Specifically, prior to the hijacking of Southern Airways Flight 49, an aircraft was considered *in-flight* even when the doors were ajar. Congress changed this and enacted law which gave the FAA authority when the aircraft was *in-flight*, re-defining the term. An aircraft was from then on to be considered in-flight, when the main cabin door was closed. This had all been changed in response to the actions of the FBI at McCoy Air Force Base, on November 10, 1972.

Another interesting thing about the Flight 49 hijacking was that it was one of the first of many threats that would be made by hijackers throughout history, of using an aircraft as a suicide-missile. This particular instance referred to flying the aircraft into a nuclear reactor. Nuclear facilities had long been aware of the threat from this type of attack, and contingencies had been included in vulnerability assessments and physical security measures at nuclear facilities for some time. This was, however, a very real and devastating form of attack, much like the Kamikaze pilots of World War II. Although this type of attack had never fully played out, civil aviation security personnel at the FAA were aware of the threat potential.[108]

By the end of 1972, more than 150 U.S. flagged aircraft had been hijacked since 1930; the majority had been perpetrated by escape artists, fugitives, and Black Panthers. Most of these had been hijacked to Cuba. Between 1968 and 1972, there was an average of 29 hijackings per year, which came out to more than two per month. Hijackings to Cuba became so-routine, that U.S. airline's and their pilots began carrying approach plans for Havana airport. The hijackings occurring in the rest of the world, however, were mostly terrorism related, while those in the U.S. were all criminal in nature. [109]

Flight 49 also forced the FAA to issue an emergency rule on December 5, 1972, calling for the mandatory inspection of *all* carry-on baggage by January 5, 1973. This rule, including the mandatory use of magnetometers, coincided with the end of the Task Force on Deterrence of Air Piracy, and seemed to send a message that this rule would be a *"cure-all"* for the violence plaguing civil aviation. If a magnetometer was not available, then, according to the rule, passengers would have to undergo a pat down and body search. Any passengers not complying with these rules, or refusing a search, would not be permitted to board.

---

[108] (Blank, 2010)
[109] (Aleman, 2012)

On March 13, 1973, the Director of the Office of Air Transportation Security thanked the *Task Force on Deterrence of Air Piracy* for their contributions to airline security, and highlighted some of their accomplishments. He said that they were, *"of paramount importance in helping to bring the hijacking menace to a halt,"* and *"they formed the spinal column of the anti-hijack program until January 5, 1973."* [110]

David Hubbard, a psychologist with the FAA at the time, had worked along-side Joseph Blank and John Marsh on the anti-air piracy task force. Mr. Hubbard worked with this team in putting together a new profile of hijackers as directed by the U.S. government. To help the task force do this, they poured over re-search material which outlined every hijacking that had occurred up to that point, for both foreign and U.S. flagged aircraft, as well as information gathered from crew and passengers that had been present during a hijacking. [111]

Hubbard found that common responses of passengers during a hijacking were: *"History is being made, and I'm part of it"*; *"Gosh, I wonder what I'll see in Cuba"*; *"If they put us in a hotel, will there be any women?"* [112]

Also in 1973, during a speech, USMS Training Chief Jack Cameron noted that deputies serving as sky marshals made 3,457 total arrests. Of these, 348 were for passengers concealing firearms. The USMS records also indicated that shortly after his speech, the U.S. Marshals Service had officially ended their sky marshal program. This was mentioned as being due to the USCS starting to board international flights at random as part of their own sky marshal pro-gram. [113]

By the middle of 1973, the many new regulations the FAA had issued were in place for passenger screening, and the CSOs of the USCS performed many of these duties as ground assignments. They were being removed from in-flight security duties at a rapid rate. The CSO Dennis Fagan was involved in carrying out ground assignments, as had his colleagues. However, when he was not per-forming CSO duties at the airport, Dennis Fagan was flying. The airline he was assigned to fly missions on was Pan Am. [114]

---

[110] (H.L. Reighard, November 1978)
[111] (Hubbard, 1971)
[112] (Hubbard, 1971)
[113] (Customs T. D., January 1971 - August 1972)
[114] (Fagan, 2011)

Flying missions on Pan Am brought Mr. Fagan to many foreign destinations; he would continue to fly and perform ground duties throughout 1973 and into 1974, fulfilling both his sky marshal and CSO functions. He flew to Tehran, Beirut, and many other cities. He never had any problems in these countries, however, he said *"We had to be careful of the PLO*, and those kinds. But, we knew we were being photographed."*

Mr. Fagan recalled *"We went into Beirut one time and we got alerted that you had to be careful when you turned your weapon in. But then, we had to turn our weapon in on the ground when we got there to their Customs authorities. So, one of the guys on one of the missions before us, he went and picked up his weapon and picked up his rounds, and they didn't feel right. So when he got on the airplane he goes into the [bathroom] and, what they did was they took the heads off the rounds and emptied the powder. So what we started to do then is you never turned in the same ammunition you carried."*

He recalled his days as a sky marshal as some of the best days of his early federal law enforcement career. Mr. Fagan would later go on to become the Special Agent in Charge (SAC) of the U.S. Customs New York field office, and the Deputy Assistant Regional Commissioner for the south eastern region.

He traces the future success of his career to having been a sky marshal with the USCS. As he stated, *"getting the [job in the] sky marshal program, well that set the tone for the rest of my life. I mean, it gave me an ability to go further than I had ever thought I would have gone career wise."*

An article from U.S. Customs archives gave some insight into the years in which the USCS ran the sky marshal program, and ultimately outlined its transfer to the FAA in June 1974.

The article discussed the beginning of USCS responsibilities, as ordered in the Master Agreement signed on October 28, 1970. This agreement was formed between the Departments of Treasury and Transportation. The article told of the agreement having been set up as a two year crash program. It was later extended until June 25, 1974, because of the *"continuing threat of air piracy and terrorism."*[115]

---

[115] (Martin J. McDonnel, 1974)
*Labeled a terrorist organization by the U.S. and Israel until 1991, the Palestinian Liberation Organization, or PLO, carried out many attacks against Israel during the 1970s'.

The problems encountered following the signing of the Master Agreement were said to be *"novel and enormous."* Many delicate negotiations were necessary to establish how Customs personnel were to be supervised under the aegis of the U.S. Department of Transportation. [116]

These negotiations had eventually resulted in a jointly published *"Manual of Air Transportation Security,"* which successfully guided FAA and Customs personnel towards *"[a] harmonious and productive working relationship."*

Since it was planned that CSOs would be added to the Customs Patrol Officer (CPO) force upon termination of the Master Agreement, emphasis was devoted to this aspect of their formal training.*

Formal training for CSOs was said to have been reinforced by field refresher and on the job training, including legal and operational aspects of the patrol function. Also, CSOs were assigned to CPO duties whenever air security needs were fulfilled.

According to the U.S. Secret Service, whose personnel provided all weapons and training at TASOS, approximately 2.5 million rounds of ammunition were expended by CSOs during their weapons training; this averages out to over 1,400 rounds of ammunition for each CSO. As an additional precaution, no CSO was allowed to carry a duty weapon with which they had not first qualified.

Within seven months of signing the Master Agreement, the Customs Bureau had fielded a trained force of 1,373 Customs Security Officer's and 125 supervisory, clerical, and support personnel, including a five-man Special Agent staff at headquarters. Included among these CSOs were the first women ever hired by Customs into its 1899 personnel series; the 1899 government series designation, at the time, was that of an entry level Customs Inspector. The first four women were hired by the Bureau of Customs in the summer of 1971.

One year after signing the Master Agreement, CSOs: [117]

- Made 800 flights,

---

[116] (Martin J. McDonnel, 1974)

[117] (Customs T. D., January 1971 - August 1972)

* Customs Patrol Officer (CPO) is a position that survives to this day, under the U.S. Customs and Border Protection (USCBP), enforcing customs and immigration laws.

- Performed 4,200 ground screening and ground inspections each week, and
- By November 25, 1973, CSOs had inspected over 100 million passengers on the ground without one of these passengers going on to hijack an aircraft.

U.S. Customs archives goes on to state, that:

- CSOs made a total of 3,828 arrests, of which
- 48 were made aboard aircraft, and
- 21 in response to an announced or threatened hijacking, with
- 27 for other causes involving safety of the aircraft such as assaults on crew members.

Further, [118]

*CSOs made 320 other arrests on the ground for bomb hoaxes, sabotage, or hijacking threats, and
*Another 484 arrests were made of passengers with weapons who attempted to circumvent screening.
*There were also 1,474 arrests for illegal possessions of narcotics,
*1,409 arrests of illegal aliens, and
*95 arrests for such causes as being a fugitive from justice or for assault on the officer or airline personnel.

In addition to these statistics, CSOs seized or detained over 66,481 potentially lethal weapons from passengers during pre-departure screening and inspection.

Except for one tragic instance at JFK, where a deranged former mental patient overpowered and wounded two CSOs after they intercepted him on the airport apron*, all of the above police actions were carried out without firing a shot in the line of duty. Dennis Fagan recalled some of the events that took place

---

[117] (Martin J. McDonnel, 1974)
*The airport apron is a specific area within the Air Operations Area (AOA). The AOA of an airport is where ground operations, and the maneuvering of aircraft, take place. The apron specifically, is the area where aircraft are being serviced, and according to ICAO, it is the area *"intended to accommodate the loading and unloading of passengers and cargo, the refueling, servicing, maintenance and parking of aircraft, and any movement of aircraft, vehicles and pedestrians necessary for such purposes."*

that day when two CSOs were injured. He had been working at one of the terminals in JFK, and was called to the scene: [119]

"We had two guys there at Kennedy airport, and I'm trying to think whether it was at the Pan Am terminal or the Eastern terminal, that were shot."

"One went on to become a DEA agent, and the other guy [sic] his name was McCarthy, I can't think of his first name, he was a retired Air Force Lt. Colonel and he went on to go with the National Transportation Safety Board. There was a guy, a nut job, a certified mentally ill person, and he went berserk in the terminal, and when they tried to control him he got hold of one of the [CSOs], and shot McCarthy."

"McCarthy got his leg shattered, because the guy shot McCarthy in the leg. And McCarthy used to tell us he had over 50 combat missions in Vietnam, and never got a scratch on him, and he goes to become a sky marshal, and is retired, and gets shot in the leg."

This was the only USCS incident during the sky marshal program which caused a weapon to be discharged in an airport. During this time, there were some gradual changes taking place in regards to ground and air security. This was in response to the investigation into the Southern Airways Flight 49 hijacking, and the FBI's handling of the incident. The changes also involved the downsizing of sky marshals, which was done due to the many successes of passenger screening implemented by airlines and airports, and the reliance on technology, such as the magnetometers by then in place at many U.S. airports. These changes would eventually lead to a halt of in-flight security duties and the very limited use of sky marshals on until the programs eventual termination. [120]

From the inception of the air security program until December 12, 1973, 153 CSOs had been converted to Special Agents, 466 to Customs Patrol Officers (CPOs), 168 to Customs Inspectors, eight to Import Specialists, and six to other positions within Customs; 137 other CSOs had accepted employment with other government agencies. [121]

Of the remaining 277 CSOs and 36 Supervisory CSOs (SCSOs), still employed after December 12, 1973, all became CPOs and Supervisory CPOs (SCPOs) prior to the program's official termination on June 25, 1974, which ended with ceremonies at Washington National Airport.

---

[119] (Fagan, 2011)
[120] (Blank, 2010), (Marsh, 2011), (Wikipedia, Southern Airways Flight 49)
[121] (Customs T. D., January 1971 - August 1972), (Martin J. McDonnel, 1974)

Customs Security Officers pioneered and proved the efficacy of the ground search procedures which are now applied to all U.S. airports. They do not deserve all the credit, however, since the U.S. Marshals Service was also heavily involved in helping set up these screening procedures. The USMS had also used the FAA hijacker profile to try and keep hijackers, or potential problem passengers, from boarding aircraft prior to flight, like their counterparts at the U.S. Customs Service.

On November 25, 1973, the Customs Air Security Division was transferred from the Office of Investigations to the Office of Operations. This transfer of responsibility within the Customs Service culminated three-years of law enforcement support to the nation's overall air security program, even though the extension called for continuing duties through June 1974, before being handed back over to the FAA. [122]

There was much work to be done before this handover would be complete. Airlines would continue flying scheduled routes, and would continue to remain vulnerable to the ever increasing terrorist threat: The two airlines with the most exposure to this threat were TWA and Pan Am.

On December 17, 1973, Pan Am Flight 110, a Boeing 707 aircraft, was scheduled to fly from Rome to Tehran. Prior to closing the aircrafts main cabin door in first class, commotion was heard from the terminal. Machine gun fire and explosions echoed through the jet bridge attached to the Boeing 707, and Captain Andrew Erbeck ordered everyone onto the floor. The noises that were heard came from six to ten Palestinian gunmen whom had removed assault rifles and incendiary grenades from their carry-on bags, firing into the air.

Some of the passengers onboard were able to catch a peak at some of the gunmen as they ran onto their flight and threw objects into the open door. Fire erupted in the first class cabin shortly after; the objects had been the incendiary devices, and smoke began to billow out into the jet bridge. In the panic and moments that followed, a flight attendant activated one of the emergency exits and passengers made a rush for the slide that would bring them to the ground, and away from the terror inside. Passengers crawled over each other, stepping on dead bodies as they moved through the thick smoke. Over twenty-nine passengers perished in the horror, including Purser* Diana Perez. [123]

---

[122] (Blank, 2010), (Noble, 2011)

[123] (Death in Rome Aboard Flight 110, December 31, 1973)

*The Purser of a flight is the lead flight attendant, responsible for managing all flight attendants onboard.

The gunmen continued their rampage in the terminal, ultimately ending up on a Lufthansa Airlines Boeing 737 aircraft. They took the plane and passengers on a long hijacking escapade, from Rome to Athens, to Syria, and finally Kuwait. They were later released by the authorities in Kuwait and returned to Palestine. [124]

With the U.S. Marshals Service having already retired its sky marshal program, and with the winding down of the U.S. Customs Service's *own* sky marshal program, the specialists within the FAA's aviation security program, along with many analysts in U.S. intelligence, still had an overwhelming concern for the threat to commercial aviation. The disturbing events happening overseas were alarming many in government. It appeared that terrorist acts against aircraft, along with the many criminal acts, would continue to be a problem as the sky marshal program was preparing to be shut down.

On February 17, 1974, a U.S. Army private, Robert K. Preston, stole a UH-1 helicopter and flew it over the White House. The private was reportedly upset over not being able to continue on with his helicopter training, and had staged the incident to show his skill. He was shot from the ground by secret service agents and forced to land. This event was said to have inspired what would happen only five days later. [125]

On February 22, 1974, a plan to use an aircraft as a weapon of mass destruction unfolded. It started when a man by the name of Samuel Byck drove to Baltimore/ Washington International Airport and shot and killed Maryland Aviation Police Officer George Neal Ramsburg, before storming onto a Delta Airlines DC-9 aircraft. [126]

The flight, Flight 523 to Atlanta, was the closest flight ready to take-off, and Byck seized this opportunity to hijack the aircraft. Captain Doug Loftin, and co-pilot Fred Jones told Byck that the aircraft could not take-off until wheel blocks were removed, at which time Byck shot them both. First Officer Fred Jones later died of his injuries.

Local police officers attempted to shoot-out the tires of the plane, but their bullets would not penetrate the thick skin. Byck's plan was to fly an aircraft into

---

[124] (Aleman, 2012), (Wikipedia, List of Aircraft Hijackings)
[125] (Holden)
[126] (Aleman, 2012), (Wikipedia, Samuel Byck), (Mueller, 2004)
* Byck committed suicide before law enforcement officers could apprehend him.

the White House to kill President Nixon. The plot was planned and inspired by the theatrics of the U.S. Army private five days earlier.

He also carried a gasoline bomb with him and threatened a flight attendant with it during the hijacking, telling her to close the aircraft door. Byck was prevented from carrying out his plan*, however it signaled a change of many past hijacking attempts and turned the FAAs profiling tools on their heads.

Byck's hijacking was a deviation from those in the past, such as those in which a hijacker usually demanded something. With Byck, the hijacker simply wanted to turn an aircraft into a large missile, in order to cause destruction through suicide. Byck's hijacking attempt was later portrayed in a movie called *"The Assassination of Richard Nixon."*

On June 11, 1974, reorganization within the Office of Air Transportation Security at the FAA began with the creation of a new position, *Associate Administrator for Aviation Safety*, which would have oversight of the newly named *Civil Aviation Security Service*. The position of Administrator for Aviation Safety, and its governing of the new Civil Aviation Security Service, would lead to later issues over *safety vs. security* and the FAA/airline relationship. The question would later be raised whether an Administrator, whose main role was geared towards *safety*, could be refrained from being cow-towed by the airlines when it came to *security* issues. [127]

Later, on June 25, 1974, all duties regarding civil aviation security were officially handed back over to the FAA. This began another transition in the history of the air marshals. With the implementation of new passenger screening procedures and the use of magnetometers, air marshals would begin seeing a decline in their numbers, as the FAA took back over the program. [128]

From their inception in 1962, to re-acquiring the program on June 25, 1974, the air marshals had seen quite a fluctuation in their numbers over the years. Starting with only 18 in-flight security personnel, to the use of hundreds of agents from various law enforcement agencies as well as military professionals, the security function saw its numbers dwindle again to pre-surge levels.

In the middle of 1974, while Moses Aleman was working as an Aviation Security Specialist with the FAA in Dallas, Texas, he was approached by FAA managers and asked to apply for a lateral transfer to FAA Headquarters in Washington DC; the FAA was interested in having bi-lingual speakers at the

---

[127] (Blank, 2010), (Marsh, 2011)
[128] (Martin J. McDonnel, 1974)

new Civil Aviation Security Service. Mr. Aleman applied for the transfer and eventually left with his family for the nation's capital. He would work closely with other aviation security professionals in this position, helping to write numerous security procedures which would eventually govern security at every airport in the world. [129]

As Mr. Aleman was moving his family east, the FAA was taking over responsibility for the only in-flight security personnel in the U.S. government; the small group of air marshals they had employed over the years would be the last of thousands flying only months before. With the close of another chapter within the air marshal history, came another change – a changing of the guard for the Director of Aviation Security – James T. Murphy would leave to work as the Deputy Director of the Metropolitan Washington airports, while Richard F. Lally would step up from his previous position as the Deputy Director, to that of Director. This would put Mr. Lally in charge of all civil aviation security, as well as the approximately 12 remaining active air marshals. [130]

A new chapter was beginning with this new handover of responsibility, and end of the Master Agreement. Airport security was surely more capable than it was at the beginning of the decade. The many civil aviation security professionals working at the FAA would continue to seek new solutions towards safeguarding commercial aviation in the United States. As hijackings and bombings would continue, these case studies would begin to suggest a need for regulation governing solutions and enhancements to airport and aviation security in general.

Richard Lally was just starting to realize this as the transition was taking place in June 1974. The dedicated team at his disposal were learning from terrorists and criminals, and their research was suggesting a need for new regulation to govern airport and aviation security in bold new ways.

---

[129] (Aleman, 2012)
[130] (Noble, 2011)

Chapter VI

Federal Air Marshal Program

FAA Civil Aviation Security Service
(June 25, 1974 – June 14, 1985)

Richard F. Lally seemed an easy fit for the position of Director of aviation security; he had worked alongside James Murphy since the inception of the Office of Air Transportation Security. Both men had worked with Joe Blank and were well acquainted with the work of the FAA task force, as well as the security procedures and regulations in place at the time. The number of air marshals would remain low, between 10 and 12, and Mr. Lally's focus would be on further shaping the Civil Aviation Security Service and its ground security programs. [131]

The newly reorganized Civil Aviation Security Service would have five divisions: intelligence, technical, air security, ground security, and administration. Richard "Dick" Noble became the manager of the ground security division and began drafting what would be called Federal Aviation Regulation (FAR) Part

---

[131] (Blank, 2010), (Marsh, 2011), (Noble, 2011)

107, which was part of Title 14 of the Code of Federal Regulations (CFR); titled *Airport Security*, FAR Part 107 would later gain traction, and eventually govern security at virtually every airport across the nation and the world.*

A man by the name of John "Jack" Hunter was part of the team writing FAR Part 107; he was an attorney by trade and had worked with Dick Noble for some time. Mr. Hunter had been brought into the aviation security domain with the help of family connections; his father was Regional Legal Counsel with the FAA. A brilliant man, *"bordering on genius,"* [130] Jack Hunter helped write numerous aviation security directives going forward and would play a momentous role over a decade later, in the expansion of the future Federal Air Marshal Program. [132]

The drafting of FAR 107 was a long process that involved numerous hurdles and a mountain of bureaucracy. While these regulations began forming, and as the official handover of all civil aviation security had just occurred, the FAA seized this opportunity to distinguish its in-flight security personnel from previous programs. In order for it not to be confused with the sky marshal program, the FAA called their in-flight security personnel, housed within its air security division, *Federal Air Marshals***. In some public articles they were still referred to as sky marshals, however, officially they were *air marshals*. [133]

The FAA had resumed command of air piracy duties mostly because of the issues that arose from the Southern Airways Flight 49 incident. Although it was

---

[132] (Vincent, 2009 - 2010)
[133] (Blank, 2010), (Vincent, 2009 - 2010)
*Title 14 (14 CFR) is titled *Aeronautics and Space*. The U.S. Code precedes the CFR. U.S. Code is enacted by Congress, and CFRs further define certain areas for interpretation by the executive branch. The *Aeronautics and Space* CFR has many chapters, and includes such topics as flight simulation training, medical standards and certification, special air traffic rules, and airport security.
Under Title 14, of the Code of Federal Regulations (CFR), CFR Part 107 is titled *Airport Security*. It covers many security functions and requirements for an airport, such as the establishment of Security Identification Display Area's (SIDA), that require badging for all employees, and specific badge markings for access control, background checks for employees, physical security systems in key locations, law enforcement duties/agreements, and other key security functions.
** As the new Civil Aviation Security Service grew other in-flight security officers would be trained as air marshals, to train a pool of Aviation Security Specialists in air marshal duties.

contractually agreed that the FAA would take over in-flight security responsibilities on June 25, 1974, the FBI's mismanagement of the Flight 49 hijacking made it that much easier. Along with the transition back to full FAA responsibility, the FAA would seek to further define their jurisdiction during a hijacking, as well as the definition of *in-flight*.

The number of air marshals that would be employed starting in 1974 would remain low; although some articles have suggested fewer than 100, making it appear as if the program was larger than it actually was, the actual number was between 15 and 20.* This would remain the case for the next decade.

The dedicated men and women re-designated as air marshals were constantly training. In the years to come, the air marshals and the FAA security program would continue to evolve. Just as the terrorists and criminals sought to learn from the weaknesses in physical security measures, the air marshals and the FAA Civil Aviation Security Service sought to meet the demands of ever changing threats to civil aviation security. The air marshals beginning in 1974 were comprised of FAA Inspectors. They came from various districts around the country, selected due to their geographic locations. For the next decade, the force would become an elite group, with a *club-like* atmosphere, and these FAA Inspectors would be trained for air marshal duties as a collateral assignment, like the FAA Peace Officers before them.

President Nixon signed the *Anti-Hijacking Act of 1974* on August 5, 1974, which would give him and other future U.S. President's, the authority to suspend air carrier service to countries that aided terrorist groups. It also further enabled the government to post warnings in U.S. airports and the *Federal Register**, notifying U.S. citizens of the countries and airports of those nation's that *did not* maintain minimum security standards.

While this was all happening, the air marshals were winding down their mission coverage of flights. The FAA inspectors designated as air marshals would fly very few missions, and in fact, would not fly at all for almost two years. However, even though there was little to no in-flight security coverage, criminal and other terrorist acts against aviation would continue.

On August 26, 1974, a Boeing 707 aircraft, originating in Athens, landed in Rome. TWA Flight 841 prepared to disembark passengers and remove baggage when smoke was seen coming from the cargo hold. After it was found that the smoke was due to a fire coming from one of the bags, the ramp workers put out the fire and notified Italian authorities. A man readily came forward to claim the bag in question and it was determined that a fire had started when the batteries of a tape player ignited lighter fluid also found in the bag. The man was released and continued on to an unknown destination. [134]

Within a week of the TWA 841 incident, and on September 2, 1974, an article came out in Time magazine talking about the end of the sky marshal program. This article, titled *The Last Marshal*, mentioned various aspects of the disbanded program and spotlighted the CSOs in-flight security roles, saying *"besides serving as plain clothes watch dogs, armed sky marshals wearing civilian clothes boarded commercial flights to thwart the would-be skyjacker."* It was also reported by the Department of Transportation in this article, that *"the last sky marshal was taken out of the air in June."* [135]

On September 8, 1974, TWA Flight 841, a Boeing 707 aircraft, departed Israel for Athens, where the plane exchanged passengers for the next leg to Rome; the final destination of the flight was JFK. After stopping in Athens, and approximately 30 minutes into its flight to Rome, TWA Flight 841 exploded and fell from the sky. All 88 persons onboard were killed, and only 24 bodies were pulled from the crash site in the Ionian Sea.

The FBI had received the bag of the passenger on TWA Flight 841, from the earlier bag-fire incident on August 26, and within ten days of the September 8, 1974 tragedy, it was determined that the bag in question had residue and particles of an unconsumed military explosive. From this evidence, it was thought that the destruction of TWA 841 over the Ionian Sea was due to a similar device, which, on September 8, had been successfully detonated.

On February 26, 1975, the FBI and FAA signed a new memorandum of understanding for hijackings and jurisdictional issues. The new memorandum further discussed the definition of *in-flight*, which had been the cornerstone of contention between the FBI and FAA for many years. This memorandum spelled out the new legal definition of *in-flight* as *"when all external doors were closed."*

Also, on April 1, 1975, the National Transportation Safety Board (NTSB), a body responsible for investigating all civil aviation accidents, finally gained separation from the Department of Transportation (DOT). It was announced by Congress that the NTSB could not properly do its job without a full separation from the DOT.

---

[134] (Board N. T.)
[135] (The Last Marshal, September 2, 1974)
*Daily journal of the United States Government.

On December 29, 1975, a bomb exploded in a coin-locker at New York's La Guardia Airport, killing 11 and injuring 75. There were no arrests made, nor a reason for why the bomb exploded, however, the bombing initiated the removal of all coin-lockers in the non-secure area of airports across the United States. [136]

Fiscal year 1975 was a quiet one for the new *FAA Federal Air Marshal Program*; there were no missions flown by air marshals during this entire reporting period.

From June 27 to July 4, 1976, the hijacking of Air France Flight 139, a Boeing A300 aircraft, played out for the world to see. The flight had departed from Tel Aviv, Israel, with 248 passengers and 12 aircrew members onboard. Shortly after take-off on June 27, two Palestinians from the PFLP and two Germans from German Revolutionary Cells, stood up and announced their intentions of hijacking the aircraft. [137]

Flight139 was initially diverted to Benghazi, Libya, where it refueled and one female passenger was released. The plane then left Benghazi on June 28, and diverted to Entebbe Airport in Uganda. [138]

At Entebbe airport, the four hijackers were joined by four others, with the support of pro-Palestinian forces on the ground. The hijackers demanded the release of 40 Palestinians held in Israel and 13 prisoners being held in Switzerland, France, Germany, and Kenya. They said that if their demands were not met, they would begin executing prisoners starting on July 1, 1976.

The hijackers separated prisoners into two groups: Israelis and others. This tradecraft by terrorist hijackers was a trend that had been seen for many years and one that would continue over the next decade, of specifically targeting Israeli and American citizens until terrorist demands were met.

Hostages at Entebbe were held for the next week, in the old terminal of the airport grounds. Some were released, but 106 still remained and the threats continued that the terrorists would begin killing hostages if their demands were not met.

Planning for a rescue operation by Israeli Special Forces had already begun; there were some diplomatic attempts to end the hostage situation at Entebbe, however these were to no avail. Instead, on July 4, 1976, a rescue operation took

---

[136] (Vincent, 2009 - 2010)
[137] (Aleman, 2012), (Wikipedia, Air France Flight 139)
[138] (Aleman, 2012), (Wikipedia, Air France Flight 139)

place. *Operation Entebbe* would use 100 commandos of the Israeli Defense Force (IDF), and would fly over 2,500 miles to rescue the hostages of Air France Flight 139. In the ninety -minute rescue mission, all hijackers were killed, along with 45 Ugandan soldiers; unfortunately, three hostages were also killed during the rescue.

The violence that ended the hijacking of Air France Flight 139 sent shock waves through the FAA and its aviation security counterparts worldwide. It signaled another violent change in hijackings and showed how far terrorists would go to further their cause.

On July 9, 1976, the only air marshal mission was flown for the entire fiscal year. It was the *first* mission flight since the FAA had resumed control over the air marshal program in 1974. The flight was from JFK to Miami (MIA), for unknown reasons. [139]

On September 10, 1976, TWA Flight 355, a Boeing 727 aircraft, was hijacked after take-off from New York's La Guardia Airport; the flight was en route to Chicago's O'Hare International Airport. The five Croatian hijackers claimed to have a bomb onboard and they also gave directions to a bomb they had planted inside a locker at Grand Central Station, in New York City. The plane was redirected to Montreal where it refueled. Here, the hijackers' demanded an appeal for Croatian independence printed in various U.S. newspapers.

While the hijacking unfolded, the bomb at Grand Central Station was found and brought to Rodman's Neck Firing Range* where law enforcement and bomb technicians tried to dismantle it. The bomb exploded instead and killed NYPD Police Officer Brian Murray. Officer Murray had been on the force for six years, and was survived by his wife and two children. Brain Murray became the first domestic death involving a terrorist act** against aviation. [140]

The hijacking ended in Paris, when the hijackers surrendered after talks with U.S. Ambassador Kenneth Rush. All passengers survived the ordeal, however

---

[139] (Administration F. A., FAA Archival Records - From 2001 Internal Report)
[140] (Murray, Brian)
*Rodman's Neck Firing Range was used by the U.S. Navy during World War I, and was later operated by the NYPD. One of the locations on the 54 acre plot is called *"The Pit"* and is used for demolitions training. This is where NYPD Officer Brian Murray was killed.
**TWA Flight 355 was not officially labeled as terrorism, although the event *was* politically motivated, and involved the death of an American Citizen.

the death of the Brain Murray underscored the lean towards violence in the hi-jackings of the mid to late 1970s', and the fact that terrorism could now be add-ed to the list of acts in the United States against a U.S. aircraft.

As the 1977 New Year celebrations came, the U.S. had already begun seeing a gradual uptick in the violence of aircraft hijackings over the past several years. These events were no longer fitting the revised FAA profile, and the trend of violent hijackings for extortion, political asylum, or by mentally deranged per-sons, continued to be a problem. The new hijackings were being well planned, by determined individuals who believed in their cause, and with the ever evolv-ing aviation security program at the FAA, and infant nature of that program at the time, criminals and terrorists had exploited the weaknesses.

As the Task Force on the Deterrence of Air Piracy had concluded in their report in 1968, "*[hijackers] apparently had concluded that it was easily possible to hijack the most impressive aircraft with very inferior weapons, that the possibility of failure was low, [and] the general public seemed to regard the matter [more] as a joke than a serious crime.*" [141]

Given the public's view that hijackings, were more of a joke "*than as a seri-ous crime,*" was another trend that appeared to continue into the latter half of 1970. Especially when the hijacked aircraft landed in other countries unfriendly to the U.S., many of the hijackers were released. The general public may not have been that concerned, since *none* of the domestic hijackings had been la-beled as terrorism. The majority of violent hijackings at this time were still oc-curring far away from U.S. soil and most Americans felt these acts would con-tinue to plague countries other than theirs. However, hijackings *would* continue to occur, and their escalating violence would challenge the FAA's aviation secu-rity program.

On October 13, 1977, at 11:00 a.m. local time, a Boeing 737 aircraft departed Palma de Mallorca, Spain, for Frankfurt, Germany. Four terrorists from the PFLP, calling themselves "*Commando Martyr Halime,*" breached the cockpit shortly after take-off, and with firearms brandished, they forced the captain to fly to Larnaca, Cyprus; Lufthansa Flight 181 would join the many others before them in the statistics of aircraft hijackings, with 36 passengers and three crew members onboard. [142]

Without enough fuel for the trip to Cyprus, Captain Jürgen Schumenn told the hijackers that the aircraft could only make Rome and would have to be refu-

---

[141] (H.L. Reighard, November 1978)
[142] (Aleman, 2012), (Blank, 2010), (Vincent, 2009 - 2010), (Tallion, 2002)

eled if the flight was to continue on. The hijackers had no choice but to allow the aircraft to fly to Rome for fuel.

The hijacking of Flight 181 was taken on a long hijacking escapade, first to Rome, then Bahrain, where a stand-off with military forces ensued, and finally Dubai, where the hijackers were provided food, water, medicine, and newspapers, as ground units were trying to figure out how to end the hijacking without bloodshed. The terrorists demanded the release of prisoners held in Italy and Turkey, and the tense stand-off in Dubai lasted until October 18, when the aircraft was allowed to depart Bahrain. The Boeing 737 lumbered down the runway and within minutes was airborne, with a destination of Aden, Yemen. [143]

Although there was an attempt to end the hijacking without military intervention, the counter-terrorist group GSG-9 (Grenzchutzgruppe 9) began training in Dubai for a rescue mission, with support from British SAS (Special Air Service) personnel. Before a response could begin, the hijacked aircraft had been allowed to take-off. As the hijackers were on the move, so was the rescue team; GSG-9 was able to get an aircraft to insert them wherever Flight 181 landed.

As rescue personnel scrambled to follow the aircraft, the Boeing 737 attempted a landing at the airport in Aden. Again, like previous landing attempts during many past hijackings, the runway had been blocked to prevent a landing. This had been a trend during the 1970s' as well, where many an aircraft had been hijacked and prevented landing, since the country *"receiving"* the aircraft did not want the problem or the international media attention that could potentially follow. Captain Schumenn was able to put the aircraft down on an adjacent strip, which was so sandy that he became concerned over possible problems with the landing gear once on the ground. Voicing this concern to the terrorists, Jürgen Schumenn was allowed to deplane to inspect the aircraft.

As the minutes passed, the hijackers became angry and worried that the captain was coordinating efforts for a rescue mission with Yemeni authorities. The leader of the terrorist team, Zohair Youssif Akache, began yelling for Schumenn to return. After several more minutes went by, the captain finally returned to the scorn of Akache. As co-pilot and First Officer Jürgen Vietor watched in horror, Captain Jürgen Schumenn was forced to kneel on the ground and was executed by a shot through the head by Akache. [144]

---

[143] (Aleman, 2012), (Blank, 2010), (Vincent, 2009 - 2010), (Tallion, 2002)
[144] (McLaughlin, 2011 - 2012)
*Operation Fire Magic.

Shortly after the brutal murder of the captain and refueling of the aircraft, the terrorists forced Vietor to make a hasty departure from Yemen. They were now headed for Mogadishu, Somalia.

On October 18, 1977, at approximately 6:22 a.m. local time, Flight 181 landed in Mogadishu; the aircraft had flown over 6,000 miles since the beginning of the hijacking. As the aircraft sat on the ground and passengers continued to fear for their lives, GSG-9 was en-route and prepared to assault the aircraft after insertion in Mogadishu.

At 8:00 p.m., the assault and rescue operation had begun. *Operation Feuerzauber** must have been quite a fireworks display for the 86 passengers that night. It was reported that the British SAS were acting as advisors and had brought their "flashbang"* devices, which they had developed in the 1960s' as non-lethal explosives, or *stun grenades*, used to disorient the enemy. The information available on whether these flashbang devices were used during the operation is conflicting; however, the name of the operation seems to suggest they were.

"*I saw the door open and a man appear. His face was painted black and starts shouting in German "We're here to rescue you, get down!"" and then he started shooting,*" reported a passenger. All eighty-six passengers were rescued in the operation, and three of the four hijackers were killed. Unfortunately, with the death of Captain Jürgen Schumenn, the hijacking was, for the FAA Civil Aviation Security Service, a signal that the terrorist hijackings occurring internationally were continuing to become ever more violent.

On December 4, 1977, another violent act occurred on a civilian aircraft. Malaysia Airlines Flight 653 was said to have been hijacked shortly after reaching cruising altitude, although to this day the case remains unsolved. During the flight, the Captain had radioed back to the tower of the Kuala Lumpur airport from which the aircraft departed and relayed that they had been hijacked by "*an unidentified hijacker.*" The captain told air traffic control, "*We're now proceeding to Singapore.*" [145]

The Malaysian Airlines flight would go on to crash, and all onboard would perish; of the 100 dead, one was a U.S. citizen. The after accident investigation report indicated that there was likely an autopilot disconnect due to "*[a] possible pitch input by someone entering the cockpit to try and control the aircraft.*" Some went on to speculate that there was a deliberate attempt to crash it. There

---

[145] (Aleman, 2012), (Wikipedia, Malaysian Airlines Flight 653)
*The stun grenade was developed by the British SAS in the 1960s'.

were noises heard in the cockpit voice recording that were indicative of a struggle, with *"[a] reasonable amount of screaming and cursing."*

In fiscal year 1977, there were no air marshal missions flown. One possible reason there were no missions, may have been due to the fact that hijackings occurring in the U.S. during this time were all criminal and *not* terroristic in nature. The FAA did not seem to see a need in using their in-flight security personnel at this time. However, criminal acts on U.S. aircraft would continue to transpire. [146]

On March 13, 1978, United Airline (UA) Flight 696, a Boeing 727 aircraft, was hijacked. The flight serviced the Seattle/Tacoma International Airport (SEA) to SFO route. The hijacking occurred shortly after take-off from SFO, and was immediately diverted to Oakland International Airport (OAK) to fuel for Cuba.

The hijacker, an American named Clay Thomas, panicked and had the captain take-off before refueling was complete. The aircraft's next destination was Denver, where the crew eventually escaped by jumping from the cockpit windows. The hijacker later surrendered due to the loss of the crew and passengers. [147]

Throughout this time period, from June 25, 1974 to 1978, and since the FAA had resumed its in-flight security responsibilities, there had been only one mission flown by air marshals. This trend was destined to continue for some time. Hijackings *were* occurring, but the advent of the various security procedures and the use of magnetometers, and statistics based on those procedures, leant 'credibility' to keeping the number of air marshals, and air marshal missions, at a low level. By late 1978, only 15-20* air marshals remained with the FAA, and were *"stationed"* throughout the U.S. at their respective FAA Inspector offices. [148]

In July 1978, a meeting in Bonn, Switzerland took place on aviation security. To further strengthen the resolve of member states against acts of air piracy and criminal and terroristic threats targeting civil aviation, it was agreed that airline

---

[146] (Administration F. A., FAA Archival Records - From 2001 Internal Report)
[147] (Aleman, 2012), (Blank, 2010), (United Airlines Flight 696)
[148] (Blank, 2010), (McLaughlin, 2011 - 2012), (Vincent, 2009 - 2010)
*Although the number of air marshals retained by the FAA was closer to a dozen. This was the case since 1970, while over a thousand sky marshals were working for the USCS and USMS. Research suggests that starting sometime in the latter half of 1978, there were 15-20 air marshals working in the Civil Aviation Security Service.

service to countries who failed to extradite or prosecute hijackers would be terminated. The ability to stop airline service in countries that were soft on air piracy, would serve as incentive for those countries to uphold the various civil aviation conventions that had been agreed upon by so many others.

On December 21, 1978, a 17 year-old girl named Robin Oswald hijacked TWA Flight 541, a McDonnell Douglas DC-9 aircraft. The hijacker sought the release of Garrett Trapnell, who had hijacked TWA Flight 2, on January 29, 1972, and was being held in prison in Illinois. TWA Flight 541 had been en route from Louisville, KY, to Kansas City International Airport, when the girl stood up and said she had a bomb. Robin Oswald was recalled by passengers as *"a beautiful, but serious girl, never showing alarm at her actions."* [149]

The hijacker had threatened to blow up the plane with dynamite she had strapped to her body if her demands were not met; she was later talked out of the plane by FBI negotiators and the bomb was determined to be a fake.

There was a definite increase in the amount of hijackings by the end of 1978; there were a total of eight hijackings of U.S. air carriers during this year. Ever since all of the changes to ground security had been put in place, claims of hijackers to have bombs or firearms turned out to be false in every case; none of them had been able to bring a real weapon or explosive past the security screening checkpoints, lending further credibility to the FAA passenger screening program. [150]

By 1979, the FAAs air marshal program was still in a fledgling state; there would be no missions flown for the entire fiscal year. There were many threats to civil aviation security at this time, but the in-flight security role was not considered an important function; terrorism was not seen as a credible threat in the continental United States. It was a matter of fact, however, that there was a wealth of information coming from U.S. intelligence pointing to an increase in international terrorism plots, and there continued to be much turmoil in the Middle East.

On November 4, 1979, the U.S. embassy in Tehran, Iran, was seized by Islamic militants and students. In what would become known as the *Iran Hostage Crisis,* these hostages would be held for a total of 444 days and the crisis would last until their release on January 20, 1981.

---

[149] (Aleman, 2012), (Wikipedia, TWA Flight 541)
[150] (Vincent, 2009 - 2010), (Coll, Ghost Wars: The Secret History of the CIA, Afghanistan, and Bin Laden, from the Soviet Invasion to September 10, 2001, 2004)

Also, on November 20, 1979, a Saudi Arabian Islamic zealot, Juhayman al-Oteibi, took over the Grand Mosque in Mecca. Iran's Ayatollah Khomeini falsely claimed that Americans were behind the takeover, and declared this a deliberate attack on Islam's holiest site, the Masjid al-Hiram.

Radio reports informed Pakistani students of the takeover and relayed Khomeini's claims; that Americans were responsible for the attack on the Grand Mosque. On November 21, 1979, a protest ensued outside the U.S. embassy in Islamabad, Pakistan. Although the protest started out peacefully, it was later joined by supporters of Jamaat-i-Islami*, a far-right political group. This group swarmed the embassy, and in the mayhem led to people climbing over the embassy walls.

In the ensuing violence, a U.S. Marine Security Guard, Steve Crowley, was killed by a gunshot wound to the head. His death was the first in what would become a struggle with Islamic terrorist groups around the world, and the beginning of what would later become known as the *"War on Terror."*

The seizure of the Grand Mosque in Mecca continued through November, and was not over until December 4, 1979, when GIGN**, a French counter-terrorism group, was flown in by the Saudi government*** to help with the problem; they ended up killing many of the terrorists, wounding several others, and taking the rest prisoner. [151]

The excellent craftsmanship of the bin-Laden family construction company actually helped repel the many initial breaching attempts of the Saudi forces. One of the sons of the founder of that Saudi Arabian company was named Osama bin-Laden. Osama bin-Laden would later reach worldwide recognition as one of the most wanted men on the planet.

The rise of international terrorism and Islamic extremism kept the FAA busy, and security experts continued to write emergency rules for civil aviation security throughout 1979. One such rule was issued on March 29, which made it a federal offense to carry a firearm or explosive into the sterile area of a U.S. air-

---

[151] (Vincent, 2009 - 2010), (Coll, Ghost Wars: The Secret History of the CIA, Afghanistan, and Bin Laden, from the Soviet Invasion to September 10, 2001, 2004), (Commission, July 22, 2004), (Coll, The Bin Ladens: An Arabian Family in the American Century, 2008)
*Jamaat-i-Islami (JI), founded on August 24, 1941, is labeled as an Islamist political party.
**National Gendarmerie Intervention Group.
***The three GIGN operators were forced by the Saudi Government to convert to Islam before they were allowed to enter Mecca.

port. Prior to this emergency ruling, it was a crime *only* if a person carried a firearm or explosive *onboard* an aircraft. This was another productive step towards better airport security during dangerous times.

Also in 1979, there was a renaming of the Civil Aviation Security Service; it would now be called the *Office of Civil Aviation Security**, a step that would begin to secure its anonymity amongst the other departments within the FAA. This began a tear away from the safety function and the Administrator that oversaw it**, although it would take other drastic and tragic circumstances to divorce the relationship completely. [152]

With the national security concern over the many violent events in the Middle East, the intelligence community turned their focus to the radical Islamic problem plaguing the world. Civil aviation security was still haunted by the Cuban hijacking problem however, and while security experts studied the terrorist problem, another incident involving Cuba would kick the Federal Air Marshal Program back into gear.

In April 1980, Embassy Row in Havana was blockaded by demonstrators seeking political asylum from the Venezuelan and Peruvian embassies. Ten thousand people had become crammed into the Peruvian embassy grounds after word had spread. People climbed trees and buildings and refused to leave.

Media accounts in 1980 had helped to dismantle the already fragile relations between Cuba and the U.S., specifically with a May 11, 1980, New York Times article, which talked of the open arms policy of the Carter administration towards Cubans. The article had stated that most Cuban refugees were *"undesirables."*

In May 1980, the U.S. Navy dispatched the *USS Saipan* to support U.S. Coast Guard efforts in assisting Cubans who were attempting to flee via the Cuban city of Mariel. Having assisted the transport of the Cuban refugees to Florida, these refugees were given food, water, and other provisions, until it could be determined what to do with them. Eventually, it was decided these refugees would be sent to holding areas in Fort Chaffee, AR, and Fort Indiantown Gap, PA, to be processed.

---

[152] (Blank, 2010), (Noble, 2011)
*Richard Lally was still Director of Civil Aviation Security at this time.
** On March 5, 1980, the FAA got rid of the Office of Investigations and Security, and transferred all responsibility to the new Office of Civil Aviation Security.

The *Mariel boatlift* would have a direct impact on the Federal Air Marshal Program within the FAA. Since the FAA only had approximately 15-20 air marshals at this time, they had to find a way to train more, in order to assign in-flight security duties and assistance in the transportation of the Cuban refugees from Florida, to refugee camps in Arizona and Pennsylvania*. [153]

In the 1980's, the FAA owned both Washington National and Dulles Airports. There were FAA Police Officers who patrolled the grounds at these airports. The FAA Police were thought of as a good force to utilize for air marshal duties. Thus, due to the Mariel boatlift crisis and the need for air marshals to assist with the transportation of Cuban immigrants taking place on government aircraft, FAA Police at Washington National and Dulles airports became Federal Air Marshals.**

As one former air marshal from the 1980s' summed up the change, *"They just came in one day and said, "OK, now you're not just FAA Police, you are FAA air marshal"."* [154]

On June 25, 1980, a Black Muslim*** hijacker commandeered a Delta Airlines L-1011 aircraft, and forced the plane to Cuba. Although hijackings of aircraft to Cuba were rare at this time, this hijacking was important, because it was the first one in which real weapons and explosives had passed through airport security undetected since the FAA emergency rule was implemented some eight years prior, on December 5, 1972, which required the mandatory inspection of all carry-on baggage. [155]

Two days after the hijacker brought weapons and explosives through a security checkpoint, and as FAA Police took to the skies to help with Cuban transport, and criminals and terrorists continued to target civil aviation, an accident involving the militaries of four countries claimed 81 lives on a commercial aircraft.

On June 27, 1980, four military jet fighters, from four separate countries, were working in concert to attempt the assassination of the President of Syria,

---

[153] (Wikipedia, Mariel Boat Lift).
[154] (McLaughlin, 2011 - 2012)
[155] (Aleman, 2012)
*The Cuban's would either be granted asylum or sent back to Cuba
**This would greatly increase the numbers of Federal Air Marshals.
***Later, Black Muslims would be targeted by terrorist groups, especially those with easy access to the target country, such as a U.S. passport holder, with free access to travel around the world. (WND, 2007)

Muammar Qaddafi*. During the operation, Qaddafi's aircraft escaped the noose that had been closing in on him, and while three of the four jet fighters returned to their respective bases, a French Mirage pursued what, the pilot thought, was the target aircraft.

At 8:59 p.m. local time, a DC-9 passenger aircraft, en route to Palermo, Sicily, disappeared from radar; Aerolinee Itavia Flight 870 had been headed to Sicily from Bologna, Italy, with 77 passengers, two pilots, and two crew members onboard. This was an embarrassing incident and a tragic one, and the attempted cover up would be a political embarrassment for the French government.

By early December 1980, there were over 100 new air marshals flying missions, working part time as FAA Police; however, some FAA Police were designated as both FAA Federal Air Marshal and FAA Police but *never flew* any missions. Also, in early December, a man by the name of Billie Vincent came onboard as the *Special Assistant of Flight Standards* for the FAA. The invasion of Afghanistan by the Soviet Union started soon after Mr. Vincent assumed this role.

Of course, the Flight Standards Division within the FAA was responsible for all aspects of aviation safety, and throughout the 1960s' had housed the original 18 FAA Peace Officers. When Mr. Vincent came onboard, he had already had an extremely successful career within the FAA for over 20 years, and he would bring a wealth of experience and contacts with him to Flight Standards as well. [156]

Billie H. Vincent was born in the hills of Tennessee, outside what is now the Kentucky Dale Hollow Resort State Park. At 17 years of age he left Tennessee to join the U.S. Air Force, where he worked as an air traffic controller for four years. After working in Tokyo, Japan, and several other locations, Mr. Vincent left the military and took a job with the CAA prior to the change to the FAA, in March of 1957. He quickly rose through the ranks of the FAA and made an unprecedented rise through the ranks as an air traffic controller, reaching journeyman status in less than a year. [157]

The typical air traffic controller took a minimum of four years to reach journeyman status, and they had a 60% failure rate. Mr. Vincent would go on to serve as a supervisor for air traffic controllers at Indianapolis Center in 1968, and then as Chief of New York Center in 1971.

---

[156] (Vincent, 2009 - 2010)
[157] (Vincent, 2009 - 2010)
*Muammar Qaddafi took office as the leader of Libya in 1969.

Eventually, Mr. Vincent ended up on the executive staff for the Director of Air Traffic Control, and worked on Capitol Hill in this capacity during 1981. Here, Mr. Vincent used his training and experience learned at the War College in Montgomery, Alabama, during the mid-1970s'.

When Mr. Vincent was placed as the Special Assistant of Flight Standards in December 1980, he became a man of many hats. He was very familiar with the processes in place at the FAA by this time, having been a veteran of the FAA, and he set out to make a difference in his newly appointed role. One of Mr. Vincent's duties was to help manage operations of the remaining air marshal force, which numbered approximately 100 at the time.

The remaining force was a small and dedicated crew. They would come to know Billie Vincent well over the next several years. Their excellent training and remarkable marksmanship can be attributed to what Mr. Vincent would implement during his tenure. Mr. Vincent believed that these dedicated men and women should get the best training necessary to perform their jobs and he would give them nothing less. Mr. Vincent began tapping sources within the military for help with training, which eventually led to cross-training and tactics development with the help of U.S. Army Special Forces. [158]

As a member of the Interagency Group on Terrorism (IGT)*, Mr. Vincent was constantly in touch with various military commanders and other people closely involved in terrorism issues, and his net of contacts grew immensely. Due to the events happening in the late 1970s' and early 1980s', in regards to international terrorism, Mr. Vincent was being briefed by the IGT on these issues since they were at the forefront of concern. As he noted, *"I was sitting their reading and discussing high grade intelligence that was sometimes outside of the classified arena. The information that I was being given was highly alarming."* He also began making some contacts in the military and the special operations community through members of the IGT.

These contacts helped Mr. Vincent draw on expertise from various specialized groups, for running mock scenarios for his air marshal force. They also began planning for contingencies in case the need arose for him to draw on contacts from the military or other law enforcement agencies in response to a hi-

---

[158] (Vincent, Interviews of Billie H. Vincent; former Director of Civil Aviation Security for FAA (1982 - 1986), 2009 - 2010)
*The IGT was a precursor to the modern day National Security Council (NSC).

jacking. It was at this time that the FAA started making plans for a coordinated response to civil aviation security threats.

There were over one-hundred air marshals across the country at this time, trained for in-flight security duty. One young air marshal assigned to the Los Angeles airport from 1980 to 1982, was a woman by the name of Lynne Osmus. Mrs. Osmus had started a career with the FAA in 1979, out of Washington DC. [159]

In early 1980, she had noticed an announcement for the air marshal force, which was advertised as a position out of Los Angeles. This was a GS-12* position; however, she was only a GS-5. She applied for the FAA Inspector position anyway, and due to a need for more manpower and not enough qualified applicants, she managed to get the job. Mrs. Osmus never flew any missions in this capacity, and mainly performed ground duties at Los Angeles International Airport (LAX) as an inspector. There were only one or two other women serving as an FAA Inspector/Federal Air Marshal at the time. Lynne Osmus would go on to play an important role in air marshals history two decades later, throughout which time she would excel at her career at the FAA.

On March 2, 1981, Pakistan Airlines Flight 326**, a Boeing 720 aircraft, was hijacked shortly after take-off from Karachi, Pakistan. Three Pakistani militants forced the pilot to divert the aircraft to Kabul, Afghanistan, and began to make demands for the release of 92 political prisoners being held in Pakistan. Five days later, on March 7, after receiving word that their demands would not be fulfilled, the militants executed Tariq Rahim, a Pakistani diplomat, and dumped his body onto the tarmac. They also began making threats of killing the three Americans onboard; they had already collected passports from passengers and had singled out westerners.

On March 9, the aircraft landed in Damascus, Syria. As negotiations for the release of passengers continued, the Pakistani government caved in to the hijackers' demands and freed 55 prisoners being held by the Zia ul-Haq*** regime.

In 1981, air marshal missions took a dip. There was only one mission flown during the year, was reported as being "*Related to the Georgetown, Guyana*

---

[159] (Osmus, 2010, 2012)
*GS-12 refers to the Government Schedule (U.S. Civil Service Pay Scale).
**The flight was a domestic one, and serviced Peshawar, Pakistan, from Karachi.
***Zia ul-Haq staged a Coup d'êtat in 1978, and ruled Pakistan until 1988.

'James Jones' cult murders of 1978." Although no specific information exists on why air marshals flew in relation to the James Jones cult murders, which occurred three years prior, there were, at the time, Hmong refugees living in the old Jonestown encampment. The flights may have been in support of these refugees, or a specific threat in regards to their presence in the camp. [160]

Going into 1982, there were again no missions flown. Having only one mission flown in the previous year, there seemed to be a return to mission trends of the late 1970s. In retrospect, this was strange amidst the international crisis and terrorist threats towards civil aviation happening at the time. The FAA was still stuck on trying to shore up ground security, and the air marshals, again, took a back-seat role, to be used rarely.

By May 1982, Billie Vincent assumed the role of FAA *Director of Civil Aviation Security*. Mr. Vincent would report directly to the Associate Administrator for Aviation Standards. This would cause problems down the road, as Mr. Vincent stated, *"my boss was tied up with the airlines on safety, and anything that could cause [him] to divert from that, from a security standpoint, caused him a problem."* Thus, there began a relationship between the FAA and the airlines *"sharing the same bed."* This would become a major hurdle for the Director of Civil Aviation Security in the future. [161]

Billie Vincent would quickly learn, through various meetings, that the world was becoming ever more violent with Islamic extremism on the rise. *"It was a fact of life that you had terrorism running all over aviation in Europe and the Mediterranean basin,"* he said. [162]

Throughout 1982, the U.S. intelligence community was getting chatter from the Middle East, and the rising terrorist threat in that region. The Soviet war in Afghanistan in South Asia was already in full swing, and the intelligence assets being used to assist the Mujahideen* were enormous. In 1982, a major war was being waged in the Panjshir valley of Afghanistan, and the Mujahideen were learning invaluable combat tactics during the intense fighting. [163]

---

[160] (Administration F. A., FAA Archival Records - From 2001 Internal Report)
[161] (Vincent, 2009 - 2010), (Steele, 2012)
[162] (Vincent, 2009 - 2010)
[163] (Coll, Ghost Wars: The Secret History of the CIA, Afghanistan, and Bin Laden, from the Soviet Invasion to September 10, 2001, 2004), (Commission, July 22, 2004)
*Mujahideen is translated as *"strugglers,"* or *"people doing jihad."*

By 1982, President Reagan had been in office for over a year, and he supported the Mujahideen, calling them '*Freedom Fighters*'. The U.S. government's support of their resistance to the Soviet Union was widely publicized. It would not become known until much later, but the events affecting the region would come to haunt the U.S. almost two decades later.

On August 11, 1982, an explosion ripped through the cabin of a Boeing 747; Pan Am Flight 830 was en-route from Narita, Japan, to Honolulu, Hawaii - at the time, it was 140 miles North West of its final destination. The aircraft went on to make an emergency landing in Honolulu, where it was found that the explosion and intense fireball had killed a 16-year old Japanese national; the young man had been with several family members, and had been prepared for a peaceful vacation. The blast also injured 15 others onboard. [164]

A man named Abu Ibrahim* was implicated in the attack, and another similar bombing of a U.S. aircraft would be linked to Ibrahim some four years later. Abu Ibrahim was part of the May 15 Terrorist Organization that was operating out of Baghdad, Iraq. The bombing of Pan Am 830 would be the beginning of a terrorist bombing campaign by Abu Ibrahim and the rest of the May 15 group, and the bomb planted on Pan Am 830, was quite sophisticated.

The bomb on Pan Am 830 was determined to have had a pressure switch as a timing device. When the device was sat on, a switch was activated which started the countdown for detonation. The so called *under the seat-cushion bomb* was ingenious, and thought to be the handy work of Abu Ibrahim, due to parts found during the investigation and a future bomb that was recovered. It was later determined in a U.S. court that an operative in Abu Ibrahim's May 15 Terrorist Organization named Mohammed Rashed had planted the bomb.

Two weeks after the Pan Am 830 bombing, the FAA received information on a *"suspicious device"* found** on a Boeing 747 aircraft, named the *"Clipper Flying Cloud,"* in Rio de Janeiro, Brazil, by a cleaning crew. The FAA scram-

---

[164] (Aleman, 2012), (Blank, 2010), (Vincent, 2009 - 2010)
*Abu Ibrahim has been wanted by the FBI for the crime, and several other aircraft related bombings, ever since.
**The device was found by the cleaning crew that was contracted out to the airline, of which would regularly look under seats for loose change and wallets. The device found on PAA 440 looked like a wallet, and had been discarded under a seat by the cleaning crew.

bled a team of experts to fly to Brazil and inspect the Pan Am aircraft, which had landed in Brazil from London and Miami, as Pan Am Flight 440 (PAA 440).

Upon inspection, the suspicious device was found to be an Improvised Explosive Device (IED), and it was hypothesized that it was likely the same type that was planted on Pan Am 830. This was a lucky break, since now the FAA had an explosive to study, not just debris. They could use the information gleaned from the device to implement security measures, in order to try and stop these bombs from getting on any other commercial flights.

By 1983, the world seemed to be moving on to other problems, and hijackings did not figure into many of those issues. By 1983, the FAA Police that had been used in the ramp-up for the Mariel boat lifts were no longer needed; with this change, the number of air marshals again dropped to between 10 and 12. The reason for the small number of air marshals being retained is unknown; however, it was a trend that was established as far back as 1974. It was a small force, but going into the next few years the government would find a use for them. [165]

Starting in 1983, there was an increase in air marshal missions for unknown reasons; there were a total of 37 missions flown throughout the fiscal year. This was a large amount of missions at the time, for such a skeleton crew. [166]

Between May 4 and 5, 1983, the International Air Transport Association (IATA) held a meeting in Montreal, Canada. This was the *21st Security Advisory Committee*, which regularly convened to discuss various aviation security measures among member airlines. During this particular meeting, the IATA discussed the varying techniques that terrorists and terror groups had started to use for circumventing airport security measures.

They discussed how terrorists employed methods that involved traveling through a *"dirty airport"* and boarded flights bound for a more secure one. Dirty airports were those with less stringent security measures. Since the majority of airports at this time allowed a person to transfer to another airline to destinations in the host country, a terrorist could use the dirty airport to gain access to an aircraft with weapons in-tow, then transfer to *"a 'target' airline and [sic] hijack the target plane."*

---

[165] (McLaughlin, 2011 - 2012)

[166] (Administration F. A., FAA Archival Records - From 2001 Internal Report)

Minutes of the 21st Security Advisory Committee meeting also stated that *"[The] would be terrorist may well have travelled on the original Carrier without any intention of committing a terrorist act against that Carrier, but with the object of a transfer to another target Carrier."* The IATA told members that the *"[only] solution to this situation is to create circumstances where some degree of reliance can be placed on the security measures of other States."* [167]

On October 23, 1983, a truck bomb destroyed the Marine barracks in Lebanon; 241 American servicemen were killed. It signaled the deadliest single-day death toll for the United States Marine Corps since the Battle of Iwo Jima. [168] The bombing was later believed to be tied to the Islamic Dawa Party, a radical Shiite platform, and one of Iraq's oldest opposition parties. The Islamic Dawa Party was eventually outlawed and crushed by Saddam Hussein in 1980. The bombing of the Marine barracks was claimed under the name '*Islamic Jihad*'. [169]

Less than two months after the bombing of the Marine barracks in Beirut, the U.S. embassy in Kuwait was attacked. On December 12, 1983, a bomb detonated in front of the building and killed five people; luckily, only a quarter of the explosives detonated due to faulty rigging. A truck had carried the explosives, which consisted of large cylinders of gas, in-concert with high explosives. It crashed through the front gates of the U.S. embassy in Kuwait, however, the suicide driver failed to hit the populated chancellery before detonating. The driver's miscalculation helped to prevent the hundreds of deaths that could have occurred, in what could have been the worst terrorist episode of the twentieth century. [170]

This incident was attributed to the Islamic Dawa Party, like the Marine Barracks bombing, and 17 members of the group were arrested and held in Kuwait for trial. The '*DAWA 17*', as they became known, would serve as a symbol of resistance for other disheartened Islamic radicals. They would also serve as the motive for kidnappings of *"westerners"* in Beirut in the mid-1980s', and numerous future aircraft hijackings as well.

In December 1983, another attempt to bomb an aircraft had been made, this time against El Al Airlines. A suitcase bomb was found by Greece, in an intelligence operation against a woman unaware that she was carrying the device.

---

[167] (United States Court of Appeals, March 11, 1996)

[168] (Coll, Ghost Wars: The Secret History of the CIA, Afghanistan, and Bin Laden, from the Soviet Invasion to September 10, 2001, 2004), (Wikipedia, Beirut Barracks Bombing)

[169] (McLaughlin, 2011 - 2012)

[170] (Wikipedia, Beirut Barracks Bombing)

During the intelligence operation the explosive device was retrieved and, although it was not until a year later, would eventually be brought to the U.S. for analysis. The explosive should have detonated on her flight from Tel Aviv to London.

Through the examination of the device, it was determined that Abu Ibrahim and the May 15 Terrorist Organization were responsible. The sophistication of the bomb showed the evolving technical skills of the terrorists. The suitcase bomb had been so well made that it was extremely hard to detect. As the terrorists continued to hone their craft, law enforcement, the FAA, and U.S. and foreign intelligence agencies tried to unravel the next plot. Americans abroad were tempting targets. [171]

On March 16, 1984, William Buckley, a Paramilitary Operations Officer working for the CIA's Special Activities Division, was kidnapped on his way to work in Beirut. Two other Americans were kidnapped at different locations in Beirut that day as well, as part of a coordinated Hezbollah effort. It was thought that one of the reasons Buckley and the others were kidnapped was because of the upcoming trial of the DAWA 17. [172]

Throughout fiscal year 1984, there were a total of 10 air marshal missions flown for unknown reasons. [173] This was an insignificant amount of flights in relation to the total number of commercial U.S. flights for even a single day, however, the fiscal year ended in September, and intelligence agencies were only just beginning to see a picture of the threat posed by the DAWA 17. It was not until December 1984, that the increasing threat to civil aviation due to the DAWA 17 started coming across U.S. intelligence networks, and FAM missions *would* increase in response to this intelligence going into the future. The intelligence chatter, which the CIA and National Security Agency (NSA) began picking up, pointed to a direct threat against commercial aircraft in general, not just U.S. flagged carriers, and this threat would rear its head in a violent manner.

On December 3, 1984, Kuwait Airways Flight 221, an Airbus A-310, was hijacked shortly after take-off from Dubai, then taken to Tehran. The flight had been hijacked by four Lebanese Shi'a terrorists. This particular flight was not very desirable among flight attendants. Kuwait Airways Flight 221 serviced Kuwait to Dubai to Karachi, then back to Kuwait, with a stop in Dubai. The

---

[171] (Vincent, 2009 - 2010)

[172] (Coll, Ghost Wars: The Secret History of the CIA, Afghanistan, and Bin Laden, from the Soviet Invasion to September 10, 2001, 2004), (Wikipedia, William Francis Buckley)

[173] (Administration F. A., FAA Archival Records - From 2001 Internal Report)

flight crew worked in one continuous shift throughout the night, since Flight 221 departed in the evening. Those that worked the flight came back exhausted. [174]

After take-off from Dubai and on the way to Karachi*, two men were seen talking in the business-class cabin; one of the men in particular appeared to have a bloody nose. A flight attendant tried to offer a handkerchief to the man during meal service, however he turned her away. Only minutes later, the same flight attendant, a young woman and American citizen, witnessed a struggle between the two men and a lady passenger.

She recalled that *"One of the men appeared to have a pistol in his hand and was waving it around. I was so frightened; I didn't know what to do. I was still a very junior flight attendant and was frozen stiff. I eventually had to be pulled away to the back of the aircraft by one of the more senior male flight attendants."*

The flight attendant, Glenda C. Ali (nee, Tan), soon heard two *"pops."* What she heard was gunfire. The hijackers had shot a security agent onboard. *"[They] told [us] that there were always two security agents, like air marshals on this route, since it was considered high-threat. I don't know what happened to the other security man, but maybe he just figured there was nothing he could do and stayed in his seat like the other passengers,"* recalled Mrs. Ali.

The wounded security man was eventually placed in a seat in the middle of the aircraft. As he was dragged down the aisle, he left trail of blood behind him on the carpet. The gunshot wound to his leg was treated by one of the male flight attendants; otherwise, the female crew members were the only crew members allowed up, in order to serve water to the passengers.

Once the aircraft landed on the ground in Tehran, the hijackers gathered passports from passengers and began singling out U.S. citizens. One of the passengers Glenda sat next to that day, in-between her flight attendant duties and while nervously awaiting release in Tehran, was a U.S. citizen named William Stanford.

Mr. Stanford told Glenda that he worked for an auditing firm; he was in fact an American diplomat. He withheld this information because he knew he would be targeted. The terrorists had already begun selecting American citizens at random to go to the front of the aircraft, where the terrorists would shut the cur-

---

[174] (McLaughlin, 2011 - 2012), (Ali, 2011), (Glenda Ali (nee, 2011), (Ali G. , 1985)
*The hijacking occurred between the second and third destination of the flight.

tains, shutting off the first-class cabin from view. They could be heard getting rough with their interrogations, yelling *"Are you CIA? We know you are CIA!"* William Stanford knew it was only a matter of time before he was selected.

"Mr. Stanford was so nice to me. I felt so useless during the hijacking and I told him this. He told me it was normal and that I would make it out just fine. He told me he was looking forward to seeing his family for Christmas. He slipped me a candy while I sat next to him and he gave me hope," Glenda recalled. [175]

As the hijacking continued on the ground in Tehran the terrorists demanded the release of the DAWA 17. In order to further help their case, the hijackers ordered the release of all women and children. Glenda Tan was notified by the male flight attendants that she needed to leave with the other women. [176]

By the fifth and sixth day of the hijacking, the terrorists were beginning to become extremely agitated. President Reagan refused to negotiate with the terrorists and their demands had not been met. They increased their torture of the U.S. and Kuwaiti citizens onboard, humiliating them and burning their hair with lighters. It was during these final days, on the 8th or 9th of December, that two U.S. citizens, Charles Hegna, and William Stanford, were murdered.

Prior to his execution, the kind and gentle Mr. Stanford had been told by the terrorists, *"I am going to count down from ten to zero. If you can run down the stairs [of the aircraft], and out of the reach of my bullets, by the time I reach zero, you will live."*

Eventually, on December 9, 1984, Iranian Commandos raided the aircraft, and the hijackers were said to have been *"brought into custody."* Other reports and information circulated that the terrorists had escaped with a cleaning crew* which had mysteriously been sent onboard that day. In the end, no investigation could be conducted on the aircraft, since it was confiscated by the Iranian government and never returned to Kuwait Airways.

This event marked yet another occurrence of westerners being targeted for violence; during the hijacking, the hijackers of Kuwait Airways Flight 221 (KU 221) intentionally sought out Americans for threat, torture, and murder. It was also another circumstance of hijackers and terrorists being released by a country sympathetic to their cause, and signaled a change in hijacker tactics. The kind

---

[175] (Glenda Ali (nee, 2011)
[176] (Ali, 2011)
*The Iranian government never explained why a cleaning crew would be sent on to a hijacked aircraft.

treatment to terrorists, by many Middle Eastern countries, strengthened the hijackers resolve. It would also spawn others to follow in their paths.

The tactics and operational planning used by the hijackers of Flight 221, showed that terrorists would go to great lengths to carry out their murderous plots. Their resolve showed that, over time, terrorist groups that target commercial aircraft would only continue to get more sophisticated and operationally prepared. The four Lebanese extremists that hijacked KU 221, had arrived in Dubai from Beirut on Middle Eastern Airlines Flight 426. They had planned to use a dirty airport to gain access to the target aircraft. By using this portal, they either came into Beirut armed, or gained access to their weapons after boarding.

The men and women working in the field of civil aviation security realized there was a new threat emerging: The Islamic radical threat. It was a trend that U.S. and foreign intelligence had been watching at the time as well. They had already managed to finger a man allegedly involved in the hijacking of KU 221, by the name of Imad Mughniyah*. [177]

The remaining air marshals were continuously training for such a hijacking. They had become highly proficient marksman and more efficient in aircraft tactics as well. They shot the PPC course of fire with their Smith and Wesson .357 caliber, 4" revolvers, and they performed the FLETC Standard for their physical fitness qualification**. They were a small group, numbering between 10 and 12 persons, and they awaited their countries call to action. [178]

Various scenarios were taught in aircraft mockups, such as one Boeing 737 that had been provided by Delta Airlines. The scenarios involved an aircraft in-flight, and ground-based scenarios that required a coordinated response, and many different agencies and various departments at the FAA took part. These exercises brought many groups together, such as local law enforcement, the FBI, Federal Air Marshals, and even the military, to prepare for the response to a

---

[177] (Vincent, 2009 - 2010)
[178] (Vincent, 2009 - 2010)
*Until September 11, 2001, Imad Mughniyah had murdered more U.S. citizens than any other terrorist alive, and was responsible for multiple kidnappings during the 1980s' including the Marine Barracks bombing; he would eventually be killed on February 12, 2008, in an Israeli/Mossad assassination.
**The FLETC Standards for physical fitness is a 1-1/2 mile run, bench press, shuttle run, and sit-and-reach. The student's score is reflective of a comparison with all prior students, given as a percentage. There are separate categories for men and women for the FLETC standards, and they are compared with their respective sex and age.

hijacking on U.S. soil. All of the men and woman that participated in this training, over the years, had become better prepared for any actual *'real-world-events'*.

Although these groups were better prepared for a potential hijacking, there were still many security issues that needed to be fixed. Airports all over the world, particularly those in third world countries, were extremely vulnerable to penetration by terrorists. It was a challenge to train personnel at these locations; the hurdles included illiteracy, lack of funding and necessary equipment, and high turnover, since those trained to U.S. standards became highly valued and usually left quickly for more lucrative positions outside their country. Athens was one such city that had major security lapses at its international airport. Athens had suffered much embarrassment among the international aviation security community. Terrorists had found bold new ways to bring weapons and explosives onboard commercial flights, and were using airports that had poor security to carry out their hijackings. The FAA and those in the Office of Civil Aviation Security, were doing their part, trying to garner support from other nations in order to improve their airport security. Moses Aleman was also trying to impart his knowledge and expertise to help these poor countries.

As Director Billie Vincent and the many others at the Office of Civil Aviation Security continued to work on improving security worldwide, another event targeting commercial aviation occurred. Although it happened far from U.S. soil, civil aviation security would have a dramatic change as a result.

Chapter VII

Evolving Threats

FAA Office of Civil Aviation Security
(June 14, 1985 - September 1992)

I n what was the middle of the night in Washington DC, on Friday, June 14, 1985, a Boeing 727 aircraft, tail number N64339, took off from Athens, Greece; the time in Athens was 10:10 a.m., and the flight was TWA 847. It was headed to London's Heathrow International Airport (LHR) and piloted by Captain John Testrake. There were 153 passengers and crew onboard, including flight engineer Benjamin C. Zimmermann, co-pilot Philip G. Maresca, and flight attendant Uli Derickson. [179]

Shortly after take-off, the flight was hijacked by two German-speaking Lebanese men, who had smuggled pistols and grenades through a security checkpoint at Athens airport. The hijackers commandeered the aircraft and demanded it be taken to Beirut. The hijackers assaulted women and children and then released

---

[179] (Vincent, 2009 - 2010), (McLaughlin, 2011 - 2012)

19 passengers in exchange for fuel. After refueling, the aircraft departed for Algiers.

For the first three years of his position as the Director of Civil Aviation Security, Mr. Vincent kept busy with many duties, and June 14 started out like any other for Mr. Vincent; like most federal employees, he was looking forward to starting his weekend the following day.[180]

This would be no ordinary day, however, and like many tragic incidents that become mostly forgotten over time, this day would later fade in the public's collective memory, but forever change the way the United States looked at the world and terrorism.

As Billie Vincent awoke, the hijackers had already brandished grenades and firearms and took control of the TWA aircraft: They would ultimately hold the passengers for 17 days; the perpetrators of which would later be identified as one Lebanese Shia extremist, and one member of Hezbollah and Islamic Jihad.

The Director of Civil Aviation Security for the FAA, Billie Vincent, was at home on the morning of June 14, and participating in his daily rituals. Mr. Vincent woke up at 4 a.m., as he had every other morning, and prepared himself for the day by doing a fitness routine that consisted of some light weights and a run.[181]

After his morning workout, Mr. Vincent made coffee and was out the door for his trip to the office in Washington DC. As he arrived, Mr. Vincent was advised of the events that had taken place in Greece. By the time Mr. Vincent was told of the hijacking, the aircraft was on ground taking on fuel, and the terrorists began releasing a number of women and children. After refueling, the aircraft departed for Beirut.

The hijackers had already begun making their demands heard, one of which was for the immediate release of the DAWA 17. After arriving in Beirut and while refueling, a Navy diver, Robert Stethem, who was already wounded from being beaten and tortured for hours, was shot and killed, and his body dumped on the tarmac. He had been targeted as a westerner, along with several other U.S. military men onboard; they had been identified by their military identification, and *all* were singled out for torture. Flight attendant Uli Derickson had attempted to hide the military IDs, but the men were discovered anyway.

---

[180] (Vincent, 2009 - 2010)
[181] (Vincent, 2009 - 2010)

Mr. Vincent had been a member of the IGT, a quasi-secret and informal organization that met monthly to discuss national security threats. Mr. Vincent had been a part of this group ever since he assumed the position as Director of Civil Aviation Security, in May 1982. During the 17 days of the TWA 847 hijacking, this group met regularly to assess the situation. The group also attempted to coordinate action plans with their foreign counterparts in Greece. One member of the IGT was a man by the name of Oliver North; a young staffer for Deputy National Security Advisor Admiral John Poindexter.

On the second day of the hijacking, Billie Vincent went to the U.S. State Department with a memorandum containing recommendations on the security problem in Greece. He had been asked to write the memo due to the country's unsatisfactory security procedures, which had allowed terrorists to bring weapons and explosives undetected through airport security. It was obvious that Greece had some major security lapses in its boarding and screening procedures. Although Mr. Vincent was not aware at the time, his memo would help the president reach a later decision, calling for security reparations in Athens.

Mr. Vincent did not think of the importance of this document he had been asked to write, however, the next morning he was contacted by Vice Admiral Donald D. Engen, the FAA Administrator, and was told that the Under-Secretary of Defense had requested a meeting; Mr. Vincent was told that a staff car would be sent to take him to an appointment at the White House. The memorandum he had written had been requested by Oliver North, to be presented to an emergency meeting with the National Security Advisor to President Reagan.

When Billie Vincent and the Administrator of the FAA arrived at the meeting, all of the IGT members were already present. A three-star Army General, a high ranking member of the FBI, the Secretary of Defense Caspar Weinberger, Oliver North, and several staff members from the White House were in attendance. [182]

All of these men would share a role in the changes about to take place within the Federal Air Marshal Program; this meeting, the crisis, and changes to occur, were in direct response to the hijacking of TWA Flight 847.

National Security Advisor John Marian Poindexter carried the meeting, and as the discussion started, the first topic was: What would be done about Greece's handling of the TWA 847 hijacking, and how would the U.S. prevent it from happening again? The paper that Mr. Vincent had prepared was the main point of discussion. It was ultimately decided to keep word for word what Mr. Vincent

---

[182] (Vincent, 2009 - 2010)

and his advisors had proposed. The recommendations included advising airlines and the public of the poor security of certain international airports, requiring airports to uphold international security standards where U.S. carriers fly, and the ability of the FAA to post warnings in U.S. airports, listing those airports and countries that did not comply.

The topic then turned to the second item: How would another TWA 847 hijacking be prevented or deterred from happening again? It was obvious to everyone in the room that there was a need to protect U.S. air carriers in-flight. Oliver North brought up the idea of re-constituting the air marshals. Don Engen became livid at this suggestion and said that there was a problem having armed people on planes, and that they should explore other solutions. Mr. Vincent bit his tongue.

Oliver North spoke of how, when he returned from Vietnam in early 1970, he had flown as a sky marshal. Don Engen was not impressed. He was resolute that there should be no armed law enforcement personnel on airplanes. This was when Mr. Vincent finally spoke up. Mr. Vincent reminded everyone, or informed those that did not already know, that the FAA already *had* air marshals, although only a handful were employed. Those that remained performed in-flight security as a small percentage of their FAA Inspector duties. He told them group that the air marshal program had been flying mostly all domestic routes, since the main threat of past hijackings was towards domestic flights. Mr. Vincent also told them that the program could quickly be expanded if this was the desire of the president. Everyone in the room listened attentively, and the speaker of the group, Mr. Poindexter, told them he would brief President Reagan: The president would make the final decision on the matter.

The hijacking of TWA Flight 847 ended after 17 days of terror and tragic circumstances for all involved, including the death of U.S. Navy Diver Robert Dean Stethem, who had been tortured and executed, then thrown overboard. Decades later, victims that had been onboard would still live with the haunting memories of the ordeal.

A majority of the passengers were later released in Beirut and held hostage in the country; many of the hijackers' demands were met: A prisoner was released by Greece, and over 700 Shia prisoners by Israel. Although most of their demands were met, the hijackers were unable to secure the release of the DAWA 17. [183]

Two days after the meeting of the IGT group, President Ronald Reagan gave a speech in response to the hijacking of TWA 847:

---

[183] (Vincent, 2009 - 2010)

"One hour ago the body of a young American hero, navy diver Robert Steth-am was returned to his native soil in a coffin after being beaten and shot at point blank range. His murder, and the fate of the other American hostages still being held in Beirut underscore an inescapable fact; the United States is, tonight, a nation being attacked by international- terrorists and wonton wanting to kill, and to seize our innocent citizens as their prisoners. "

It was clear to the members of the IGT assembly, by President Reagan's decision, that an event like the hijacking of TWA 847, could never be allowed to happen again. The decisions made by the IGT and carried out by President Reagan, would insure that there was a plan in place to allow a stand up of sufficient personnel to react to, or thwart, a hijacking.

On June 18, 1985, President Reagan further elaborated on the changes to take place in civil aviation security: [184]

" In response to this situation I am directing that the following steps be taken: I have directed the Secretary of Transportation, in cooperation with the Secretary of State, to explore immediately an expansion of our armed sky marshal program aboard international flights of U.S. Air Carriers for better protection of passengers; I have directed the Secretary of State to issue an immediate travel advisory for U.S. citizens travelling through the Athens international airport, warning them of dangers. This warning will remain in effect until the Greek government has improved the security situation there, and until it has demonstrated a willingness to comply with the security provisions of the Greek Civil Aviation Agreement, and the Tokyo-Montreal and Hague Conventions regarding prosecution and punishment of air pirates. I have asked for a full explanation of the events surrounding the take-over of the aircraft in Athens. I have appealed to the Department of Transportation and the Federal Aviation Administration for all U.S. air carriers to review the wisdom of continuing any flights into Athens until the security situation there improves. And further, I have asked Secretary Shultz and Dole to report to me on whether we should terminate the service of foreign air carriers whose governments do not honor appropriate international conventions or provide adequate security at their airports. I am calling upon all allied and friendly governments to redouble their efforts to improve airport security and take other measures to prevent the hijacking of aircraft. "

By the time of this speech, Mr. Vincent had already been approached by Oliver North at an IGT meeting. He told Mr. Vincent that he had been tasked with writing three National Security Decision Directives (NSDDs) by the National

---

[184] (Reagan on Hijacking of TWA Flight 847, 1985)

Security Advisor. One of these was on aviation security. Mr. North asked Billie Vincent if he could help him with the NSDD, since this was his area of expertise; Mr. Vincent was also the only person within the FAA, besides the Administrator, that could work with certain classified material. Mr. Vincent told him, *"I can do better than that, I'll write it for you."* [185]

Billie Vincent handed the project to Jack Hunter, who was still working in the Office of Civil Aviation Security. By this time, he had been helping to write numerous emergency security rules. The emergency rules he had written and that were issued by the FAA throughout the years, had been a point of contention between the FAA and U.S. airlines; the FAA was trying to take a stand on security, while the airlines were trying to protect their bottom line.

Mr. Hunter took the NSDD project on with a vengeance. Within this document he would include, not only an expansion of the Federal Air Marshal Program, but also the building of a *'crisis center'*,* with a SCIF, or Sensitive Compartmented Information Facility, built-in. A SCIF would enable the new program to be tied into U.S. intelligence agencies and other sensitive departments. With the help of Jack Hunter, an expansion of the Federal Air Marshal Program at the FAA, and the model for the modern Federal Air Marshal *Service*, would be drafted and later signed into effect by President Ronald Reagan on July 22, 1985.

Hiring for the air marshals happened quickly, due to the TWA 847 hijacking and response by President Ronald Reagan. The president signed an executive order and National Security Decision Directive, NSDD 180, to have air marshals fly on international flights of U.S. air carriers.

Along with NSDD 180, Public Law 99-83 was enacted, which called for an International Anti-Terrorism Committee, as well as increasing the number of air marshals in the FAA Federal Air Marshal Program; Public Law 99-83, or the *International Security Development and Cooperation Act of 1985*, also established requirements to assess security at foreign airports, gave $5 million to the Federal Air Marshal Program, and provided additional funds for research and development of airport security devices and explosives detection techniques. [186]

---

[185] (Vincent, 2009 - 2010)
[186] (National Security Decision Directive - 180), (S. 2268 - Public Law 87-197, 2010)
* The nature and details of the 'crisis center' remain classified.

By the end of June 1985, the FAA had started hiring air marshals; they would hire approximately 150 over the next two years. One former air marshal that was hired immediately after TWA 847 reported:[187]

> "*[T]here were a number of things that happened; first of all the president directed that the air marshal program be re-instituted in the FAA, so they hired about 150 of us, and just about all of us were former law enforcement, or military. That's when I was hired.*"

> "*We went through about six-weeks of basic training out at a place called Marana, Arizona. Most people are familiar with Artesia, in New Mexico: Marana was in between Tucson and Phoenix, Arizona, in the middle of the desert.*"

> "*Well that was 'FLETC West', if you will, and we trained there; that was where our basic training was, and then we returned there [sic] every six-months for weapons requalification, physical fitness requalification, that kind of thing.*"

> "*The other important part of this response to TWA 847 was the primary focus was overseas, [on] international flights.*"

By late 1985, air marshals were being trained at Marana, Arizona. Every six months, the FAA would send the air marshals through recurrent training at Marana. They would qualify with their weapons with the PPC qualification and make sure they could pass the physical fitness requirement, which was still the FLETC standard. The training in Marana was run by the U.S. Department of Treasury. This was a continuing trend, since Treasury agents had been used in the past, during the sky marshals program as instructors at TASOS. [188]

In 1985, the position of an air marshal was only a portion of the duties of an FAA Inspector; air marshals flew missions 40% of the time and performed FAA Inspector duties for the other 60%, approximately. The new post-TWA 847 air marshals were assigned the title *Civil Aviation Security Special Agents*. [189]

The new changes to occur within the Federal Air Marshal Program, including the signing of NSDD-180, were still in a premature state on the morning of June 23, 1985, as the hijacking of TWA 847 was still underway. This particular day

---

[187] (McLaughlin, 2011 - 2012)
[188] (McLaughlin, 2011 - 2012)
[189] (McLaughlin, 2011 - 2012), (Administration D. o., Semi Annual Report to Congress on the Effectiveness of the Civil Aviation Security Program, January 1, 1988 - June 30, 1988)

was an important one to aviation security professionals: On this morning, a Boeing 747, Canadian Pacific Airlines Flight 003, quietly sat at an arrival gate at Tokyo's Narita International Airport. It was off-loading baggage and passengers from a long flight over the pacific from Vancouver. At 7:03 a.m. local time, an explosive detonated in the cargo hold, killing two baggage handlers and seriously wounding four others. Had the flight not been ten-minutes behind schedule, the aircraft would have been destroyed while still in the air; 390 people were to be onboard the next flight that day, which was to be an Air India flight, and were spared a sure disaster.

Fifty-five minutes later a bomb exploded in the cargo hold of another aircraft: Air India Flight 182. The aircraft, also a Boeing 747, broke up over Ireland on its way to London Heathrow, plunging into the Atlantic Ocean* and killing all 329 people onboard.

The prosecution of this attack would take 20 years, and attain notoriety as one of the most costly legal investigations of the Canadian government. Initially, the bombing in Narita was thought to have been carried out by angry locals, who had been opposed to the building of the Narita airport in rural Japan. Later, however, after the Flight 182 bombing, and upon further investigation of Flight 003, a Sikh extremist group was implicated in both terrorist acts.

The hijacking of TWA 847 and the bombings of Flight 003 and 182, respectively, had major repercussions in regards to aviation security. The response by the Reagan administration for the hijacking of TWA 847 had already been issued, but the bombings of the other two flights had involved baggage being checked on a flight without a passenger accompanying those bags. After the bombings, the U.S. government decided that ICAO should help train air marshals, aviation security managers, and third world countries, in Annex 17 security procedures. [190]

Standards and Recommended Practices (SARPs), are considered the most important legislative function** performed by ICAO. They are incorporated into 18 technical annexes to the *Convention on International Civil Aviation*, also known as the Chicago Convention. SARPs for international aviation security

---

[190] (Aleman, 2012)
*The aircraft has never been recovered, and lies over two miles down, on the Atlantic Ocean sea floor.
**Although ICAO annexes are followed at most all airports in the world, they have no actual governing authority, as they are not a governing body.

were first adopted by the ICAO Council in March 1974, and designated as Annex 17* to the Chicago Convention, as part of 18 technical annexes.

In August 1985, Moses Aleman, by then one of two U.S. ICAO representatives in the world, was sent to Oklahoma City to help train air marshals in Annex 17 procedures. The FAA also required aviation security supervisors to watch closed circuit broadcast of the presentations. This was the beginning of a push towards giving air marshals the tools to perform airport security inspections overseas, since law for this had just been passed with Public Law 99-83. [191]

"The idea was to have the FAMS who escorted flights overseas, & had to remain there until another flight could be assigned to them to work back, could use the time there conducting the foreign airport security assessments that later became SOP. This is before there were CASLOS (Civil Aviation Security Liaison Officers)."

Moses Aleman had been selected by ICAO to help teach Annex 17 procedures all over the world in October 1980. His bi-lingual ability, and his knowledge of aviation security as a specialist in the field, was very attractive to ICAO. By 1985 and 1986, Mr. Aleman had already been teaching these procedures on loan from the FAA and in a host of third world countries, and was one of very few individuals doing so. He represented the FAA's early attempt to teach aviation security procedures to poor and fledgling countries, which were the weakest links in the aviation system. By doing this, they were trying to shore up all civil aviation security *worldwide* in the process. Before the FAA had allowed Mr. Aleman to do this, he had asked ICAO *"Is that even possible, for me to be on loan from the FAA to teach for you guys?"* The representatives at ICAO were quick to reply, *"When we want someone we usually get them. We go directly to the top of the FAA."* This showed that the FAA was trying to help improve security throughout the entire aviation system. Also, by training their air marshals in these procedures, the U.S. would have another tool at their disposal for improving airport security, and overall aviation security worldwide, by giving them the means to evaluate airport security as they traveled abroad. [192]

---

[191] (S. 2268 - Public Law 87-197, 2010), (ICAO Home Page)
[192] (Aleman, 2012)
*Annex 17 is titled, *Security: Safeguarding International Civil Aviation Against Acts of Unlawful Interference,* and was developed by ICAO, providing *"the standard procedures and guidance for the Civil Aviation Industry, on how to safeguard the industry against acts of unlawful interference."*

By the end of 1985, there were a total of 32 air marshal missions flown for the year; all of these flights were on international routes and intelligence driven.

A typical air marshal during this time would fly to Bombay, Kuwait, Dubai, Karachi, and other volatile Middle Eastern countries; the majority of these routes had been targeted by hijackers and terrorists in the past. There were some teams that covered flights to Lebanon, up until October 1985, when the route was shut down. All the flights being covered by air marshals at this time were tied directly to specific threats, and a specific aircraft or airline: This was referred to as *Risk Based Security*. The information came directly from the intelligence community, and was a direct result of the Anti-Terrorism Committee meetings set-up by President Ronald Reagan. Missions were based on U.S. and foreign intelligence, and signed off by the Director of Civil Aviation Security.[193]

A former air marshal that flew missions during this time recalled: [194]

> *"[J]ust about all of our flights were on TWA or Pan Am, and occasionally we used to fly on Eastern, but that was primarily down to South America. I never went on those flights, but I know that some FAMs did. All of these flights were based on specific threats and intelligence."*

The weapon carried by the air marshals in 1985 was the Smith and Wesson .357 caliber, 4" revolver. The PPC* qualification test, required by air marshals at the time, was designed for a revolver, with six-shot stages of fire. The air marshals continued to use the PPC as their standard, as they had since the mid-1970s, and most continually practiced to be proficient with their weapons. The air marshals of this era were made up of FAA Inspectors that were required to perform in-flight security duties as part of their job, and some ended up having trouble qualifying, yet were able to keep their guns, credentials, and air marshal status.

In the first week of November 1985, the first class of Federal Air Marshals graduated training since June 25, 1974, when the program was taken back from the U.S. Customs sky marshal program. Before this class graduated, the total

---

[193] (McLaughlin, 2011 - 2012)
[194] (McLaughlin, 2011 - 2012)
* Practical Pistol Course (PPC) is a course of fire used for firearms qualification. It is based off of the National Rifle Association (NRA) PPC course of fire. Initially developed for a revolver, the PPC was later used with semi-automatic pistols as well, with 6-shot stages of fire (again, originally developed for a 6-shot revolver).

number of air marshals had remained stagnant, with approximately one-dozen over the previous decade.

A Washington Times article, in November 1985, discussed the five-week training course for air marshals, and also outlined the FAA security measures ordered by President Reagan in response to TWA 847. [195]

On Thanksgiving Eve, 1985, a team of air marshals travelled on mission to Cairo. Shortly after arrival, the team met up with the TWA flight crew. Joining them was Uli Derickson, who was on her first trip back to the Middle East since she had been a crew member serving on TWA 847; Uli Derickson had been a flight attendant on that flight and was credited with helping protect some of the Israeli and American passengers from being targeted by the hijackers. The air marshal team had Thanksgiving dinner with Mrs. Derickson and the flight crew at the Sheraton Heliopolis Hotel in Cairo. The next day, the crew returned to JFK, and the air marshal team continued on to Kuwait and Bombay.

For their Thanksgiving dinner, all at the table talked about a hijacking which had occurred only five days earlier. On November 23, 1985, three hijackers had taken control of Egypt Air Flight 648. The aircraft, a Boeing 737, had been scheduled to depart from Athens, at 8:00 p.m. local time, and the intended destination was Cairo.

Approximately ten minutes after take-off, the aircraft was hijacked by three members of Abu Nidal*. They were armed with grenades and firearms. The aircraft was later forced to land in Malta, where there was a standoff with authorities on the ground; during the standoff, the hijackers killed an American woman and shot four others, in order to have their demands met for fuel.

A raid took place by Egyptian commandos, whom had been flown in specifically for a rescue mission; the group's name was Task Force 777. In response, the terrorists lobbed grenades at the passengers and shot others. In the ensuing violence, the Egyptian commando snipers mistakenly shot some passengers as they tried to escape; 55 out of the 88 passengers were ultimately killed in this incident. [196]

---

[195] (McCaslin, November 8, 1985)
[196] (Aleman, 2012), (McLaughlin, 2011 - 2012)
*The Abu Nidal Organization (ANO) was a militant Palestinian splinter group. Founded by a man named Abu Nidal in the early 1970s', the ANO was responsible for numerous terrorist attacks on Israel and other western targets.

One of the terrorists was eventually put on trial by the Maltese government, but retribution by the terrorists was feared. The hijackers were given a light sentence, said to be due to inadequate laws in the country to prosecute crimes against civil aviation. As the air marshals and TWA flight crew gave thanks at the Sheraton in Cairo, families from nine nations*were preparing to bury the dead.

On December 27, 1985, coordinated terrorist attacks in the airports of Rome, Italy, and Vienna, Austria, ended up killing 19 and wounding over one hundred; five of the dead were American citizens. The terrorist group Abu Nidal Organization later took credit for the bloody attacks, which were said to be in response to Israel's bombing of the Palestinian Liberation Organization's (PLO's) headquarters in Tunis. Muammar Qaddafi of Libya praised the terrorists, further stressing relations between the U.S. and Libya. [197]

The coordinated attacks on these two airports alarmed civil aviation security experts within the FAA. The terrorist problem in Europe was beginning to spread at an alarming rate and it did not appear to be slowing down. Due to the problems between the U.S. and Libya, the FAA issued an emergency rule which suspended all aviation relations with the country; no U.S. air carriers could go into Libya, and no aircraft leaving Libya could enter the United States.

The tension between the U.S. and Libya was setting the stage for an explosive situation in need of just one more spark; that spark came on April 5, 1986. On that date, U.S. servicemen, locals, and others, were enjoying an evening out in Berlin, at a discotheque called Le Belle. At approximately 1:30 a.m. local time, an explosion rocked the establishment, sending people flying and debris littering the street. By the time the dust settled, 230 people would be found injured and three dead**.

This event was blamed on Libya, of which had been determined by U.S. intelligence through an intercepted cable. The cable was from the Libyan government to the Libyan embassy in East Berlin, congratulating them on a job well done.

---

[197] (Wikipedia, Rome and Vienna Airport Attacks)
*Citizens from Austria, Belgium, Egypt, Greece, Israel, Philippines, Palestine, United States, and Mexico were killed in this vicious terrorist hijacking.
** Two U.S. servicemen were killed in this incident; one would die instantly and one would die of injuries two months later; (Wikipedia, 1986 Berlin Dicotheque Bombing)

Joseph and Viola

First Communion

Joe Pontecorvo (Left), Viola (2nd from Left), and Friends

FAA Peace Officers Training – 1962

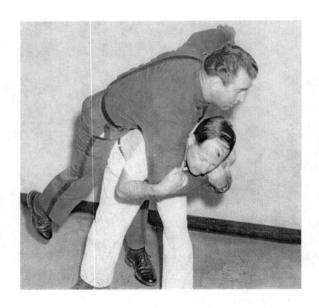

Joseph Pontecorvo – Defensive Measures Training

Photos Courtesy of Joseph A. Pontecorvo

Swearing in of the First Air Marshals: FAA Peace Officers

Photos courtesy of Joseph A. Pontecorvo

D L TION	(2) QUANTITY	(3) UNIT	(4) ARTICLE	(5) FUNCTIONAL CODE	(6) UNIT PRICE	(7) AMOUNT
	1	ea.	Revolver, Colt "Cobra" .38 Cal. Special s/n 120096 6 shot, 2" Barrel			56.45
	1	ea.	Holster, Buckheimer, B-825, .38 Cal. 2" Barrel, RH draw, Plainfinish			3.06
	1	ea.	Billy, (Blackjack) Buckheimer #207 7-1/2", 6 oz, shot filled			2.28
	1	Pr.	324455 Handcuffs, Peerless, 10 oz. w/keys			11.25
	1	ea.	Fountain Pen Teargas Gun .38 Cal.			4.00
	1	ea.	Cleaning Kit, Revolver, .38 Cal. "PCO" Hoppes			1.30
	1	c	Ammunition, .38 Cal. Winchester		7.02	7.02
	4	ea.	Cartridges, .38 Special Gas		.45	1.80

I hereby certify that the above articles were received
d condition, except as noted hereon.

FUNCTION CA62-282-1	TOTAL COST		TOTAL	87.16

| DATE 3-27-62 | SIGNATURE | | | |

Region

POSTED (Date Initial)
Personally Charged Property

REQUISITIONING OFFICE COPY   FORM CA-10-8 (8-61)

FAA Peace Officers Issued Equipment
Courtesy of Joseph A. Pontecorvo

FAA 'SKYJACK' UNIT READY TO GRAPPLE

First group of FAA Peace Officers in meeting with Attorney General Kennedy.   Ke

A special group of FAA peace officers, organized last year to help prevent aircraft hijackings, has completed a one-week refresher course in law enforcement techniques and procedures at the United States Border Patrol Academy in Port

1961. It was signed by nedy September 5, 1961.

The marshals will be airline flights on request management or the FBI. civilian clothes and may

"Skyjack" Article – FAA Horizons
Courtesy of Terry Kraus, PhD

Joseph Pontecorvo – FAA Flight Standards Division

FAA Peace Officer Recurrent Training, 1968

Photos Courtesy of Joseph A. Pontecorvo

1970s' Passenger and Baggage Screening System

Sky marshal Firearms Training, c. 1970s'

Photos Courtesy of Terry Kraus, PhD

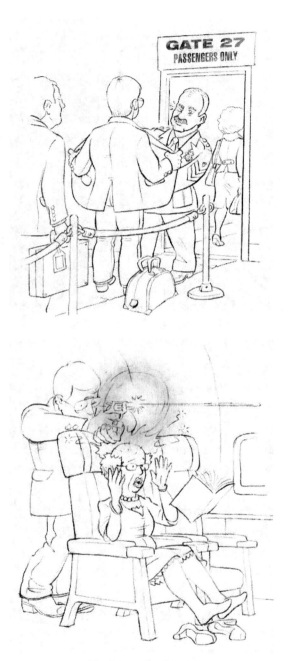

Sky Marshal Cartoons
Art Work Courtesy of Steve Rustad

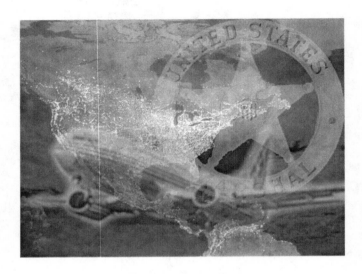

Sky Marshal Tribute
1969 - 1973

Before the days of airport passenger screening detectors and Federal Air Marshals, the Nation relied on the expertise of 1,500 Customs Security Officers to protect the aviation system from hostile acts. We admire the dedication and contributions of these *Sky Marshals* who laid the groundwork for the force currently in place today. The Nation owes a debt of gratitude for their service and for passing the mantel to a new generation of Federal law enforcement officers to promote confidence in the aviation system. The Federal Air Marshal Service honors and remembers these *Sky Marshals* who have inspired excellence in aviation security.

FAA Federal Air Marshals recognition of Sky Marshals
Courtesy of G.M. McLaughlin

FLETC Training

Skills Upgrade Training - 1992

Photos Courtesy of G.M. McLaughlin

Firearms Training at Mid-South Institute

Tactics Training with FBI Hostage Rescue Team

Photos Courtesy of G.M. McLaughlin

FAA Federal Air Marshal Training

Photos Courtesy of G.M. McLaughlin

Post – 9/11 Federal Air Marshal – Firearms Training

Photos Courtesy of G.M. McLaughlin

A response came from the U.S. only ten days later; over 60-tons of explosives were dropped on various targets in Libya during *Operation El Dorado Canyon*. Over twenty-five years later, some victims of the discotheque bombing would seek damages from frozen assets of the Libyan leader. [198]

As the year turned to 1986, a mixture of the increasing terrorist threat and insufficient power of the FAA to put in place adequate security controls was about to become the perfect combination for a very combustible environment for commercial aviation.

By 1986, the increased threat to civil aviation was keeping air marshals very busy. Even though they were only working as air marshals for 40 percent of the time, the missions began to increase due to the increasing threat stream that was being generated by U.S. and foreign intelligence. For the fiscal year of 1986, air marshals would fly 216 missions, all on international flights and all based off of credible intelligence. [199]

Even though air marshal missions were increasing at this time, there was still not a true specialization of in-flight security functions for the typical air marshal, since these duties were split between flying missions and performing security inspection duties. The collateral duties of an air marshal were also *non-voluntary*, since the job was required of all FAA Inspectors. The routes being flown during this time were also extremely vulnerable ones: This, in combination with air marshals that were concerned for their own safety and security, meant security lapses were bound to follow. [200]

On April 2, 1986, a Boeing 727, TWA Flight 840, was en-route from Athens to Rome. A team of air marshals were reported to have been travelling on this flight, which was frequently covered at the time; they would be connecting in Rome to continue on to New York. The TWA 840 route serviced Rome from Athens and Cairo every day, and returned to Athens after passengers disembarked in Rome. A woman onboard Flight 840 earlier that day had sinister intentions, and had brought an explosive device with her onboard a previous leg of the flight.

After setting an explosive under her seat on the initial flight from Cairo to Athens, the woman went about her business and prepared for arrival; she would

---

[198] (Aviation Security Chronology - taken from DOT website), (Wikipedia, Operation El Dorado Canyon)
[199] (Administration F. A., FAA Archival Records - From 2001 Internal Report)
[200] (McLaughlin, 2011 - 2012)

be getting off the flight and following her escape plan. Upon arrival in Athens the woman-terrorist calmly entered a transit lounge to prepare for her flight to Beirut. She would go on to elude foreign and U.S. intelligence agencies, only to be questioned later, then released. The team of air marshals on the flight from Athens to Rome, had not known an explosive was onboard the aircraft, and they boarded the flight and continued on unaware. After landing in Rome, the team checked in for another flight going back to New York's Kennedy airport, on a Boeing 747. On its way back to Athens, TWA 840 exploded.

TWA Flight 840, and the attempted destruction of the aircraft and murder of all onboard, was another story showing bravery in the face of danger for the pilots of the aircraft, although tragic. Upon detonation, the force of the explosive ejected four American passengers through a nine-foot by three-foot diameter hole in the cabin, including a nine-month old infant. Five other passengers were injured; the 110 others survived, as pilot Richard "Pete" Peterson made a heroic emergency landing. About the explosion, he reported, *"It sounded like a shotgun went off next to [my] ear."* [201]

A group calling itself the Arab Revolutionary Cells claimed responsibility for the bombing, and said it was carried out because of *"American Arrogance."* The woman-terrorist was suspected of belonging to the Abu Nidal Organization, a militant Palestinian group. Regardless of what terrorist group or cell she belonged to, she was ultimately another courier for Abu Ibrahim's May 15 Terrorist Organization bombing campaign. [202]

The woman, travelling under the name May Elias Mansur, had sat in seat 10F, on the in-bound flight from Cairo to Athens. She had reportedly listened to music the entire flight and had her tray table extended over her lap for the majority of the flight as well. Investigators later hypothesize that she had placed an explosive device in the life-preserver under her seat at some point during the flight, using the tray table to conceal her actions and arming it before departing the aircraft. The device, which was similar to ones found with a pressure switch attached, appropriately named the *under the seat-cushion bomb*, had been seen before in connection with the bombing of Pan Am 830, and the attempted bombing of Pan Am 440. The device that killed four Americans onboard TWA Flight 840 had not exploded while the air marshals were on their way to Rome, it was hypothesized, because the lady that was sitting in seat 10F, the wife of an Italian politician, had been out of her seat repeatedly; the switch in the explosive device stopped the timing mechanism whenever pressure was taken off of it, such as when someone stood up from their seat. The unfortunate man sitting in seat 10F

---

[201] (William E. Smith, April 14, 1986)
[202] (Vincent, 2009 - 2010)

on the trip back to Athens, remained in his seat for the entire trip, thus allowing the timing device to countdown. He was later violently ejected from the aircraft and found in a field among littered debris and the bodies of other victims. The people who had sat within the immediate area of the blast and died, it was reported, were *"not wearing their seatbelts at the time of detonation."* One man recalled, *"We heard a big bang outside the window, and then I saw the man sitting next to me disappear and I felt myself being pulled out."* Luckily for him, he had been wearing his seat belt. [203]

Whether the bombing was responsible by the May 15 group or Abu Nidal, both had been on the radar of U.S. intelligence for some time. Abu Nidal had been implicated in many of the attacks towards civil aviation during the 1980s' and other U.S. and foreign ally targets as well. The Abu Nidal Organization was a militant Palestinian group founded by a man named Abu Nidal. It was later claimed by the U.S. State Department, that the group was responsible for attacks in over 20 countries and killing or injuring over 900 people.

All but one of the air marshals that were on TWA 840 resigned when they returned home. Again, at this time, air marshal duty was a requirement as an FAA Inspector. The violence of the hijackings and bombings of the time period hit home with some, and many decided they were not prepared for a counter-terrorism engagement. However, the violence was just beginning to heat up. [204]

On April 17, 1986, a bomb was discovered by an Israeli air marshal during a profiling search. The bomb was discovered prior to boarding for a flight from London Heathrow to Tel Aviv, Israel; the aircraft was a Boeing 747. A woman, Anne Marie Murphy, was duped into carrying a suitcase given to her by her boyfriend, and the explosive was found inside. The explosive was sophisticated, with a sympathetic detonator* concealed in a calculator, along with an electronic fuse. The boyfriend was ultimately arrested, charged, and convicted by British authorities. Again, this bomb resembled those made by Abu Ibrahim, and he was immediately suspected after the bomb was looked at by explosives experts. The May 15 Terrorist Organization continued their bombing campaign, specifically targeting the aviation system.

---

[203] (Vincent, 2009 - 2010), (Administration F. A., FAA Archival Records - From 2001 Internal Report)
[204] (McLaughlin, 2011 - 2012)
*A Sympathetic Detonator, or sympathetic detonation, is one in which a smaller explosion is set off, which in-turn sets off the main explosive charge.

This incident became known as the *Hindawi Affair*. The perpetrator, Hindawi, subsequently appealed the sentence of 45 years. His appeal was rejected by the Lord Chief Justice, who noted that,

> *"Put briefly, this was about as foul and as horrible a crime as could possibly be imagined. It is no thanks to this applicant that his plot did not succeed in destroying 360 or 370 lives in the effort to promote one side of a political dispute by terrorism. In the judgment of this Court the sentence of 45 years' imprisonment was not a day too long. This application is refused."* [205]

While the FAA Inspectors/ air marshals were apprised of these events, many continued to question their positions, especially those that put their lives in danger on some of the more risky flights. With the rising tide of terrorism being discussed by many air marshals, other events would cause more of the FAA Inspectors to resign.

On July 3, 1986, Billie Vincent formally stepped down as the Director of Civil Aviation Security and retired from the FAA. After his departure, Richard Noble stepped in as the *Acting Director for Civil Aviation Security* until a long term replacement could be found. Richard Noble had worked in aviation security for nearly two decades, and had served as Mr. Vincent's Deputy Director for several years. [206]

In 1986, due to a number of security lapses in Manila, Philippines, the Secretary of Transportation announced that the Manila airport had not maintained effective security standards. An incident involving the attempted smuggling of weapons to the Japanese Yakuza, showed another example of terrorists and criminals using *'dirty airports'* to bring prohibited items into more secure ones, and showed a need for security revisions in Manila. Four Filipina barmaids were found transiting an airport in Okinawa with hundreds of rounds of ammunition and over twenty handguns strapped to their bodies. It was later determined that the barmaids had met with an airport official, who had coached them on how to accomplish their goal. The following day, they had walked through security and were handed the prohibited items by an airport employee.

In response to this example of a criminal or terrorist element using a dirty airport to defeat airport security, the FAA continued its support of foreign airports, in order to improve overall aviation security and the closing of security loopholes. At the end of the day, each country is responsible for ensuring security of its own aviation system and airports. The people within the Office of Civil

---

[205] (Wikipedia, Hindawi Affair)
[206] (Vincent, 2009 - 2010)

Aviation Security had known for some time that the *"spoke-and-wheel effect"* of civil aviation was the blue print for any security fixes, and required the help of all nations for the whole system to become more secure. [207]

The spoke-and-wheel effect took into account that there were certain hubs for air carriers located all over the world. These hubs were the starting point for all aircraft going to multiple destinations around the world as well. With aircraft going out, they were also coming in from other hubs, and thus the spoke and wheel system as it pertained to aviation security, had to account for all aircraft leaving and arriving; security was only as good as the weakest link in that chain. If a poor nation with poor security was part of the chain, then that partner nation's airport would need to be evaluated and bolstered to ensure that security procedures were being followed, or else all other links in the spoke and wheel would weaken. [208]

These security lapses were not only happening in Manila, but at numerous airports around the world. The gaps in security at these more vulnerable *'portals'* were being highlighted as one of the major reasons that hijackings were able to be carried out, such as the TWA 847 hijacking in Athens. Another hijacking would only further stress the need to enhance and monitor security at all airports within the reach of the FAA.

On September 5, 1986, Pan Am Flight 73, a Boeing 747, was stormed by four men during boarding in Karachi, Pakistan. The men, dressed as airport security personnel, exited an "airport security" marked van, firing into the air. During the confusion, the pilots escaped through the overhead hatch. The hijackers demanded a crew to fly them to Cyprus, and a U.S. citizen was killed and dumped on tarmac to emphasize the request. [209]

Negotiations for release of the passengers lasted 17 hours, during which time a Ground Power Unit (GPU) was hooked up to supply power to the lights and air conditioning. During the hijacking and stand-off on the ground, passengers and crew were herded into the center of the aircraft by the terrorists.

When the power to the GPU failed (it ran out of gas) and the lights went out, the hijackers, fearing an assault, began shooting and lobbing hand grenades into the mass of people. Amidst the screams and commotion, 22 were killed and 125 injured. The four hijackers and one co-conspirator were tried and jailed in Pakistan, however, they were subsequently released.

---

[207] (McLaughlin, 2011 - 2012)

[208] (McLaughlin, 2011 - 2012)

[209] (Aleman, 2012), (Wikipedia, Pan Am Flight 73)

The events of Pan Am Flight 73 rocked the non-volunteer force of air marshals, and this caused many more to question the work they were doing, worrying more for their own personal safety than the safety and security of those they were supposed to protect. Although there were no air marshals on this fateful flight, it was a frequently covered route, and this made many question the collateral, non-voluntary duty they were assigned to.

On November 23, 1986, a man named Raymond A. Salazar assumed the role as Director for Civil Aviation Security. Mr. Salazar came into the Office of Civil Aviation Security at a crucial time. With the constant battle of trying to prop up security at airports, not only in the U.S., but abroad as well, and trying to implement the security procedures still being unwound after the fallout from TWA 847, the new Director would be a very busy man. The strengthening of airport security would remain Mr. Salazar's focus over the next several years. Like other Director's before him, Mr. Salazar had been a career employee. This small detail would become a sore that, by Mr. Salazar's appointment, had begun to fester. [210]

By appointing FAA employees, the system was setting itself up for failure, in the respect that these Directors of security were easily manipulated by the lobbying process that constantly pushed back on security reparations for U.S. airlines. Unfortunately for Raymond Salazar, a light would soon be focused on this glaring oversight.

On July 24, 1987, Air Afrique Flight 56 was hijacked by a lone hijacker while over Milan, Italy. The hijacker demanded he be flown to Beirut. The flight had been operating on the Brazzaville (Republic of Congo) to Rome, to Paris route. The hijacker turned out to be a 21 year-old member of the Party of God, named Hussein Ali Mohammed Hariri. [211]

The pilot convinced the hijacker that the plane needed to be refueled and that they needed to land at Geneva International Airport (GVA) in Switzerland. While on the ground, Hariri shot and killed a French citizen and seriously wounded a flight attendant. Swiss forces eventually stormed the aircraft and arrested the hijacker. Shortly after the hijacking, Hariri was tried and sentenced to life in prison by a Swiss court.

---

[210] (Vincent, 2009 - 2010)

[211] (Aleman, 2012), (Wikipedia, Air Afrique)

By the end of fiscal year 1987, the air marshals had flown 268 missions. All of these flights were international and were conducted based on specific threat intelligence. [212]

On November 12, 1987, a flight left Pyongyang, North Korea, carrying two Japanese passport holders, a father and daughter. Hachiya Shinichi, and Hachiya Mayumi were leaving North Korea for Europe, on a trip they had taken two-years prior for shopping and sightseeing. On their previous trip, they had also met with some business contacts. These business contacts were not from a reputable practice; they were members of the North Korean intelligence service. The Hachiya's, in fact, were not Japanese tourists, but North Korean intelligence agents. [213]

Only four months prior, in July 1987, the two North Korean intelligence agents had been to a one-month training course in the use of a specially designed explosive device, one that had been developed by the direct order of Kim Jong II, the self-pronounced *'Supreme Leader of North Korea'*. Kim Jong II's desire was to blow up a South Korean passenger aircraft, to *"discourage other Nation's from participating in the 1988 Seoul Olympics."* By November 12, 1987, the two agents and their handlers were well on their way to executing a plan to carry out these orders.

On November 27, 1987, the two intelligence agents were in Belgrade, Yugoslavia. They had already been given an explosive device and carried two sets of airline tickets: One pair of tickets had the couple routed from Baghdad, Iraq to Seoul, South Korea, and another pair had the two routed from Abu Dhabi, in the United Arab Emirates (UAE), to Amman, Jordan. Both pairs of tickets were booked under the alias Hachiya.

On November 29, 1987, Korean Air Flight 858, a Boeing707, was boarded in Baghdad after the intelligence agents arrived from Belgrade. Korean Air Flight 858 (KAL 858) would depart Baghdad for Abu Dhabi, UAE, with a final destination of Seoul, South Korea. The two North Korean agents also boarded Flight 858, with their explosive in-tow; they did not intend to remain for the entire flight.

The elder intelligence agent was questioned by Iraqi security at Baghdad International Airport (BIA) prior to boarding: It was standard procedure during this time for airport security to confiscate batteries in electronics, in an attempt

---

[212] (Administration F. A., FAA Archival Records - From 2001 Internal Report)
[213] ((Various)), (Aleman, 2012), (McLaughlin, 2011 - 2012), (Wikipedia, Korean Air Flight 858)

to remove the power source from potential explosive devices, and the security agent wanted to perform the procedure on the intelligence agent's radio. The crafty old intelligence officer was quick to respond and turned on the clock radio to show that it worked. He pleaded that the flight was a long one, and that the radio would keep him occupied. His ploy worked, and the clock radio was returned intact.

The intelligence agents left the aircraft in Abu Dhabi, leaving a handbag containing the bomb in an overhead compartment, above seats 7B and 7C. The explosive was sophisticated and consisted of a main charge of liquid explosive concealed in a whisky bottle, with a sympathetic detonator and digital watch delay fuse mechanism concealed in a clock radio.[214]

As the plane prepared to land in Bangkok, Thailand, it's final leg prior to continuing on to South Korea, it exploded somewhere over the border between Thailand and Burma, killing 115 passengers and crew.

Both subjects were arrested in Bahrain, as they attempted to make their way to Amman. They had been forced to fly to Bahrain by the authorities in Abu Dhabi, due to some concerns over their passports. In Bahrain, the woman, later identified as Kim Hyon Hui, was suspected of traveling under a false passport; the passport for the man was real, having been procured by the intelligence agent from an unknowing former business partner. During interrogation in Bahrain, the male committed suicide by biting down on a cyanide capsule concealed in a cigarette. The female attempted the same, but only ingested enough of the poison to put her in the hospital for two weeks. She was eventually turned over to South Korean authorities and confessed details of the entire incident, including the North Korean government's involvement in the plot, and the explosive's composition. The agent, Kim Hyon Hui, later wrote a book on how the government trained her as a North Korean spy, called *"The Tears of My Soul."* She was later pardoned of a life sentence by the President of South Korea, Roh Tae-woo, who stated *"she is as much a victim of this evil regime as the passengers aboard KAL 858."*

The FAA conducted a test on the validity of the terrorist's statements in regards to the radical new Improvised Explosive Device (IED) used on KAL 858. The FAA concluded that the IED the terrorist had described could have caused the destruction of the aircraft.

---

[214] ((Various)), (Aleman, 2012), (McLaughlin, 2011 - 2012), (Wikipedia, Korean Air Flight 858)

The attack on Korean Air Flight 858 took 3 years to plan, and showed the determination and patience of terrorist organizations in planning and attacking their targets. Due to the bombing of KAL 858 the air marshal program decided to man all U.S. air carrier flights going in and out of South Korea for the upcoming Summer Olympics in Seoul.

On December 7, 1987, Pacific Southwest Airways Flight 1771 crashed in Cayucos, California, in San Louis Obispo County. The voice recorder onboard was found in the wreckage and implicated a murder-suicide of a former employee of the parent company for Pacific Southwest Airways. [215]

The murder-suicide and likely hijacking, of Southern Airways Flight 1771, demonstrated the *'insider threat'* from within airlines and airports. Over time, the insider threat had been the cause of many security failures around the world, leading to many prior hijackings and bombings, along with the smuggling of contraband. This would continue to be a threat to aviation security, and experts in the field were constantly trying to find ways of mitigating the insider threat risk.

With the continuing of the FAA's attempt to strengthen civil aviation security, the baggage screening system had caught the eyes of those within the Office of Civil Aviation Security as a possible weakness, and on December 17, 1987, a rule was put in place requiring *'positive bag match'* with passengers before a flight departed. According to this emergency rule, the positive bag match system was required of all international flights of U.S. airlines. The rule required that all bags be accompanied with a passenger onboard before the aircraft closed its doors and pushed back from the gate; if the passenger was not on the aircraft, the bags were required to be removed. [216]

On April 5, 1988, Kuwait Air Flight 422 was hijacked four hours into its flight from Bangkok to Kuwait. Two men burst into the cockpit with guns drawn, and instructed the pilots *"to not touch any instruments;"* the aircraft was a Boeing 747.

Within minutes, they instructed the captain to disengage the auto pilot, change course to a specific heading, and re-engage the auto pilot. The two men were part of a team of seven to nine hijackers*. The aircraft was flown under

---

[215] (Aleman, 2012)

[216] (Aleman, 2012)

*The total number of hijackers remains unknown. The impact of the hijacking of Kuwait Air Flight 422 on the FAM Program was immense. Some of the same tactics used on KU422 would again be seen during the hijackings on 9/11.

supervision of one of the hijackers, later believed to be a trained flight engineer, to Masshad, Iran.

Like other previous aircraft hijackings, there was a demand for the release of the DAWA 17. The hijackers demonstrated a professional, highly trained, and disciplined behavior throughout the event. They exhibited a keen awareness of special operations rescue techniques and anticipated responses of law enforcement and security personnel.

During the 16 day incident, the aircraft left Mashhad International Airport (MHD), then stopped and refueled in Cyprus, where the bodies of two Kuwaiti citizens were removed. The aircraft then departed Larnaca International Airport (LCA) in Cyprus and continued to Algieria. During the night of April 22, with the international media covering the event at Hourari International Airport (ALG), Algeria, the hijackers left the aircraft and were never heard from again.[217]

A former air marshal working at the time commented on the terrorists change in tactics, saying *"this one we referred to as the "A-Team" and our tactics and deployment strategies were significantly adjusted/ upgraded accordingly."* Congress approved an additional 300 FAM positions because of the Kuwait Air Flight 422 episode*.

On March 4, 1988, a Delta Airlines passenger set off the metal detector at Atlanta's Hartsfield International Airport (ATL). He refused the request of police officer's to search his person. He was later found to be armed with a .25 caliber pistol. Although it is hard to prove a negative, this incident was documented as a prevented hijacking. [218]

By the end of fiscal year 1988, there had been 368 FAM missions flown. A report also stated that between January 1 and June 30, 1988, FAMs flew 4,250,000 nautical miles and conducted 95 security assessments at airports overseas. These assessments were being done pursuant to the International Security and Development Cooperation Act of 1985, or Public Law 99-83.

---

[217] (McLaughlin, 2011 - 2012)

[218] (Administration D. o., Semi Annual Report to Congress on the Effectiveness of the Civil Aviation Security Program, January 1, 1988 - June 30, 1988)
*The fact that the U.S. Congress approved so many new FAM positions due to this hijacking, shows the gravity of the KU422 hijacking. By using their own trained pilot to steer one of the aircraft, the terrorists had proven, by 1988, that they were becoming technically proficient to carry out very elaborate attacks on civil aviation interests.

The bi-annual report to congress on civil aviation security, had the following to say about the air marshal program: [219]

"We continued to assign Federal Air Marshal Teams to U.S. air carriers on selected flights operating in especially sensitive or threatened areas throughout the world."

"Although there were no hijackings or attempted hijackings of U.S. air carriers during the reporting period, hijackings conducted in other countries continue to demonstrate the vulnerability of civil aviation aircraft."

"The missions, all flown with U.S. air carriers, were selected based on analysis of worldwide terrorist activities. Since civil aviation continues to represent an attractive target to terrorists, FAM's will continue this very effective countermeasure of providing in-flight security."

By the latter half of 1988, terrorist hijackings around the world began to increase, and a new tactic began to emerge with multiple bombings and attempted bombings*. The death and destruction that had been a hallmark of the terrorist campaign caused many in the FAM program to reassess their commitment. However, 300 new positions became available, and many more men and women signed on as FAA Inspectors.

There was also a change in the use of firearm for the FAMs in the latter half of 1988. Due to a study conducted by the USSS, the air marshal program shifted to a Sig Sauer P226, 9mm firearm. This shift was significant, in that the air marshals went from using a revolver to a semi-automatic pistol. Although it was a revolver qualification course, the Practical Pistol Course, or PPC, would continue to be the Federal Air Marshal firearms qualification standard. [220]

The move to semi-automatic pistols and more powerful weapons was being carried out by many law enforcement agencies at the time. Two years prior, on April 11, 1986, a shootout between two bank robbers and the FBI forced a review of handgun policies across the United States. The tragedy of this shooting, in an unincorporated region of Miami-Dade County, Florida, left two FBI agents

---

[219] (Administration D. o., Semi Annual Report to Congress on the Effectiveness of the Civil Aviation Security Program, January 1, 1988 - June 30, 1988)
[220] (McLaughlin, 2011 - 2012)
*Hijackings were becoming ever more violent at the time as well, however, in the late 1980s' the focus was on bomb threats against the aviation sector.

dead and five others injured, due to the heavily armed actions of bank robbers Russell Matix and Michael Platt.

The air marshals had carried a revolver for so long that it was a major change to go to the semi-automatic Sig Sauer. Although the revolver would, within a year or two, be phased out completely, for the first couple of years a FAM could choose to carry either the Sig Sauer P226, or the six-shot revolver.[221]

On October 2, 1988, Israeli intelligence officials notified the West German Intelligence Service, Bundesnachrichtendienst (BND)* that a General Command (GC) PLFP cell (PLFP-GC) was operating throughout Europe, including West Germany. Details of safe houses were given, along with other information regarding the operational planning of these cells.

The BND sought approval for a surveillance operation on PFLP-GC safe houses in West Germany, and by October 10, 1988, *Operation Herbslaub*, or *Autumn Leaves*, had begun. Sixteen targets in West Germany were watched 24-hours per day, seven days a week. This surveillance and the information reaped from it, would later become the subject of much controversy.

On October 16, two of the men under surveillance went shopping for electronics. Marwan Khreesat and Haffez Dalkamoni were looking for items that they could use for hiding explosives. They had been tasked with building an IED out of common electronics, and Khreesat was a master bomb builder, with plenty of experience and many murders on his hands. Khreesat was looking for older model electronics; one's that he knew he could manipulate for their destructive purpose, but would leave them operational: Terrorists knew they may be asked to prove that electronics worked before they were allowed past security check points; this had been done in Baghdad prior to the Korean Air Flight 858 bombing.

On October 26, sixteen terrorists from the PFLP were arrested in West Germany. A flat in Neuss received much of the attention, when numerous items were found for bomb making. Electronics in the apartment had been modified as IEDs, and it appeared that the PFLP was in the final stages of a major attack. Missing from the apartment in Neuss that day was a Toshiba Bomb Beat cassette player. It was not known at the time, but this particular cassette player would find its way onto a commercial aircraft with disastrous consequences.

---

[221] (McLaughlin, 2011 - 2012)
*The Bundesnachrichtendienst, or BND, was formed on April 1, 1956, as the German Federal Intelligence Service. In 1988 the BND was heavily involved in the Cold War effort, and were severely limited on manpower.

During questioning, Dalkamoni would say, *"under my supervision and responsibility, Khreesat modified into bombs one Toshiba radio recorder."*

On December 5, 1988, the FAA issued a security bulletin; they had received information from U.S. intelligence that a Pan Am flight would be blown up from Frankfurt to the United States within two weeks. This bulletin was taken very seriously and was sent to all U.S. air carriers, including Pan Am.[222] On December 21, 1988, a flight originating in Malta landed in Frankfurt, and exchanged passengers and baggage to an aircraft on its journey to London, before exchanging baggage and passengers to New York's JFK airport on Pan Am 103. It was not yet realized, but this particular flight would cause major security changes in civil aviation throughout the world.

Pan Am 103, a Boeing 747, was scheduled from London Heathrow to JFK, however, the flight would never make its final destination: While over Lockerbie, Scotland, the plane exploded, killing 259 onboard and another 11 on the ground.

There were immediate calls claiming responsibility for the attack. It was first thought that the Iranians were behind the bombing, due to the accidental downing of an Iranian airliner by the U.S. five months prior. One day after the attack, the most credible claim of responsibility, according to the Central Intelligence Agency, came from a group that called themselves the *Guardians of the Islamic Revolution.*

The security bulletin, which had been issued 16 days prior, was later found under a pile of papers on a security desk at Frankfurt airport; it appeared that the threat was not taken seriously at Pan Am.

Not long after the tragedy, debris began being collected by investigators on the ground in Scotland. Laboratories at Boeing in Kent, Washington, had figured out that Pan Am 103 had been downed by a high-explosive of some kind. Also, early on was the realization that terrorists were getting ever more sophisticated in their operational planning and knowledge of the aviation system. As one Boeing employee and expert pointed out, *"It was a diabolically well-planned event, handled by experts in the knowledge of the aircraft, its structure, the flight plan – the works."* [223] The explosion that brought down the Boeing 747 aircraft had immediately severed the cockpit from the fuselage and the communications and control systems. The significance of this event was not lost on security experts at the FAA; a new committee formed in the disasters wake would lay blame on both the FAA and the airline industry.

---

[222] (McLaughlin, 2011 - 2012), (Steele, 2012)

[223] (Magazine, Diabollically Planned: Pan Am's Flight 103, January 9, 1989)

One of the many findings that would arise from the Congressional Committee of the Pan Am 103 bombing investigation was that the FAA was '*in-bed*' with the airlines. Their recommendation was to have a security person come from outside the FAA from now on*. [224]

Before the bombing of Pan Am 103, every former Director of Civil Aviation Security, respectively, was hired from within the FAA; after Pan Am 103, this would not be the case. There would be a re-structuring and reforming of the FAA's aviation security capabilities, and the Office of Civil Aviation Security would spend much of the next decade trying to implement all of the numerous recommendations that would be spawned from the committee's meetings. [225]

The bombing of Pan Am 103 was, for 1988, of the same magnitude of the terrorist attacks that took place over a decade later, on September 11, 2001. December 24, 1988, was a tragic day for the country, and civil aviation was forever changed because of Pan Am 103 in many regards. The investigation was just beginning in late 1988, but there would be much more information gleaned for a decade to come. It would later be determined that the terrorists had *again* used a dirty airport to insert their explosive. In Malta, the terrorists were able to obtain baggage tags from an insider, to place on the luggage which would contain the bomb and facilitate its transfer. Later, when the baggage transited the airport in Frankfurt, the man screening bags in the x-ray machine had only been on the job for a few months, and the package containing the explosive, housed in a radio, was also missed by screeners in London. [226]

By then, in late 1988, the number of hijackings and bombings targeting civil aviation were still flourishing, and the world was reeling from the bombing of Pan Am 103. This had been a recurring problem for three-decades, and the numbers of disasters related to these events were on the rise. As this steady rise in terrorism took place, air marshals continued to cover international flights on U.S. air carriers.

In regards to civil aviation security and the Federal Air Marshal Program, the following statistics were made public in the *Semi-Annual Report to Congress on*

---

[224] (Vincent, 2009 - 2010), (Agency C. I., December 22, 1988), (Commission, July 22, 2004)
[225] (Steele, 2012)
[226] (Aleman, 2012)
*Along with the FAA, Pan Am took much of the blame for numerous failures as well, and was later convicted of gross negligence on June 10, 1992.

the Effectiveness of the Civil Aviation Security Program, covering the period ending December 31, 1988: [227]

- Federal Air Marshal teams flew over 7,200,000 nautical miles, and
- 45 assessments of foreign airports were conducted.
- Also, the following actions were mandated by the FAA in response to the Pan Am 103 bombing:

    1. 100% x-ray or inspection of all checked baggage,
    2. Prohibiting passenger access to checked baggage after security inspection,
    3. Positive matching of all passengers and checked baggage, and
    4. X-ray or physical examination of small packages or parcels shipped through passenger counters.

In 1989, in the wake of the Pan Am 103 bombing, the Aviation Security Advisory Committee (ASAC) was established by the U.S. Secretary of Transportation. The committee's responsibilities were said to be *"an important partnership of FAA and representatives of other government agencies, the aviation industry, and the flying public. The Secretary of Transportation established ASAC in 1989 in the aftermath of the bombing of Pan Am Flight 103 as a forum for improving civil aviation security. Plenary sessions offer the opportunity to exchange views and information. Members also sit or. topical subcommittees and working groups that focus on specific security issues; the BWG (Base line Working Group) was one such working group. "*

For the decade leading to Pan Am 103, bombings of aircraft had been on the rise. The Director of Civil Aviation Security, Raymond Salazar and others within the Office of Civil Aviation Security, remained focused on looking for ways to help shore up ground security abroad after the tragedy. Enhancing security on the ground would help hinder the ability of terrorists from bringing explosives onboard aircraft in the future.

Aircraft hijackings throughout 1989 were scarce. Due to intelligence chatter on possible threats to civil aviation, there were a total of 241 missions flown during the entire fiscal year; all missions were international. [228]

---

[227] (Administration D. o., Semi Annual Report to Congress on the Effectiveness of the Civil Aviation Security Program, July 1, 1988 - December 30, 1988)
[228] (Administration F. A., FAA Archival Records - From 2001 Internal Report)

Between 1988 and 1989, a group called al-Qaeda was being organized by Osama bin-Laden, a Saudi dissident that had helped organize fighters for the Afghan resistance during the Afghan-Russian War. With the war in Afghanistan over, Osama bin-Laden turned his focus on forming a radical Sunni Muslim movement calling for his own form of *global jihad*, or war against non-practicing Muslims*. The forming of al-Qaeda was meant to facilitate the movement of personnel and expand jihad operations to other areas outside Afghanistan. However, al-Qaeda would begin planning and carrying out terrorist acts against many western targets shortly after their founding. [229]

From 1989 to 1990, U.S. intelligence began receiving an overwhelming amount of information on the threat of Middle East terrorism. The Office of Civil Aviation Security was slowly becoming more closely associated with the intelligence community and was apprised of the threats. The security experts at the FAA continued putting together new procedures to help prevent other tragedies, such as had befallen Pan Am 103.

For many in the security office, it seemed like they were constantly fighting a losing battle with the airlines. Shortly after the bombing of Pan Am 103, the FAA required all U.S. air carriers to have a positive match for bags and passengers. This meant that, throughout Europe and the U.S., all airlines would have to ensure passengers were onboard if their checked luggage was to remain on the flight. This was a repeat of a prior emergency FAA rule, put in place on December 17, 1987, one year prior to the tragedy of Pan Am 103, requiring airlines originating from an international airport to *physically search* all bags transiting through the system before they were loaded; the failure of Pan Am to follow this emergency rule had led to the many deaths over Lockerbie and on the ground.

Amidst these changes and sometime between 1989 and 1990, the air marshals made a switch from the Sig P226 semi-automatic handgun, to the Sig P228. The Sig P228 was a more compact version of the P226. The FAM program would use the Sig Sauer P228 firearm for nearly a decade. [230]

On May 9, 1990, Raymond Salazar stepped down as the Director of Civil Aviation Security and was reassigned to a post in Florida; his resignation came just six days before the release of the *Presidential Commission on Aviation Security and Terrorism* investigation report. This commission and report were prepared in response to the Pan Am 103 bombing. Joseph K. Blank, a former anti-air piracy task force member, summed up the resignation of Raymond Salazar: *"I don't remember [Salazar's] name, but Busey (the Administrator of the FAA)*

---

[229] (Coll, The Bin Ladens: An Arabian Family in the American Century, 2008)
[230] (McLaughlin, 2011 - 2012)
*Mostly, westerners were targeted.

really rode him hard due to the Pan Am 103 bombing, and he eventually left the position." [231]

An article from the Washington Post summarized the recommendations of the commission, on May 15, 1990:

"[A] top-to-bottom revamping of the government's airline security apparatus, [and] threats to civil aviation should be made public if they are deemed sufficiently credible." It also called for *"[a] thorough assessment of the security threat at domestic airports."*

The commission also recommended *"that a new assistant secretary of transportation for security and intelligence [needs to be] created to oversee aviation safety, and that the FAA's security division be elevated to report directly to Busey (Administrator of the FAA). It also recommended that a federal security manager be created at each major airport."*

On October 2, 1990, a Boeing 737, Xiamen Airlines Flight 8301, veered out of control during approach, causing the aircraft to hit a Boeing 757 on the ground. Seven of the nine crew, and 75 of the 93 passengers, were killed. Flight 8301 had been hijacked, and the hijacker had managed to gain access to the cockpit. After negotiations between the hijacker and the ground failed, it is believed the hijacker attempted to take control of the aircraft and was responsible for the death of most onboard. [232]

Once again, a lone wolf had successfully hijacked an aircraft, only this time deliberately crashing it. Air marshals practiced for such events, and throughout this time they continued providing in-flight security as directed by the FAA. They knew that one of the biggest threats to the hijacking of an aircraft came from the lone wolf.* By this time, with hijackings and bombings becoming ever more a national security threat, air marshals were steadily increasing their mission flight coverage.

By the end of the 1990 fiscal year, 343 missions had been flown by air marshals. This number was a significant increase from past missions, and can be directly contributed to the threat at this time. [233]

---

[231] (Blank, 2010)

[232] (McLaughlin, 2011 - 2012), (Xiamen Airlines Flight 8301)

[233] (Administration F. A., FAA Archival Records - From 2001 Internal Report)
*Lone wolf hijackers are harder to detect prior to attack. Because of their limited contact to others, in comparison to a terrorist organization, they have a better ability to go undetected while gathering information on the target.

In light of the Pan Am 103 investigation and demands by the Congressional Committee, the appointment of retired U.S. Marine Corps Major General O.K. Steele, as the Associate Administrator for Civil Aviation Security, had been secured on November 1, 1990. [234]

Although O.K. Steele had been the first appointed to the position of Associate Administrator for Civil Aviation Security, one that would later be referred to as ACS1, he was not the first in mind for the position.

A man named Cathal Flynn, who grew up, and was educated in, Ireland, was offered the job by his old friend, the Administrator of the FAA, James Busey. Mr. Flynn had served in the U.S. Navy and retired as a one-star Vice Admiral, and had known Mr. Busey in the military.

Due to family obligations, and since staying in the Washington DC area was not an option at the time, Mr. Flynn recommended an old colleague, Orlo Steele. The two had worked together when Mr. Flynn was working for the Naval Criminal Investigative Service (NCIS). Mr. Steele had helped Mr. Flynn set up physical security training while the two were in the military working on a joint project.

Orlo Keith (O.K.) Steele was born in Oakland, CA, on October 28, 1932. He later graduated from Stanford University, with a B.A. degree in political science. He entered the Marine Corps in 1955, and was later designated an infantry officer and assigned to the 3rd Marine Division, where he served as Platoon Commander. He also served as the Assistant S-3 (the operations officer in military units), in 2nd Battalion, 9th Marines. [235]

O.K. Steele later found himself ordered to the Marine Corps Mountain Warfare Training Center in Bridgeport, CA. He served there for two years, as the Officer-in-Charge/ Senior Instructor Guide of the Mountain Leadership School. Mr. Steele would become very fond of the Mountain Warfare Training Center, and he would eventually write a book about its history. He went on to attend training at the Amphibious Warfare School in Quantico, VA, and after graduating in July 1967, was ordered to Vietnam, where he served with the 1st Marine Division.

Mr. Steele went on to further his education between 1979 and 1980, when he again became a student, this time at the National War College in Washington, DC.

---

[234] (Steele, 2012)
[235] (Steele, 2012)

Later in his career, he was assigned duty as the Deputy Naval Inspector General for Marine Corps Matters/Inspector General of the Marine Corps, on September 29, 1989. He served in this capacity until his retirement from the Marine Corps, on October 1, 1990.

Mr.. Steele's personal decorations and awards included: The Distinguished Service Medal; Bronze Star Medal with Combat "V"; Combat Action Ribbon; Presidential Unit Citation with one bronze star; Navy Meritorious Unit Citation with one bronze star; National Defense Service Medal; Vietnam Service Medal with four bronze stars; Sea Service Deployment Ribbon; Overseas Service Ribbon: Republic of Vietnam Cross of Gallantry with gold star; Republic of Vietnam Meritorious Unit Citation Gallantry Cross with Palm, and Republic of Vietnam Campaign Medal with device.

After retiring from the Marine Corps, and upon recommendation from Cathal Flynn, Major General (Ret.) O.K. Steel was given the position as the Associate Administrator for Civil Aviation Security (ACS1). He understood terrorism as a military officer, with his many ties to the intelligence community and special operations. In this position, Mr. Steele would begin to develop a vision for the Federal Air Marshal Program; this vision would further strengthen the bond between FAA security and the intelligence community, and would eventually turn the future air marshal force into the most specialized experts in civil aviation security the world had ever seen.

As the world moved into 1990, there was a rift between Iraq and Kuwait which would lead to the Iraq-Kuwait War. The rift resulted in a seven-month - long occupation of Kuwait, which subsequently led to the direct military involvement of the U.S. and coalition forces.

U.S. intelligence agencies during this time were essentially fighting two wars; they were fighting the ground war in Kuwait and a new terrorist threat in Europe. This terrorist threat, and the intelligence agencies efforts to thwart it, carried through 1990 and into 1991. Although some of the circumstances leading to the heightened threat towards civil aviation are still classified, it placed an immense strain on aviation security and drastically changed the position of Federal Air Marshal.[236]

In fiscal year 1991, there were 258 FAM missions flown. These missions were all threat generated and fed to civil aviation security professionals directly from U.S. intelligence agencies. All of the missions covered during this period were on international, U.S. flagged flights

---

[236] (McLaughlin, 2011 - 2012)

Chapter VIII

Counter Terrorism Specialization

FAA Office of Civil Aviation Security
(September 1992 - September 10, 2001)

W hile living in Germany and working as a Civil Aviation Security Liaison Officer (CASLO) for the FAA in Frankfurt, Germany, and shortly after helping to investigate the Pan Am 103 crash in 1988, Gregory Murray McLaughlin was getting ready to take vacation with his wife in Europe. They were joined that spring by the newly appointed Associate Administrator for Civil Aviation Security, O.K. Steele. During his trip to Germany, the retired Major General would extend an offer that McLaughlin couldn't refuse. [237]

Mr. McLaughlin had worked as an air marshal ever since he was hired in the aftermath of TWA 847. He was in the air flying by October 1985, after being hired and trained in Marana, Arizona. Mr. McLaughlin had seen the ups and downs of the air marshal program, and had flown countless missions in support

---

[237] (McLaughlin, 2011 - 2012)

of in-flight security duties, before being sent to Frankfurt as part of the Pan Am 103 investigation team.

Gregory M. McLaughlin grew up in Northern New Jersey, and enjoyed what most young men did in the early 1960's; he played football and spent time with his neighborhood friends. The McLaughlin family moved to Illinois while Greg was still in High School, and he graduated in a new state, then rushed off to college in Kentucky, graduating in 1969.

Mr. McLaughlin was immediately drafted into the U.S. Marine Corps and went through boot camp in 1969. When it became known that Mr. McLaughlin had a degree from college, he was sent through Officer Candidate School (OCS). After OCS, he was assigned as an infantry officer in Vietnam until 1972, after which he returned to Illinois and found a job with the Skokie Police Department, in a large suburb of Chicago.

For thirteen years, until 1985, he would serve on the Skokie Police Department for the last five years, he would serve as a violent crimes detective; some capitol cases brought by Mr. McLaughlin caused him to make a name for himself in law enforcement.

Later, in 1989, when Mr. McLaughlin had already been an air marshal for four years, a man named Monte Belger, who would later go on to serve as the Associate Administrator for the FAA, knew of McLaughlin's investigative experience as a law enforcement officer in Illinois. Thus, he was selected to help with the investigation of Pan Am 103, and would later become one of the first CASLOs assigned overseas to help evaluate the security of foreign airports. [238]

By 1992, when O.K. Steele began having his vision for a new, stronger air marshal program, Mr. McLaughlin had already contributed enormously to the field of civil aviation security. He had worked on many classified projects in Germany, and had made many contacts in the aviation security and intelligence communities abroad. This caused O.K. Steele to visit McLaughlin in the spring of 1992.

The FAA Associate Administrator for the Office of Civil Aviation Security, O.K. Steele, came to Mr. McLaughlin because of his reputation, and told him about his plan to try and make the Federal Air Marshals a *voluntary force*, with tougher firearms qualification and physical fitness standards for all who wanted to stay onboard.

---

[238] (McLaughlin, 2011 - 2012)

Mr. Steele told McLaughlin that he envisioned the air marshals flying 60% of the time, as opposed to the 40% they had as FAA Inspectors throughout the 1980s' and early 1990s'. O.K. Steele had a vision of a FAM program that was modeled after what can be seen with a lot of tier-one groups* in the military today. The Associate Administrator told McLaughlin that he wanted him to be the Director of this new force; Greg McLaughlin accepted. [239]

In September 1992, Greg McLaughlin returned from Germany and went to work in Washington DC for the FAA, as the new Director of the Federal Air Marshal Program. Orlo Steele wanted McLaughlin to make the new staff of air marshals *the* experts in civil aviation security and hijackings. He began by ordering McLaughlin to send out letters to all the current Federal Air Marshals throughout the FAA, notifying the force that, in order to stay in the position, they had to write back and tell McLaughlin they wished to volunteer.

The letter would state that the position of a FAM would be 60% of their duties, and only 40% would be that of an FAA Inspector/ security specialist. Mr. McLaughlin was given the authority to keep 55 part-time employees (air marshals) and 11 staff.

In 1992, there were between 250 and 300 FAMs. The replies that came back in response to the letter were not many, and after receiving these, McLaughlin began tasking managers with putting together a training program for the "new FAMs." He called this training *"skills upgrade training,"* but as he recalled, it was more like a *"skills upgrade try out."*

Before the new training program started, Steele told McLaughlin he wanted him to find the best pistol shooters in the world to help get their firearms program running; he wanted the new FAMs to be the best. McLaughlin found a man by the name of Tom Bullins to revamp the entire FAMs firearms program. Tom Bullins was the owner and operator of *Trigger Time*, a shooting school located outside the back gate of Ft. Bragg, NC, which trained some of the most elite soldiers found in the U.S. military. [240]

Mr. Bullins helped to develop the firearms qualifications course for the new air marshal program. This qualification standard would become known as the Tactical Pistol Course, or TPC.

---

[239] (Steele, 2012)
[240] (McLaughlin, 2011 - 2012), (Trigger Time)
* Tier-one military groups are those such as U.S. Special Forces, U.S. Navy SEALs, Delta Force, etc.

The TPC consisted of the following course of fire, shot from seven yards:

- From Concealed Holster – fire one round in 1.65 seconds (this was done twice).
- From Low Ready – fire two rounds in 1.35 seconds (this was done twice).
- From Low Ready – fire one round, reload and then fire one additional round in 3.25 seconds (this was done twice).
- From Concealed Holster - 180° pivot, one round each at three targets in 3.50 seconds (done twice; turning left first and right second).
- From Low Ready – fire one round, drop to one knee, emergency reload, fire one additional round in 4.00 seconds (this was done twice).

Mr. Bullins also helped bring instructors from some of the special operations groups that trained with him, such as Delta Force and SEAL Team Six. These instructors would help train the new air marshals and assess them during the skills upgrade training.

The TPC was somewhat of a misnomer. There was no *'tactical'* thought process that had to be applied to the qualification course, since all times and standards were given to the shooter beforehand. The TPC was more of a *'mechanics course'* in which the shooter demonstrated the fundamentals of marksmanship within a given time constraint.

Most of the air marshals that had volunteered and were able to pass the TPC, had some form of military background. Only one woman passed the skills upgrade training, and this would come to cause problems for Mr. McLaughlin due to Equal Employment Opportunity (EEO) complaints; Mr. McLaughlin would deal with the EEO complaints for over a year.

Most of the EEO complaints that were filed stemmed from the changes made to the physical fitness qualification standard, which was a two mile run, a certain fixed number of pull-ups, fixed number of sit-ups, and a fixed number of push-ups; the standards were the same for both men and women. The TPC was the most difficult obstacle for candidates to pass during the skills upgrade training, and McLaughlin would later testify in court: "*I failed people for missing the standard by a fraction of a second. This was the standard, and I would not sacrifice the standards.*"[241]

The group of air marshals to complete skills upgrade training in late 1992 numbered 55. Although the air marshals still resided in various offices through-

---

[241] (McLaughlin, 2011 - 2012)

out the U.S., Major General Orlo Steele had envisioned a permanent home for the force. This would come later, but the program would start to look at possible locations for a home early on in their reorganization.

The air marshals that were in place by the end of 1992 began conducting most of their training at Quantico, VA. They shared a range with the FBI Hostage Rescue Team (HRT) and developed close ties there. The shoot house and training facility consisted of 360-degree live-fire ranges, shoot houses, and airplane mockups. [242]

During this time, on paper, if one looked at an organizational chart of the air marshal program within the FAA, there were three people between Greg McLaughlin and the Associate Administrator for Civil Aviation Security; however, this was not the way it worked. All the missions being handed out to the air marshals during this time came directly from the Associate Administrator, and Mr. McLaughlin would answer only to him.

All of the missions going forward were on international routes, as they had been since the hijacking of TWA Flight 847 in late 1985, and were directly tied to the intelligence community. During this new transition, Director McLaughlin would work on getting all air marshals and staff SCI (Sensitive Compartmented Information) clearance for their Top Secret (TS) classifications. This would bring the Office of Civil Aviation Security and the air marshals ever closer to the intelligence community. The director would also have a staff member within civil aviation security that worked full time at Langley, and missions for FAMs would be tasked based on information coming through these networks. By the end of 1992, there were a total of 251 missions flown.

Going into the year 1993, the new air marshal program under O.K. Steele, as Associate Administrator of Civil Aviation Security, and Greg McLaughlin, as Director of the Federal Air Marshal Program, was starting to thrive. The new force of 55, throughout 1993, would make a name for themselves as being extremely proficient pistol shooters.

Between 1992 and 1993, if an air marshal was called for a mission they were brought in to Washington DC, one to two-days prior. The air marshal(s) would demonstrate their proficiency by passing the TPC and doing a Physical Training (PT) fitness test. If the air marshal did not pass, they didn't go on the mission. However, McLaughlin elaborated *"again, now you are talking about all volunteers; they were people that were already in shape and had the right attitude,*

---

[242] (McLaughlin, 2011 - 2012), (Steele, 2012)

and [if] you told them they had to go to Saudi Arabia they didn't go crazy about it. "[243]

Throughout 1993, the air marshals continued looking for a home. They had looked at building a facility at Quantico, but it was too cost prohibitive. The air marshals enjoyed training with the HRT team, however, it was a shared facility and they wanted a place of their own to train in their highly specialized field.

Contacts grew during this time, and there was cross training from various military groups at Ft. Bragg, NC. Starting in 1993, McLaughlin started sending a team every year to attend the John F. Kennedy's School of Special Warfare and other related counter-terrorism specific training venues.

In October 1993, Major General O.K. Steele decided to retire back to California. He had only planned on staying for a few years, and by 1993 he had finally decided to move on towards a well-deserved retirement. [244]

After Mr. Steele announced his retirement, retired U.S. Navy Vice Admiral (VADM), Cathal Flynn decided to put his name back in for the position of ACS1. Mr. Flynn ended up securing a consulting position with the FAA for November and December 1993. In January 1994, Cathal Flynn was confirmed as the new Associate Administrator for Civil Aviation Security. [245]

Cathal Flynn came into this position with numerous contacts throughout the military special operations and intelligence communities. The air marshals that were under Cathal Flynn and Greg McLaughlin, operating as a small, close-knit organization, would continue to specialize in the field of aviation security and counter-terrorism throughout the decade. Cathal Flynn had worked with Orlo Steele in the past, and he bought into the vision that Steele had for the air marshal as an *all-volunteer* force. The FAMs would continue to benefit from this vision, and the traditions carried on by Cathal Flynn.

Cathal "Irish" Flynn was born in Dublin, Ireland, in 1938. He went on to graduate from the University of Dublin, Trinity College, in 1959. He came back to the U.S. in 1960, and decided that he should join the draft. After a friend told him about the Navy, he signed up. He was later commissioned as an officer, and it was during his officer training that he saw a demonstration by a petty officer from the Underwater Demolition Teams (UDT) in Little Creek, Virginia. Cathal Flynn thought it looked interesting and joined the elite group.

---

[243] (McLaughlin, 2011 - 2012)
[244] (Steele, 2012)
[245] (Flynn, 2012)

Mr. Flynn went to the training for UDT, and upon graduation was sent to UDT-11 in Coronado, CA. Shortly before the Vietnam War, Mr. Flynn went to work with the newly formed SEAL Team One, also in Coronado. After serving in Vietnam, Mr. Flynn decided he would stay in the Navy, and in 1965 he went on to serve as an officer in the regular U.S. Navy, where he spent 30-years before retiring in 1990.

When VADM Cathal Flynn joined the FAA as the Associate Administrator for Civil Aviation Security, he had amassed numerous contacts with his work at the Naval Investigative Service (NCIS) and the Joint Special Operations Command (JSOC). He would use these contacts to help boost the image, and help enhance the already stellar training, of the air marshal program.

As Cathal Flynn settled into his new position, the air marshals continued to be fed intelligence on threats to commercial flights, and accordingly ramped up their missions. During the fiscal year of 1993, there were a total of 266 missions flown. [246]

On February 26, 1993, a bomb was detonated in the parking structure of the World Trade Center's North Tower, in New York. The bomb was 1,336 pounds, and killed six people. Although the bomb left a 30 meter crater, it failed to bring the North Tower down, as was the terrorist plot. The event was perpetrated by men that had trained at al-Qaeda camps in Afghanistan; the mastermind was a man from Kuwait named Khaled Sheikh Mohammed (KSM)*. The World Trade Center Bombing would not be the last time the iconic building would be targeted by terrorists; terrorists had built a habit in the previous decade of returning to a target to attack again, if the first attack was not as successful as they had intended. [247]

The air marshals continued to train with various military units, cross-training in skills related to counter-terrorism. Some of the training they conducted with HRT was very demanding. The air marshals by this time, however, "*knew the proper end of a gun, and weren't just a rag tag kind of an organization.*"

By 1994, the air marshals had gained much respect in the shooting community, but they were still borrowing training facilities from various specialized mili-

---

[246] (Administration F. A., FAA Archival Records - From 2001 Internal Report)
[247] (Commission, July 22, 2004)
*KSM was not initially connected to this incident. His uncle, Ramsi Yousef was seen as the mastermind, until it was found later that KSM had sent funds to one of the operatives.

tary groups and the HRT team at Quantico. The search for a permanent home resumed and started pointing towards possible space on FAA owned property.

At this time there was talk amongst some of the air marshals, in which they referred to themselves as somewhat of a counter-terrorism/ special operations team. This alarmed upper management at the FBI. Some of the HRT team members that the air marshals had trained with began relaying these concerns at training venues.

The FBI/ HRT team took their concern to Mr. Flynn, saying that the air marshals should be disbanded; they were concerned over *blue on blue* situations* on aircraft. Cathal Flynn took this information and complaint to Richard A. Clarke, of the National Security Council (NSC), and told him of the concerns.

Mr. Clarke wanted to know how many FAM missions were flown per year to try and get a sense of the size of the program. Mr. Flynn replied that there was something in the neighborhood of one-half of a mission per day, which was mainly due to the small size of the force and the operational nature and procedures of FAM missions during 1994; he also explained some of the missions and the nature of the program, from the history of the early 1960's to the current state of the program.

Richard Clarke told Mr. Flynn he did not see any potential for "blue on blue" scenarios that the FBI had been concerned about. Mr. Clarke brought this Federal Air Marshal issue up as an agenda item during a meeting one day, and said only one thing: *"The FAMs stay."* [248, 249]

Also in 1994, Khaled Sheikh Mohammed (KSM) started testing airport security with his uncle, and a co-conspirator of the World Trade Center bombing, Ramsi Yousef. The pair had booked separate flights, in which they both carried fourteen bottles of contact lens solution containing nitroglycerin; they were beginning to test security measures for a sinister plot. [250]

On December 11, 1994, KSM and Ramsi Yousef were ready to move into the next stage of their terrorist campaign. They had been planting homemade bombs in various locations as their operational planning and readiness continued, and had reached a critical stage: They were ready to test their bombs on a flight. On

---

[248] (Clarke, 2004)

[249] (Flynn, 2012)

[250] (McLaughlin, 2011 - 2012), (Wikipedia, Bojinka Plot), (Commission, July 22, 2004)

* *"Blue-on-blue"* refers to shoot-outs between police officers.

this date, Yousef, travelling under an alias, left a bomb inside the life jacket of an aircraft* he had been on, and then disembarked in Cebu. Cebu was a stopover on the aircrafts flight from Manila, Philippines to Narita, Japan.

The bomb was placed under seat 26K of a Boeing 747, and exploded enroute to Narita; a Japanese businessman sitting in the seat was killed and an additional ten were injured: The captain then went on to make an emergency landing in Okinawa. This was a tragic event that the terrorists had deliberately planned as part of a larger operation. The next phase of the operation being planned by KSM and Ramsi Yousef had started to take shape. U.S. intelligence was aware of the increase in the threat of bombings towards commercial aircraft at the time, but hijackings were not about to slow down either, nor was their potential for violence.

On December 24, 1994, Air France Flight 8969, an Airbus A300 aircraft, boarded its passengers for its flight from Houari Boumedienne Airport in Algiers, Algeria, to Orly International Airport in Paris. As the aircraft was boarding, four men dressed as Algerian police came onboard. The men carried weapons and asked passengers for their passports. [251]

These four men ended up hijacking the aircraft after some crew became suspicious that they were not police officers**. The hijackers brandished assault rifles, grenades, dynamite, and detonation cord. These particular hijackers were part of a terrorist group from Algeria, the Armed Islamic Group (GIA), which was opposed to the French government; their wish was to destroy something in symbolism of their hatred.

The hijackers appeared to be tactically aware of law enforcement capabilities and they went to great lengths to disguise themselves, such as putting on the uniforms of the crew to confuse police snipers. They also forced the women to make veils for their heads with blankets. The 200 plus passengers and crew onboard then heard the hijackers make the following statement: [252]

---

[251] (McLaughlin, 2011 - 2012), (Wikipedia, Air France Flight 8969)
[252] (Wikipedia, Air France Flight 8969)
* This was Philippines Airline Flight 434. Yousef was witnessed as having bounced around to various unoccupied seats in the aircraft. It was hypothesized that his desire was to place the explosive near the centerline fuel tanks, however his placement was wrong and did not do sufficient damage to bring down the Boeing 747.
** Algerian police did not carry firearms in the airport at the time.

"We are the soldiers of mercy. Allah has selected us as his soldiers. We are here to wage war in his name."

The hijackers demanded that members of a party called the Islamic Salvation Front be released, and when their demands were not met, they started getting rough with the passengers. When the hijackers had checked passports and other passenger identification, they had come across an off-duty Algerian police officer. To get the Algerian government to cave-in to their demands (fuel and clearance to take-off), they shot and killed the man. Shortly after the murder, a commercial attaché for the embassy of Vietnam was also shot and killed. [253]

The French government began planning a military operation in the early stages of the hijacking. They were scrambling to try and determine the best course of action for the problem, and began alerting special groups that trained in counter-terrorism missions.

On Christmas day, the French government found out through an informant that the true purpose of the hijacking was to fly and crash the aircraft into the Eiffel Tower in Paris. This was an alarming realization, and the French government stepped up plans for a rescue.

The hijackers had released some passengers, such as some women, children, and sick people, however by Christmas day, approximately 170 passengers still remained onboard. The hijackers then began threatening, that if they did not get clearance to take-off by that evening, they would start executing one passenger every half-hour. The hijackers eventually felt that their demands were not being met and executed a chef.

The aircraft was soon given clearance to take-off and headed to Marseilles. While the aircraft was airborne, the French commando team GIGN started training on an empty Airbus A300, at the airport where Air France Flight 8969 was due to land. They practiced their movements and rehearsed for a rescue attempt.

The flight landed at 3:30 a.m. local time, in Marseilles; in a stroke of luck for the French government, the aircraft had landed at GIGN headquarters. Negotiations took place over the next twelve hours between the hijackers and law enforcement. The raid began by GIGN, when a hijacker fired at the control tower, and after a twenty-minute gun battle, all four hijackers were killed. All passengers survived the ordeal, however some were injured.

---

[253] (McLaughlin, 2011 - 2012), (Wikipedia, Air France Flight 8969)

This hijacking could have ended much worse. This was a new type of attack plan, in that a terrorist organization planned to use its enemies flagged air carrier to fly it like a missile into a target within the enemy country. This plan would be used later, with much deadlier consequences.

Shortly after Air France Flight 8969, Director Greg McLaughlin received approval to send an air marshal out to France, to interview the GIGN commandos and crew involved in the hijacking, in order to gain as much information from the event as possible. This authorization was gained through Cathal Flynn, and an air marshal was sent out to do a classified debrief of the incident.

While this was all going on, talks continued on finding a home for the air marshals. The FAMs continued flying and training for their missions, while some were prepping their families for the commitment they would have to make, when the FAA moved the FAM program and all its personnel to one centrally located facility somewhere in the United States.

There were a total of 139 missions flown by air marshals for the fiscal year of 1994, and all were on international routes. The international flight coverage during this time was directly influenced by intelligence and threat information that came from groups such as the CSG*, CIA, NSA, and foreign counterparts. The CSG was meeting on numerous terrorism issues, and they were fully aware of KSM, Ramsi Yousef, and al-Qaeda. They were starting to get other intelligence chatter on possible airline plots. [254]

Going into 1995, there were a lot of things happening in the intelligence community. With terrorist attacks overseas starting to become a trend, as well as domestic attacks, such as the World Trade Center bombing in New York, terrorist plots began to be picked up by intelligence agencies. Attacks against civil aviation, such as the one targeting Philippine Airlines Flight 434, began to be seen as a viable threat to national security.

The air marshal force continued fulfilling their mission of protecting U.S. air carriers on international flights deemed a threat, and as directed by the Associate Administrator for Civil Aviation Security. All the threat intelligence for air marshal missions at the time was out of the FAA intelligence center, which had contacts with all of the various intelligence agencies; there were also still meetings at the CSG, or Coordinated Sub-Group, which focused on terrorism and which had members attached to the FAA's Office of Civil Aviation Security. The focus

---

[254] (McLaughlin, 2011 - 2012)
*The CSG, or Coordinated Sub-Group, was a carryover from the IGT, and worked closely with the NSC.

of this group, and the various intelligence agencies, would continue to be concentrated on international threats, such as those being perpetrated and planned by Ramsi Yousef and KSM.

In fact, Ramsi Yousef and KSM were busy getting ready for their next terrorist act, which would involve attacking the U.S. directly through the use of commercial aircraft. The plan was for five terrorists to set bombs on 12 U.S. bound aircraft. [255] These bombs, like the ones in the previous test run, would be planted inside life jackets on U.S. flagged aircraft, routed with multiple leg flights heading towards the United States; bombs would be placed on the first leg of the aircrafts flight. The terrorists had the added benefit of not having to have a visa, since the flights that were selected were all originating and ending in Asian countries. The bombs for this plot would be placed on January 21, 1995.

On January 7, 1995, a chemical fire erupted in a Manila apartment that Ramsi Yousef and his team of terrorists were using as a safe house and for mixing explosives. Several people were injured by the fire; however, both Ramsi Yousef and KSM avoided capture. The airline plot was exposed due to documents and other intelligence information found in the apartment. The plan to blow up multiple U.S. flagged aircraft became known as the *Bojinka plot*. The estimated death toll of this attack, had it been carried out successfully, was 4,000. The fire in the safe house caused the disruption of the terrorist cell before the plot could be carried out, which was a lucky break for civil aviation security. [256]

Admiral Flynn was aware of the Bojinka plot at this time, as he recalled: [257]

"[S]ome things were really hitting the fan in aviation security during my time, notably in the Bojinka plot of the Ramsi Yousef attempt to bomb several U.S. airliners all at once."

In the spring of 1995, there was an emergency response at the FAA due to a bomb threat from the "*Unabomber**." In August, the Secretary of Transportation announced a heightened state of alert for the U.S. transportation system. Even more stringent enforcement procedures, however, also started being implement-

---

[255] (Vincent, Bombers, Hijackers, Body Scanners, and Jihadists, 2012)
[256] (Wikipedia, Bojinka Plot)
[257] (Flynn, 2012)
*Ted Kaczynski was called the "Unabomber" by the media, based off the FBI case which they called UNABOM, which stood for "University and Airline Bomber." Between 1978 and 1995, Kaczynski sent a total of 16 bombs to targets, which included universities and airlines.

ed in October 1995, which would last through 1996, due to the Atlanta Olympics.

In 1995, the Federal Air Marshal Program finally found a permanent home; an FAA facility in Atlantic City, NJ, next to the Atlantic City Airport, would become the new air marshal headquarters. This new facility would be referred to as ACY, named after the local airport designation. They built a linear range and a shoot house, and secured the use of an FAA aircraft for training with non-lethal training munitions and for practicing tactics. Although tactics were evolving with the threat to civil aviation, the air marshals still did not have an official lesson plan for their specialized aircraft tactics. [258]

Now that the air marshals had a home, they started standardizing their training. Air marshal training would consist of three phases:

- The first phase was a Criminal Investigative Training Program (CITP) at FLETC, which was approximately 11-weeks in length.

- The second phase was seven-days, spent at either United Airlines in Chicago, or Delta Airlines in Atlanta. Here, air marshals would climb in, under, and around various aircraft for familiarization.

- The third phase was five-weeks in ACY, for FAM specific training. This training included the Tactical Pistol Course (TPC), defensive tactics, legal considerations, general topics (explosives, anti-terrorism, trade craft), and a tactics culmination exercise with role-players in a mock aircraft.

Air marshals attending training during this time would also learn to operate radios inside the aircraft, and some would get cockpit simulator training.

By 1996, the force of air marshals had found a home in the Atlantic City area. These air marshals were all volunteers, in extremely good shape, excellent pistol shooters, and were considered some of the world's aviation security and hijacking experts. Many of the air marshals had uprooted their lives from other parts of the country to move to Atlantic City for a job that they believed in. Major General O.K. Steele had a vision, and Vice Admiral Cathal Flynn bought into it as well; they had both turned the air marshal program into an extremely capable force, and they had a team of air marshals that would follow them anywhere.

---

[258] (McLaughlin, 2011 - 2012)

By the end of the 1995 fiscal year, the FAMs had flown 130 missions; all were intelligence and threat driven, and all were on international flights.

One of the men that Vice Admiral Flynn had regular meetings with during his tenure was Richard Clarke, the chairman of the CSG. The two would meet to discuss various national security issues that could potentially affect civil aviation security, and information derived from foreign allies which could impact U.S. interests.

The CSG was under the National Security Council (NSC) Deputies Committee in the organizational U.S. government structure to combat terrorism. The NSC is responsible for coordinating policy on national security issues and is staffed with senior-level officials from military, diplomatic, intelligence, law enforcement and other government entities.

While the CSG worked on terrorism issues going into 1996, the FAA and FBI teamed up to conduct a joint threat and vulnerability assessment at high risk airports, under the federal aviation reauthorization act of 1996. This was an attempt to help better understand security vulnerabilities in order to fix them, and to identify high risk airports for implementing state of the art solutions at these key facilities.

In addressing the FAA's Civil Aviation Security effectiveness and training, a 1996 report stated that *"the FAA develops an extensive training program for FAA personnel and others for responsibilities for civil aviation security. Aviation security training for FAA special agents is generally conducted as resident training at the FAA academy in Oklahoma City."* It goes on to say that *"the FAA trained 286 FAA students in basic and advanced aviation security and internal security programs in 1996."* [259]

In addition to adding almost 300 new FAA special agents for civil aviation security duties at airports across the U.S., by 1996, the FAA reported that there was a Computer-Assisted Passenger Screening (CAPS)* system in place. CAPS applied an automated profiling system, which had been started through a joint project of Northwest Airlines and the FAA. Much like the profiling system used by sky marshals in the 1970s', it was different in the respect that CAPS used computers, instead of people, to select passengers for additional screening. The

---

[259] (Administration U. D., Annual Report to Congress on Civil Aviation Security, January 1, 1996 - December 31, 1996)
*The use of the CAPS system would be immediately discontinued after the September 11, 2001 attacks (9/11); this automated profiling system would fail to detect the majority of the terrorists on 9/11.

report said that the development of CAPS had proceeded to the point that full operational capability for Northwest airlines was anticipated for 1997.

At a time when the human element was being taken out of the intelligence gathering process as well, such as the downsizing of intelligence officers at the CIA, CAPS was just one more example of computers replacing human thought, insight, and instinct.

In 1996, another improvement that the FAA report spoke of was a *passenger-baggage match* protocol that ensured no unaccompanied bag entered the aviation system, and that a passenger's bag be removed if the passenger was not onboard. This was a byproduct of the Pan Am 103 bombing, and past failures of airlines, such as Pan Am, to follow FAA emergency rules.

It was reported on the Federal Air Marshal Program during this time, that the program *"provides an armed force whose mission is to protect the travelling public and flight crews on U.S. carriers by deterring criminal and terrorist acts which target aircraft in flight."* The FAA report went on to state that, the *"operational training facility is located at the William J. Hughes Technical Center in Atlantic City, NJ. The force is capable of rapid deployment worldwide. During 1996, FAMs provided in-flight security on flights of all major air carriers to and from 74 cities in 43 countries. Just knowing that FAM's could be onboard may deter someone who is planning to interfere with a flight."*

The head of FAA security, Cathal Flynn, said in a statement during the Atlanta Olympics in 1996, that *"we could ban aircraft over the stadium,"* in response to concerns of someone possibly blowing-up an aircraft over the stadium during the ceremonies. The security concerns and focus that went into the Atlanta Olympics that year were huge. In preparing for the Olympics, the air marshals started to adopt new strategies to add to their deterrent factor; this led to the group doing demonstrations and interviews for international media, such as CNN, NBC, and BBC, in order to get the word out that air marshals could be on any plane at any time. [260]

The Atlanta Olympics was a major security undertaking and was designated as a National Security Event; FAMs assisted in security operations during the Olympics doing various flights in and out of Atlanta's Hartsfield Airport, making them a visible deterrent.

Also in 1996, Osama bin-Laden issued a statement that al-Qaeda would wage jihad on foreign troops, and that he would use all his resources in an attempt to force westerners from what al-Qaeda considered Islamic lands. This statement

---

[260] (Multiple news broadcasts on the FAA Federal Air Marshal Program, 1996)

comes shortly before a devastating attack in Saudi Arabia by al-Qaeda and its affiliates. [261]

On June 25, 1996, a car bomb exploded at the Khobar Towers in Riyadh, Saudi Arabia, outside a complex housing foreign military personnel; the attack was a deliberate one against foreigners. The terrorists that perpetrated the attack had stated that their goal was to get the U.S. military to leave the country.

The attack on the Khobar Towers was believed to have been perpetrated by al-Qaeda, by some; however, the official U.S. statement on the bombing, dated June 25, 1996, stated that Hezbollah was responsible. This attack showed a continuing threat of terrorist activity on western targets abroad, regardless of who was responsible.

On July 17, 1996, only two-days prior to the Atlanta Olympics opening ceremonies, TWA Flight 800 exploded shortly after departure from JFK airport; the flight was bound for Paris. [262]

This particular flight had originated as Flight 881 in Athens, which had been the focus of security issues in the past, and after refueling and a crew change at JFK, the flight was scheduled to depart for Paris at 7:00 p.m. local time, but was delayed a little over one-hour.

Shortly after being ordered to climb to 15,000 feet, the aircraft disappeared from radar. Reports began flooding in about an explosion being seen from a nearby aircraft. Later reports also came forward from witnesses, saying they had seen some kind of missile going up towards the aircraft. The National Transportation Safety Board (NTSB) later finished their report, with the hypothesis that there was some sort of short circuit within the fuel compartment that caused the explosion of TWA Flight 800.

The investigation of TWA 800 never found conclusive evidence as to what truly brought down the flight. At the time of the disaster there was significant information pointing towards threats against JFK airport. It was known that terrorist groups had placed operatives at the airport as workers, to learn the aviation system and map its weaknesses. Although the panel investigating TWA 800 reported the short circuit hypothesis, the evidence was not enough for a final determination surrounding the circumstances that killed so many innocent lives: Terrorism could not be ruled out.

---

[261] (Coll, Ghost Wars: The Secret History of the CIA, Afghanistan, and Bin Laden, from the Soviet Invasion to September 10, 2001, 2004)
[262] (Aleman, 2012), (Steele, 2012)

Retired Major General O.K. Steele came on as a consultant for the investigation of TWA 800. It was just one of many instances in which the former Associate Administrator for Civil Aviation Security came back as an expert to help out in an investigative capacity, or as an expert witness. [263]

By the end of the fiscal year 1996, FAMs had flown 187 missions. All missions were on international flights and all were in regards to specific, risk based intelligence.

During 1996 and 1997, the FAA's Office of Civil Aviation Security stated in a report that its mission was, *"to protect the users of commercial air transportation against terrorist and other criminal acts."* It elaborated, saying *"because terrorist and other criminal acts seek to destroy public confidence in the safety of air travel and disrupt this vital segment of the U.S. and world economies, the continued growth of commercial air transportation hinges on the effectiveness of aviation security measures. Protecting the infrastructure – FAA facilities and equipment and the employees who operate them – is a critical part of the FAA's aviation security mission."* [264]

In 1997, the FAA gave Director Greg McLaughlin authority to hire his own people from outside the FAA for positions as air marshals: *"Up until this point I was not allowed to hire them. Once I had the authority to hire who I wanted, that's when we had a pretty sophisticated group of people that came out of the special operations community."* [265]

At the time, the air marshals adopted the use of three teams of 12, with three teams of 36 flying FAMs. As McLaughlin recalled, *"We instituted a program where FAMS had an operational cycle of 25 days, where FAMs were out in the world somewhere. Then there was an administrative cycle, where FAMs could take leave or do some non-FAM training for the FAA, and then there was an alert cycle. When FAMs were in the 25 day alert cycle, FAMs came to work every Monday through Friday, but they were on a four-hour window, which meant four-hours after I was told that something was going on FAMs were moving."*

Early in this reorganization, a team was in the alert cycle, when there was a threat that had to be covered immediately. The team had to be flown out of Atlantic City by a government aircraft in order to not miss their mission. The state of aviation security and the terrorist threat at this time had an effect of panic at

---

[263] (Steele, 2012)
[264] (Administration U. D., Annual Report to Congress on Civil Aviation Security, January 1, 1996 - December 31, 1996)
[265] (McLaughlin, 2011 - 2012)

the Office of Civil Aviation Security: These experts knew who they were up against, and the seriousness of that threat.

While in the alert cycle, FAMs would train. All of the FAMs were expert marksman, and they trained at the firearms range and shoot house while in their alert cycle; they dry-fired their weapons at least one-hour per day*, and practiced various scenarios with their simmunitions, based on past hijackings and potential terrorist tactics, as dreamt up by think tanks at the FAA.

By the end of 1997, air marshals continued to train and mature in their specialized fields. FAMs had flown 184 missions for the year, all on international flights, and all based on specific threat intelligence. [266]

In 1997, a new Director of Training** was promoted within the air marshal ranks. He would fill this position until late 2001. His promotion would bring valuable counter-terrorism experience to the FAM program and further standardize the expert training FAMs received. [267]

The new Director of Training began to use his contacts in the special operations community to develop a lesson plan for air marshal tactics. This began by evaluating future training instructors in order to expand the capabilities of the force. The Director of Training became the first civilian to attend the first week of training with the Naval Special Warfare Development Group (DEVGRU), also known as SEAL Team Six. This was done in order to evaluate Duane Dieter, a civilian Defensive Tactics instructor. Upon completion of this evaluation, Duane Dieter was brought in as a civilian instructor for the FAM program, establishing lesson plans for the Defensive Tactics curriculum during the initial FAM training program and their bi-annual refresher training.

In late 1997, the Director of Training was given a white paper to read by Israeli Shin Bet. This document was called the *Foreign Air Security Manual*. Israel had the second oldest air marshal service, second to the U.S., and had invaluable counter terrorism experience. El Al Airlines had developed the security manual with their own unique experiences in regards to aviation security threats. The manual had many case studies, including changes in terrorist trends over many decades. One case study included information on a German citizen that had been used to carry out attacks, and was ultimately picked up by Shin Bet.

---

[266] (Administration F. A., FAA Archival Records - From 2001 Internal Report)
[267] (McLaughlin, 2011 - 2012)
*This was required of all FAMs in an *alert* status.
***Name withheld** due to current affiliation with the FAMS.

This manual served as an excellent guideline for developing the FAM tactics lesson plan that would become the Director of Training's legacy.

Starting in 1998, the Director of Training also started sending teams of air marshals to train at Ft. Bragg, for one or two weeks, with various foreign military units. They trained at Ft. Bragg with groups like the German Federal Police SWAT (Special Weapons and Tactics), Austrian and Israeli air marshals, the Swiss military forces, and many other foreign counterparts.

The pistol shooting prowess of the U.S. Federal Air Marshals had become well known by 1998. They were cross-training with specialized counter-terrorism groups, and held the highest firearms qualification standard in the world, and word had gotten around about their skills.

This was a big year for the firearms program of the air marshals. The switch was made in 1998 to the Sig Sauer P229, which fired the .357 sig cartridge. The FAMs were continuing to model their firearms program after that of the secret service, as they had for nearly three decades. Going back to the sky marshal era, the air marshal's firearms program had followed that of the secret service. By 1998, the presidential security detail was using the Sig P229, and the FAMs followed suit and made the switch.

In 1998, Cathal Flynn called Director McLaughlin and told him that they needed to figure out a way to have their firearms program evaluated. They could not go with the FBI or the Federal Law Enforcement Training Center (FLETC), since both the FBI and FLETC had previously wanted to be taught, and possibly adapt, the air marshal TPC qualification. The FAM program had sent instructors to the FBI and FLETC in previous years, and had even taught instructors for the respective departments the TPC: Not one of them had passed. [268]

The new Director of Training told Mr. McLaughlin that he knew some people that might be able to help with evaluating the program. Finally, in 1998, a team of personnel from the Joint Special Operations Command (JSOC) came to the air marshal training facility to evaluate their shooting program. [269]

The report that was generated from the three weeks that JSOC spent evaluating the air marshal shooting program, stated that, in their opinion, *"air marshals were among the top 1% of shooters in the world."* This was an ego boost for the FAMs, and further added credibility to the small team.

---

[268] (McLaughlin, 2011 - 2012), (Flynn, 2012)
[269] (McLaughlin, 2011 - 2012)

On August 7, 1998, between 10:30 and 10:40 a.m. local time, two suicide truck bombs were detonated outside the U.S. embassies in Dar es Salaam and Nairobi, Kenya, with a total of 223 killed and over 4,000 wounded at the two sites. The attack was carried out by the terrorist group al-Qaeda. [270]

The terrorist attacks showed a trend in international terrorism threats against national security interests. The focus, however, for U.S. intelligence and law enforcement, remained more on *international* risks to facilities, military personnel, and commercial aviation. In the attacks wake, a special section of the CIA would be organized to specifically target and track Osama bin-Laden, and the al-Qaeda network.

By the end of fiscal year 1998, FAMs had flown 137 missions: All of these were on international flights. FAM missions would continue to target specific flights, or specific individuals, following the threat stream fed to the FAA by U.S. and foreign intelligence. Air marshals knew of al-Qaeda, and the rise in attacks on western targets.

In 1999, there was a shift towards more mission flight coverage: Over the next three years, the missions flown by air marshals would almost double. The program would, however, lose three team members over the same number of years. This increase in mission coverage was a direct reflection of the increasing threat of terrorism, specifically terrorism targeting the aviation sector. However, this increase in missions led to numerous hurdles and logistical problems.

Greg McLaughlin reported one those logistical problems, stating, *"It was hard; one of the problems I had was my operational team was already gone, and it seemed like about three months out of four the alert team would never complete a true 25 day alert [cycle], they would be alerted and have to go deploy. The world didn't know, but we certainly did, of Osama bin Laden and al-Qaeda, and we were chasing people all over the planet."*

The training the air marshals had developed by this time ensured that they were experts on the platforms they were working on. The increased mission tempo, due to the intelligence on terrorism threats, was calling on all of their skills, patience, and training, to protect the public, and in their attempt to disrupt terrorist plots.

---

[270] (Coll, Ghost Wars: The Secret History of the CIA, Afghanistan, and Bin Laden, from the Soviet Invasion to September 10, 2001, 2004), (Commission, July 22, 2004)

The Office of Civil Aviation Security at the FAA knew terrorism and other aviation related security issues would remain to be a plague to the industry. Hijacking remained a tempting act, not just the bombings that had become so prevalent over the years. A lone hijacker proved this on July 23, 1999. On this date, the attempted hijacking of All Nippon Airlines (ANA) Flight 61 took place, by a man armed with a large knife. [271]

The Boeing 747 aircraft was en route from Tokyo International Airport to New Chitose Airport, in Chitose, Japan when the attempted hijacking began; the flight carried 503 passengers. Approximately twenty-five minutes into the flight, a man named Yuji Nishizawa brandished a kitchen knife and forced his way into the cockpit by threatening a flight attendant. The man was 28-years old, unemployed, and had taken a very large dose of an anti-depressant. In his delusional state, he wished to fly the aircraft into the Rainbow Bridge in Tokyo.

Mr. Nishizawa carried out a series of threats while in the cockpit, and in the process had stabbed the captain in the chest. Nishizawa then took control of the aircraft, forcing it into a steep dive. The man's actions resulted in a loss of altitude, of over 300 meters.

Eventually the crew members were able to control Nishizawa, and then prepared for what would be an emergency landing back at Tokyo International Airport. Nishizawa was later sentenced to life in prison. This event proved the need for the Federal Air Marshal Program and the air marshal's extensive training. It also showed the bravery of the flight crew, which had been a recurring theme over the decades in in-flight emergencies.

By 1999, the air marshals on duty were all highly skilled and specialized. McLaughlin recalled that he had four former members of the SEAL teams, along with former Air Force PJs and Army Rangers as well. The few remaining members that had no military experience, were also extremely fit and thoroughly trained. Those with no military backgrounds had been sent to the same schools and held to the same standards, and all of the air marshals thrived and excelled in their positions. They were proud of being experts in their fields.

In late 1999, some of the non-military FAMs found themselves at training courses; with bags packed, checked out of their hotels and ready to depart the classroom with plane tickets in hand, when men would come rushing through the doors, throw burlap sacks over their heads and take them off to a two, to three-day, SERE (Survival, Evasion, Resistance, and Escape) course. Here they were taught the necessary skills for survival if they were jailed somewhere, or

---

[271] (Wikipedia, All Nippon Airlines Flight 61)

ended up in a country in which a coup was taking place: This had apparently happened to one FAM team in a South American country, and it was at that time that the new Director of Training and Director McLaughlin felt obligated to give the non-military people skills that could potentially save their life. As McLaughlin put it, the thinking at the time was, *"[W]e were sending people to some very hostile countries, and you have to ask yourself. Can you honestly say you have prepared these [FAMs] to survive if they are thrown in jail during a coup or some other dangerous situation?"* [272]

Due to the increase in intelligence on terrorism threats, the FAMs flew on 265 missions throughout the fiscal year of 1999. Going into the new millennium, and fiscal year 2000, there was another thwarted civil aviation terrorist attack plot, this time on a major U.S. airport.

On December 14, 1999, Customs officials questioned a man arriving from Canada in his vehicle, as he was crossing through to the U.S. after being transported via ferry. Due to inconsistencies in his questioning, U.S. Customs officials searched his vehicle and found a major cache of explosives. The explosives were to be used to bomb the Los Angeles International Airport around the turn of the millennium. [273]

Ten days later, on Christmas Eve, a bespectacled man onboard India Air Flight 814, stood up and threatened to blow up the aircraft, an Airbus A-300. The lead flight attendant onboard recalled, *"The moment I turned my face towards the galley, I saw somebody wearing a mask."* The hijacker was heard saying the following:

"There should be no movement. This is a bomb, to blow up the plane." [274]

At the time, the aircraft was somewhere between Kathmandu, Nepal and Delhi, India, and was just entering Indian airspace. Four other militants joined the man, and they ordered Captain Devi Sharan to *"fly west."*

Harkat-ul-Mujahideen, a Pakistan based organization, was involved in this hijacking, in an attempt to negotiate the release of three militants being held in India.

---

[272] (McLaughlin, 2011 - 2012)
[273] (Coll, Ghost Wars: The Secret History of the CIA, Afghanistan, and Bin Laden, from the Soviet Invasion to September 10, 2001, 2004)
[274] (Wikipedia, Air India Flight 182), (McLaughlin, 2011 - 2012)
* The Taliban is an Islamic fundamentalist militant group. The Taliban ruled Afghanistan in 1999.

After having the aircraft fly to Amristar, India, narrowly missing a truck intended on blocking the aircraft, the plane was forced to land in Lahore, Pakistan, where the aircraft was refueled rapidly then departed. The hijackers then had the aircraft flown to Dubai, where 27 passengers were released. One of the passengers released was Rupin Katyal; Rupin had been stabbed multiple times by the hijackers, most likely in order to gain cabin compliance. The hijackers were sending a message to other passengers onboard that may have been intending to take action towards the militants. The message was simple: *"Try anything, and we will kill you."* Mr. Katyal later succumbed to his wounds, and the aircraft then headed for Kandahar, Afghanistan.

In 1999 Afghanistan, the Taliban* were trying to show cooperation with other foreign governments, in order to try and gain recognition as a legitimate government of Afghanistan. In this attempt, the Taliban agreed to mediate between the hijackers and the Indian government; however, instead, they surrounded the aircraft with other Taliban fighters, in order to prevent the Indian military from attempting a rescue operation. Eventually, on December 31, 1999, all remaining passengers were released and flown back to India. The five hijackers were released through Pakistan, after being taken across the border by the Taliban. This was not the last time the five hijackers, Ibrahim Azhar, Shahid Sayed, Sunny Qazi, Mistri Ibrahim, and Shakir were heard of from U.S. and foreign intelligence agencies; most would be killed in drone strikes many years later by the United States and its allies.

Three days after the Flight 814 hijacking, on January 3, 2000, an explosive-laden boat sunk in Yemen, after trying to bomb the *USS The Sullivans* at port. This would lead to another similar incident with disastrous and deadly consequences. The group responsible for planning the bombing, and attempting to execute the attack, had affiliations with al-Qaeda. [275]

At the end of September 2000, which was the last month of fiscal year 2000, FAMs had flown a total of 254 missions, all on international flights. [276]

On October 12, al-Qaeda struck again, targeting another U.S. flagged ship at port. The *USS Cole* was moored in Yemen when it became the target of a suicide attack. Another explosive-laden boat, similar to that which attempted to sink the *USS The Sullivans*, was steered towards the *USS Cole*, however, this time the bomb exploded and ripped through the hull of the guided missile destroyer. Seventeen sailors were killed and thirty-nine injured in this sinister act.

---

[275] (Wikipedia, USS The Sullivans (DDG-68))
[276] (Administration F. A., FAA Archival Records - From 2001 Internal Report)

Terrorists were learning from their mistakes, and were becoming ever more bold and vigilant in their planning and operational effectiveness. [277]

Al Qaeda in the Arabian Peninsula (AQAP), a terrorist group with roots to al-Qaeda and Osama bin-Laden, took responsibility for the attack on the *USS Cole*. Al Qaeda had been on the radar of U.S. and foreign intelligence agencies for some time, going back to the World Trade Center attack in 1993, in New York. This would not be the first or last time the world heard the name al-Qaeda mentioned in regards to terrorism. [278]

On November 21, 2000, the Administrator of the FAA, Jane F. Garvey, named U.S. Lieutenant (Lt.) General Michael A. Canavan as the new Associate Administrator for the Office of Civil Aviation Security. This ended the tenure of Vice Admiral Cathal Flynn, who retired to California.

Lt. General Michael Canavan, like Vice Admiral Flynn, was not new to the problems faced by international terrorism. He, like Flynn, also bought into the air marshal program that was envisioned by O.K. Steele in 1992, and he was determined to see that the program stayed like it was. He was determined to promote the use of air marshals and to continue to support the training which had made them the world's experts in aviation security and hijackings.

"I am extremely pleased that Mike Canavan has accepted this important position with the FAA," said Mrs. Garvey. She went on, further highlighting his background, saying *"His vast experience in overseeing the defense of our nation will make him a strong leader as we work with industry to ensure security for the flying public."*[279]

Michael A. Canavan came from a distinguished military career and a specialized background, much like the FAMs he was now coming to be ultimately in charge of. Director Gregory McLaughlin was now working for his third boss in almost a decade, and he came to respect each very highly, for their knowledge and dedication to the mission. Michael Canavan was no exception.

Mr. Canavan enlisted in the U.S. Army in 1966, and went on to have numerous command and staff positions with various Special Forces groups. He also went on to become General of the U.S. Army Training and Doctrine Command

---

[277] (Wikipedia, USS Cole Bombing)

[278] (Wikipedia, Al Qaeda in the Arabian Peninsula)

[279] (Administration F. A., Press Release - U.S. Army Lt. General Michael Canavan Named to Head FAA Office of Civil Aviation Security, 2000)

(TRADOC). Lt. General Canavan retired on January 1, 2001, just prior to his appointment as Associate Administrator of Civil Aviation Security for the FAA.

By June 2001, Lynne Osmus was appointed the Deputy Associate Administrator of Civil Aviation Security (ACS2) at the FAA. This would put Lynne Osmus in the number two position in the Office of Civil Aviation Security, under Michael Canavan. [280]

By September 10, 2001, there were approximately twenty CASLOs working for the FAA at airports around the world. The CASLO position came from the Pan Am 103 investigation and the International Civil Aviation and Cooperation Act of 1985, mainly for ensuring security procedures were followed at foreign airports, and to perform vulnerability assessments of those airports. Mr. McLaughlin had carried out this very mission in Frankfurt, in the early 1990s'. [281]

The CASLOs were also used to liaison with foreign governments that the United States wanted an air carrier security presence. The CASLOs were in place in these foreign locations and would be available in case of any catastrophes in their area of operations. One of their many duties was to report adverse findings of security problems with the host countries air security program. Although they *were* trained in air marshal duties, they were *not* air marshals in the literal sense.

On the FAM side, there were 33 air marshals working for the Office of Civil Aviation Security for the FAA by September 10, 2001. The force was a dedicated one. They were experts in their field, chasing the threat stream on multiple missions. By this time, according to a report prepared for the FAA in March 2001, there had already been 346 mission flights for fiscal year 2001; however, these were only on international routes. [282]

In less than six months, by September 2001, the air marshals were doing 500% more flights than in previous years. This is a direct reflection on the intelligence coming in at the time and the events happening in regards to international terrorism and national security threats. As of September 10, 2001, the Federal Air Marshal Program had a budget of $4 million. [283]

---

[280] (Osmus, 2010, 2012)

[281] (McLaughlin, 2011 - 2012)

[282] (Administration F. A., FAA Archival Records - From 2001 Internal Report)

[283] (Commission, July 22, 2004)

By the evening of September 10, 2001, as the men, women, children, and citizens of the United States prepared for bed, the Office of Civil Aviation at the FAA was very much aware of the dangers of terrorism targeting commercial aircraft. Their main focus however, over the past decade, had been towards the increase in bombings of aircraft, such as the multiple bombing attempts of the early 1980s', like the one that destroyed Pan Am 103. Although it had been almost 12 years since the bombing over Lockerbie, the repercussions were still being felt in aviation security in the last month of fiscal year 2001, and that focus had been on bombings. No one at the FAA, or any other government post, was prepared for the events that would occur the next morning.

Chapter IX

9/11 Attacks

(September 11, 2001)

On the morning of September 11, 2001 (9/11), four commercial passenger jet aircraft were hijacked by 19 al-Qaeda terrorists. The hijackers went on to intentionally crash two of the airliners into the World Trade Center towers in New York City, killing all onboard and many inside the buildings. Both towers later collapsed within two hours, destroying nearby buildings and damaging others. The hijackers crashed another aircraft into the Pentagon in Arlington, Virginia. A fourth plane crashed into a field near Shanksville, Pennsylvania, after some of the passengers and crew attempted to retake control of the aircraft. Nearly 3,000 people died as a result of the attacks on 9/11. [284]

All of these aircraft held a considerable amount of fuel. The hijackers on 9/11 had intentionally hijacked flights that were transcontinental and carried the most fuel in order to use the aircraft as a pilot-guided suicide missile. The aircraft that

---

[284] (Commission, July 22, 2004)

were hijacked that day were made by Boeing: two 767s, and two 757s, which both carried up to 11,500 gallons of jet fuel*.

Attack on the World Trade Center (New York)

Five al-Qaeda terrorist hijackers took part in the hijacking of American Airlines (AA) Flight 11 (AA11), which departed out of Boston's Logan International Airport (BOS). AA11 was scheduled for departure on the morning of September 11, 2001, at 8:00 a.m., local time**, with an intended destination of Los Angeles International Airport (LAX). The hijacking is believed to have started just shortly after take-off, at approximately 8:14 a.m.

The hijackers used strong arm tactics and claimed to have a bomb. They also stabbed two flight attendants. An ex-Israeli military officer Daniel Lewin was stabbed as well, and it is believed, due to his seating assignment near some of the hijackers, that he may have tried to stop the hijacker in front of him, not realizing another hijacker was positioned behind him. Much of this and other information in regards to the hijacking came from two flight attendants in the cabin, who had contacted their company (United Airlines) via the air phone.

The hijackers were successful in their attempt to gain access to the cockpit, and commandeered the aircraft through the use of their own trained pilot***. The hijacker-pilot steered the aircraft towards New York, and eventually crashed the Boeing 767 into the north tower of the World Trade Center. The pilots, Captain John Ogonowski and First Officer Thomas McGuiness, nine flight attendants, and eighty-one passengers (including the five hijackers) died upon impact, as well as a number of unknown persons in the north tower. [285]

---

[285] (Commission, July 22, 2004), (McLaughlin, 2011 - 2012)

* Going back into the early 1970s' criminals and terrorists had targeted mostly wide bodied aircraft, which carried a considerable amount of fuel as well. This was mostly done in the past however, to take the aircraft on longer flights, furthering the hijacker's time to negotiate. In the case of 9/11, it was to have a larger guided missile, with more fuel, for a larger explosion.

**The attacks on 9/11 all occurred on the Easter Seaboard, on Eastern Standard Time (EST).

***The same had been done in 1988, during the hijacking of Kuwait Air Flight 422 (KU422). By 1988, terrorist groups had proved to have the potential of piloting large aircraft (the hijacked KU422 was a Boeing 747, wide bodied aircraft).

United Airlines (UA) Flight 175 (UA175) was scheduled to depart out of BOS, and like AA 11, was also bound for LAX; UA175 departed at 8:14 a.m. At approximately 8:42 a.m., the crew reported hearing a *"suspicious transmission"* from another plane; that plane was the hijacked flight of American Airlines Flight 11. This was UA175's last transmission, and it is believed that the flight was hijacked by five al-Qaeda terrorists at approximately 8:45 a.m.

The tactics used on UA175 were similar to those of the AA11 hijacking. The hijackers claimed to have a bomb, stabbed flight attendants, and killed both of the pilots.

The hijackers were successful in gaining access to the cockpit and commandeering the aircraft with the use of their own trained pilot. The hijacker-pilot of UA175 steered the aircraft towards New York City, and struck the south tower of the World Trade Center at approximately 9:03 a.m. All fifty-seven passengers (including hijackers), seven flight attendants and both Captain Victor Saracini and First Officer Michael Horrocks, were killed on impact, including an unknown number of people in the south tower.

Attack on the Pentagon

American Airlines Flight 77 (AA77) departed Washington Dulles International Airport (IAD) for LAX at 8:20 a.m., ten-minutes past its scheduled departure time. It is believed that, between 8:51 and 8:54 a.m. the aircraft, a Boeing 757 aircraft, was hijacked just shortly after making its last radio transmission.

There were five al-Qaeda terrorist hijackers on AA77, and they used the same tactics as the other two hijackings. The use of strong arm tactics was a similarity, and phone calls made to the ground by passengers relayed that the terrorists had in their possession knives, or box cutters, and had breached the cockpit. Under threat of violence, the terrorists had moved all of the passengers to the rear of the plane.

The hijackers of AA77 also brought a trained pilot, who took control of the aircraft immediately after the murder of the pilots; shortly after the terrorist-pilot took control, the aircraft turned and headed towards Washington DC. At approximately 9:37 a.m., the Boeing 757 crashed into the Pentagon, killing four crew members, two pilots, Captain Charles F. Burlingame and First Officer David Charlebois, and fifty-eight passengers (including hijackers). An additional 125 persons inside the pentagon were also killed, due to the hijacking and deliberate crash of American Airlines Flight 77. [286]

Thwarted hijacking by passengers

United Airlines Flight 93 (UA93) departed for San Francisco from Newark Liberty International Airport (EWR) in New Jersey, at 8:42 a.m., more than 25 minutes after its scheduled departure time. At approximately 9:28 a.m. four al-Qaeda terrorist hijackers initiated the hijacking of Flight 93.

The hijackers used similar tactics as the other three hijackings; they claimed to have a bomb, they used violence, had stabbed two people, possibly Captain Jason Dahl and First Officer Leroy Homer, and used their own trained pilot to steer the aircraft towards a target for deliberate attack.

At approximately 9:32 a.m., the Boeing 757's auto pilot was reprogrammed to head east towards Washington DC. From reports received on the ground, by some of the loved ones of passengers onboard UA93, the passengers intended to attempt to retake the aircraft and storm the cockpit; by 9:57 a.m., the passengers began their assault.

At approximately 10:02 a.m., United Airlines Flight 93 crashed into an empty field in Shanksville, Pennsylvania. All five crew members, as well as the thirty-seven passengers (including hijackers) perished in the crash. The brave passengers of Flight 93 attempted to take back over the aircraft, and prevented an unknown number of casualties, had the hijackers been able to carry out their plan; the Capitol Building or the White House was said to have been the intended target.

The death toll of the September 11, 2001 attacks was over 3,000 persons, and the tragic event had a deep impact on the nation. While the world was mourning, U.S. intelligence and law enforcement agencies kept functioning; they were busy investigating the coordinated attacks and trying to figure out who may have perpetrated them. In the immediate aftermath of 9/11, U.S. intelligence began honing in on al-Qaeda as a likely suspect organization.

---

[286] (Commission, July 22, 2004), (McLaughlin, 2011 - 2012)

Chapter X

New Beginnings

(September 11, 2001 – November 19, 2001)

On September 11, 2001, the Director of the Federal Air Marshal Program, Greg McLaughlin, was as alarmed as anyone to see the country attacked so deliberately, and was surprised that intelligence agencies and law enforcement departments had not seen the plot coming. Although U.S. intelligence was very much aware of Osama bin-Laden and al-Qaeda, it was still focused on international threats as far as civil aviation security was concerned, and the threat of explosives on aircraft. [287]

McLaughlin spoke with Lynne Osmus by telephone later that day about the future of the air marshal program. Mrs. Osmus had been sick the morning of the attacks, and had come into the command center at FAA headquarters after receiving a call from Claudio Manno*. She had received a call immediately after the first two aircraft hit the north and south towers. After the attacks had oc-

---

[287] (McLaughlin, 2011 - 2012)

Director of Emergency Operations and Communications for the FAA.

curred, and later that same evening, Osmus and McLaughlin had a chance to talk: Since Michael Canavan was out of the country at the time, Mrs. Osmus had assumed the role as ACS1 in his absence. [288]

Mr. McLaughlin was told that Canavan wanted to see him on Thursday, in Washington DC. The men would have to find a way to get there on Thursday, whether the airports in the Nation's Capital were open for business or not. Micaheal Canavan had a more pressing and immediate problem just to get back to the United States: Later in the evening of September 11, Mr. Canavan was forced to use his contacts as a retired military general, to hop a military flight back from San Juan.

Mr. McLaughlin acquired approval to fly up to Dulles airport that Thursday in an old FAA instruments plane. On September 13, he packed his large frame into the back of an aircraft so tightly stuffed with instruments that the pilot and Mr. McLaughlin barely fit. The short flight was strange, only two days after the worst aviation related terrorist attack in the world, and Mr. McLaughlin found an eerie sight at Dulles, as one of the only aircraft active on the runway. After landing at Dulles, he was picked up by a staff car and drove to Washington DC, for meetings with Mr. Canavan and several others; the talks would involve discussions on carving out the security response to the 9/11 attacks. [289]

Present at the meeting that day were Michael Canavan and Greg McLaughlin, along with the Administrator of the FAA Jane Garvey. Also present were the Deputy Secretary of Transportation Michael Jackson, White House Chief of Staff Andrew Card, many White House staffers, and Deputy Administrator of the FAA Monte R. Berger.

One of the major decisions that came out of this meeting, was the need to rapidly build up the Federal Air Marshal Program. Within a few days of the September 13 meeting, a number was given to Mr. McLaughlin, in regards to how many air marshals would need to be trained and flying in the air within one month: That number was 600.

Director McLaughlin was surprised when Mr. Canavan told him this. He was reassured when he was told that he could hire whoever he wanted to help him stand up the force. He was also told that the government and the FAA were already trying to work on the issue of hiring and training 600 air marshals within the one-month time frame. The idea for this was already being rigorously discussed, and the plan was to enlist current law enforcement officers, so that they

---

[288] (Osmus, 2010, 2012)
[289] (Osmus, 2010, 2012), (McLaughlin, 2011 - 2012)

could be taught the essential aircraft specific aspects of the job and skip the legal and law enforcement training.

Immediately after the terrorist attacks, the focus of the Federal Air Marshal Program would continue as it had for nearly a decade: Counter-terrorism. Although new laws would quickly be passed giving Federal Air Marshals a much broader law enforcement capability, not only on the aircraft while in-flight, but in other circumstances as well, they continued to focus mainly on countering terrorist acts. As McLaughlin stated, they were not *"air cops."* [290]

With this in mind, and the direction given to him from the September 13 meeting, Director McLaughlin began contacting old associates from the aviation security sector. Some of these were former air marshals, or others that McLaughlin had known and respected for their knowledge of aviation security. He immediately summoned his former Operations Officer and Director of Training from other civil aviation security positions. One man that was hired during this time was a former air marshal that had been sent out to debrief the commandos involved in the assault on the Air France 8969 hijacking. These were people with expertise in aviation security, and they would remain on the job until McLaughlin was seen through the tough work ahead.

After the 9/11 attacks, there were to be swift changes to civil aviation security. This happened rapidly in a matter of the first few months following the attacks. These changes, like many after 9/11, would begin to shape the Federal Air Marshal Program into the *Federal Air Marshal Service*, and the new agencies that would be associated with it.

To meet the huge demand of interviewing and processing thousands of air marshals, a hotel in the Atlantic City, New Jersey area, was converted into a quasi-indoctrination center for candidates. An application and interview process was set up by a woman named Christine Grecko, who had been handpicked and sent with her team to the William J. Hughes Technical Center, to help with the hiring. The gravity and importance of this mass hiring of air marshals was underscored by the fact that Mrs. Grecko and her team had been sent directly by the Administrator of the FAA, Jane Garvey. [291]

This was a monumental task to hire the number that would later be demanded of McLaughlin and the FAM program. What is now known within the Federal Air Marshal Service as *'The Number'*, or the number of air marshals in service, is classified. It is rumored to be around 4,000 strong, however, the number was,

---

[290] (McLaughlin, 2011 - 2012)
[291] (McLaughlin, 2011 - 2012)

and still *is*, likely in the thousands, and the fulfillment of such manpower was a logistical problem of magnificent proportions. The hotel processing center for new FAMs and the team of personnel at the FAA Technical Center helped relieve this burden, and thousands of applications of those wishing to serve their country poured in.

Since the logistics of hiring had been worked out, the operational task of training the air marshals was taken on by Director McLaughlin and his new team of managers, along with other personnel familiar with the their function and needs. A contractor was brought in to handle the initial training. Most of the instructors from the contract company Science Applications International Corporation (SAIC) were former U.S. Army Special Forces operators, bringing serious experience and skills necessary for the new FAMs. The training received by the first classes post-9/11 covered the essentials, such as aircraft tactics and combat shooting. Since most of the new FAMs hired immediately after 9/11 were former or current law enforcement officers, there was no need to teach certain skills, such as arrest procedures or handcuffing techniques. This allowed McLaughlin and the FAM program to push forward in meeting their deadline of 600 flying air marshals within 30 days: By the end of the one-month deadline, this goal had been met.

Due to the rapid standup of air marshals, and the use of instructors mostly from the military sector, there were rifts at times between instructor and student. Since most of the FAM candidates in the initial two-week training course were prior or current federal employees, there were certain things that could and could not be done, in order to ensure fair and equal treatment for all. Also, some of the initial classes shot 10,000 rounds of ammunition, for example, while another class may only have shot 5,000 rounds; there was much inconsistency. Also, over the course of two or three classes, the TPC, or Tactical Pistol Course, dating back to the latter part of 1992, was phased out, due to the high attrition rate of those attempting it; early on in the training process for the post-9/11 FAMs, there was a shift away from the TPC to the PPC, or Practical Pistol Course: The PPC was a carryover from the days of revolvers, and the same qualification standard shot by the 1980s' era FAMs.

The inconsistency of the initial training courses was apparent to many of the new air marshals, many of whom had come with an extensive range of experience. However, this was to be expected with the speed in which the program was expected to grow.

The first mission flights took to the post-9/11 skies manned by people from various law enforcement agencies, such as the U.S. Secret Service, U.S. Customs and Border Protection, and numerous others. The use of these personnel helped to augment the training of a permanent work force, as had been done in 1961, 1970, and 1985. It was understood that, as in the past, to stand up such a large force, it would take a long time for background investigations, training, equipment issue, etc. In the meantime, there would need to be a sense of security for the general public, in order to restore confidence in the U.S. civil aviation system.

The first personnel to be hired as air marshal's post-9/11 were, in the first months, issued credentials that stated they were FAA *Civil Aviation Security Specialists.* [292]

Jane Garvey, the FAA Administrator, had appointed Michael Canavan to the ACS1 position within the Office of Civil Aviation Security, in January 2001. One of Mr. Canavan's jobs was to act as *"hijack coordinator,"* and his having been out of the country during the attacks was brought into question. Also, during discussions of the number of air marshals to be trained post-9/11, Mr. Canavan made some enemies within the Bush administration, when he expressed his opinion that it would be impossible to put air marshal coverage on *every* flight in and out of the U.S., as had been suggested by some; if this *had* been done, the new Federal Air Marshal Service would outnumber the U.S. Army in manpower.

There were many security issues being brought up by people in the government that had no knowledge of the aviation industry, and as the tension mounted with the hiring of so many air marshals, along with the major changes that were to occur within the FAA and civil aviation security, the environment became a pressure cooker from which Mr. Canavan could not escape.

On October 4, 2001, it was announced that, in reference to Michael Canavan, *"[H]e and administrator Jane Garvey mutually agreed that he would look elsewhere,"* said a spokesman from the Department of Transportation. This change left Lynne Osumus as the Acting Associate Administrator of civil aviation security for the FAA. [293]

Around this time, there were some scheduling conflicts that needed to be resolved in day to day operations that, normally, Messrs. Canavan and McLaughlin would handle. Mrs. Osmus called Director McLaughlin to try and coordinate some of these changes due to her new position. Mr. McLaughlin respectfully advised her that he needed clearance from *"The General"* first. It was

---

[292] (McLaughlin, 2011 - 2012)
[293] (Wald, October 5, 2001)

at this time that Mr. McLaughlin first heard the news of Mr. Canavan having *"stepped down"* as ACS1.

On November 12, 2001, one of the first incidents took place onboard a flight in which air marshals had to become involved. After the attacks of 9/11 a new security rule had been put in place, requiring passengers to remain seated, and to not use the bathroom during the last 30-minutes of flight: [294]

"A US Airways plane from Pittsburgh to Reagan Washington National Airport was diverted to Washington Dulles International Airport because of an unruly passenger, the Federal Aviation Administration said Monday."

"US Airways spokesman Richard Weintraub said air marshals on board Flight 969 ordered the plane to Dulles rather than National. Dulles is 40 miles farther outside the capital than Reagan National. The plane landed without incident at 5:08 p.m. EST, the FAA said."

"The passenger, Raho Ortiz, 33, of Washington, was arrested, law enforcement and airport officials said. Law enforcement authorities said the man ignored warnings to stay in his seat on Flight 969. Passengers cannot leave their seats during the last 30 minutes of any flight into Reagan National under new security rules imposed when the airport reopened after the Sept. 11 terror attacks."

"Another passenger, Robert Gorence, a former assistant U.S. attorney for New Mexico, said he saw a man "making his way toward the cockpit" when "an air marshal jumped up with his gun and subdued him."

"Gorence, in a cell phone call from the plane to Albuquerque television station KOAT, said all the passengers "were ordered to put our hands above our heads, and then we were quickly diverted to Washington-Dulles." [295]

Situations like this were to be common place at first, although not always quite this dramatic. There were many tense moments within the first months that the new surge of air marshals took to the skies. The alert for terrorist activity was extremely high initially, which was to be expected. After the initial stand-up however, things eventually started to come into place, and the 600 new air marshals began to find comfort in their positions. [296]

---

[294] (Press, D.C. Man Arrested on Flight, November 12, 2001)
[295] (Press, D.C. Man Arrested on Flight, November 12, 2001)
[296] (McLaughlin, 2011 - 2012)

On November 19, 2001 the Aviation Transportation Security Act (ATSA) was signed by President George W. Bush, establishing the Transportation Security Administration (TSA). Lynne Osmus, working as the acting-ACS1 for the FAA, began a liaison relationship with the TSA, and began helping with a hand-over of security duties from the FAA. Although this process would start with the November 19, 2001 establishment of the TSA, it would be some time until all security duties were transferred. The exact date of which the TSA officially took over responsibility for the Federal Air Marshal Program, on paper, is unknown; however, it likely occurred between November 19, 2001 and January 2002.

Chapter XI

Federal Air Marshal Service under TSA

U.S. Transportation Security Administration
(November 19, 2001 – November 2, 2003)

N ot long after the TSA was brought into existence, Mrs. Osmus began helping the TSA assume all aviation security duties. Around this same time, a man named Kevin Houlihan took over the duties of ACS1. Although this was the traditional title, and the role had been more or less fixed since O.K. Steele had first been appointed in 1992 to the position, in the post-9/11, FAA/TSA transition, the ACS1, Federal Air Marshals, and the duties of the Office of Civil Aviation Security, began breaking away from the FAA and started taking their guidance from the Department of Transportation (DOT). By March 2002, Kevin Houlihan would be referred to as the *"TSA Undersecretary"* in official memorandums. [297]

During the early beginnings of the TSA, Mr. Houlihan, a twenty-five year veteran of the USSS, had been brought in by a man named John Magaw, another

---

[297] (Stefani, March 6, 2002)

former secret service agent, and former head of President Bush's security detail; Magaw had been appointed to head up the new TSA, officially as the *Undersecretary of Transportation for Security*. The post-9/11 lineup of managers from the secret service would later become a sore subject for air marshals, and would bring rumors of the program having been taken over by the secret service. Other future choices of lead positions within the ranks of the FAMs would reinforce this idea, although as Director McLaughlin later pointed out, *"[when] you are put in charge, you are going to surround yourself with people you are comfortable with. It could have been anybody, it just happened in this case to be the secret service."* [298]

With the work having already begun on the transition from the FAA's Office of Civil Aviation Security, to what would eventually be called the Office of Law Enforcement (OLE) within TSA, there were many legalities to be worked out. Mrs. Osmus and a team of others within the Office of Civil Aviation Security, worked day after day from November 2001 through January 2002, writing memorandums that spelled out each and every responsibility of the new TSA, and all the inroads that would be shared with the FAA. These memorandums had to take into account the various new requirements for aviation security that were being piled on by the U.S. government, in response to the terrorist attacks on 9/11.

The tireless efforts of these men and women, both within TSA and the FAA, helped make possible an undertaking never before attempted. Not since the joint cooperation between the FAA, DOT, USCS, and USMS, during the *'sky marshal'* days of the early 1970's, had something like this been done. The legal paperwork alone required teams of lawyers and persons with specialized knowledge in the plethora of civil aviation security requirements; this was an area where the FAA's team from the Office of Civil Aviation Security, along with their own legal counsel, leant their expertise. The FAA team helped vet any documents before they were implemented within TSA.

While the legalities were sorted out in Washington DC for the security handover, there was still much work being done operationally. In order to stand up the thousands of other air marshals as required by the Bush administration, Mr. McLaughlin was busy trying to hire and train the new Federal Air Marshals as efficiently as possible given the time constraints. [299]

---

[298] (McLaughlin, 2011 - 2012)
[299] (McLaughlin, 2011 - 2012)

While the training of the new air marshals continued and airlines tried to resume their global and domestic service, another attempt was made to kill innocent people onboard an aircraft.

On December 22, 2001, American Airlines Flight 63 was en route to Miami, Florida, from Paris, France. The aircraft was carrying 197 passengers and crew, when a man named Richard Colvin Reid was confronted by a flight attendant, as he attempted to ignite a wire protruding from one of his shoes. A man of French citizenship held Reid's arms, as other passengers grabbed his legs. A doctor on the aircraft sedated Reid and another armed himself with a fire extinguisher. The response by the passengers onboard Flight 63 that day was instrumental in saving the aircraft from sure destruction. What could have been a catastrophic event, if the explosives in Reid's shoe had been detonated successfully, turned into another example of heroics by passengers. Richard Reid would become internationally known as the *"Shoe Bomber"* because of this wicked plot. [300]

This incident was proof that terrorism targeting aviation would continue to be a problem going forth into the year 2002. The hiring and training of thousands of air marshals continued into the New Year. Also, in January 2002, a man named Thomas Quinn was selected as the new Director of the Federal Air Marshal Service (FAMS).

Thomas Quinn came to the FAMS from many years of service with the U.S. Secret Service (USSS). Prior service with the USSS was one commonality shared between Quinn, Magaw and Houlihan. Like Magaw, Thomas Quinn would also choose to surround himself with people he knew and had associations with; he would pick prior secret service agents like himself to help build up security operations at the Federal Air Marshal Service.

The new Federal Air Marshal Service under TSA was beginning to form with Director Quinn in place. Greg McLaughlin would stay on as *Deputy Director* to assist Mr. Quinn, and to use his contacts in aviation and intelligence while the TSA gained footing. [301]

Aviation continued to be a tempting target for terrorists, and airport terminals would continue to serve as a fertile hunting ground, as had been the case for decades. On July 4, 2002, an air marshal assigned to the Los Angeles Field Office (LAFO) heard shots fired within the airport terminal. The FAM had been

---

[300] (Programs, January 16, 2002)
[301] (McLaughlin, 2011 - 2012)

patrolling an area near the food courts of the international terminal, adjacent to the El Al ticket counters, when the shooting started. [302]

Drawing their weapon and finding cover, the air marshal assessed the scene and went on to interview witnesses and cordon off the area. A later bomb scare and rumors of a *"dirty bomb,"* placed other concerns on the situation, and the FAM was involved in that response as well. The air marshal later received a commendation by the Los Angeles Police Department (LAPD) for their actions that day.

Not only were airports still tempting targets, but aircraft continued to have credible threats against them as well. Air marshals' onboard Delta Airlines Flight 475 on August 31, 2002, found themselves utilizing the training they had learned at the FAA Technical Center. This incident served to demonstrate the capabilities of FAMs when they are called to action.

Delta Airlines Flight 475 departed Atlanta for Philadelphia at 11:10 a.m. local time; FAMs Mumma and McCullers were onboard for the quick trip. [303]

At approximately 11:55 a.m., a passenger named Steven Feuer was observed entering the first-class cabin by the FAM team. This was a violation of security protocol in place at the time, and remains a rule to this day that is announced by all airlines before take-off. Later in the flight, the lead flight attendant asked for assistance in dealing with Mr. Feuer. The FAM team ended up arresting Mr. Feuer, after the man acted aggressively towards one of the FAMs.

After Mr. Feuer was subdued and seat-belted into one of the front row seats, the air marshals drew their weapons after trying repeatedly to gain control of passengers. The FAMs ultimately gained compliance of all individuals onboard the aircraft, and upon landing, they decided to detain another individual that was believed to be watching their actions prior to landing.

Air marshals were being asked by their country to make split-second decisions in regards to aviation security, as the nation's last line of defense in preventing aircraft from becoming weapons of mass destruction. Not even one year had passed since the attacks of September 11, 2001, and the men and women working in the national security arena were ever sensitive to the increasing threat of terrorism.

---

[302] (FAM A. f.)

[303] (McCullers, August 31, 2002): *Open Source Document*

By 2002, Osama bin-Laden had been implicated in the terrorist attacks on 9/11. War had begun with the first air strikes taking place in Afghanistan in October 2001. The *"War on Terrorism"* was in full swing, and U.S. intelligence agencies would continue to see aviation as a tempting target by terrorist organizations. The chatter coming in from the various intelligence networks, as well as the history of terrorist organizations, pointed to the terrorists desire to use their previous reconnaissance of aviation targets, in order to perpetrate other attacks. This surely caught the eye of the Federal Air Marshal Service.

Director Thomas Quinn, with the help of Deputy Director Greg McLaughlin and his numerous contacts in the aviation security industry, started figuring out the organizational structure of the Federal Air Marshal Service and how to deal with the rising threat of terrorism for aviation. The problem was not a new one, however, the program was much larger than it had ever been, and it would be up to these men to decide how to use the thousands of new air marshals. [304]

The mass hiring of air marshals brought other challenges as well; in September 2002, air marshal's started complaining about the need to wear suit jackets on flights, which affected their anonymity. Thus began a four-year battle with air marshals, with legal representation from the Federal Law Enforcement Officers Association (FLEOA), and TSA. Air marshals voiced concern that the attire they were required to wear, under the dress-code policy, affected their ability to blend in with the flying public*. One air marshal commented on national television that, *"even a four-year-old could tell who we are."* Some air marshals refused to follow policy and instead wore clothes matching their environment.

The assignment of mission flights, post-9/11, was a work in progress. FAMs would get a phone call prior to their work week, and would be given their respective schedules for a one-week time period; the initial work week, during the first eight-months to one-year, was four-days on, three-days off. This later changed to a five-day work-week.

It was up to Messrs.' Quinn and McLaughlin to come up with the scheduling system for missions, and the assigning of new field offices to the layered security system that was TSA's Office of Law Enforcement. McLaughlin explained to Quinn about the spoke-and-wheel system of aviation security; Thomas Quinn's expertise was not in aviation security, and he relied on Mr. McLaughlin for his experience and knowledge in this highly specialized field.   The spoke-and-

---

[304] (McLaughlin, 2011 - 2012)

*Air marshals were required to wear a suit-jacket while on-duty per FAMS policy.

wheel system described the relationship between the interconnectivity of the various airports domestically and internationally, and the airlines and their respective hubs that feed in and out of that system. The spoke-and-wheel model would be used to assign field offices and to plan missions accordingly, along with other variables that are classified.

In September 2002, shortly after the one-year anniversary of the 9/11 attacks, a man named Hussein Ali Mohammed Hariri, the hijacker of Air Afrique Flight 56 in 1987, escaped custody with the aid of accomplices. On December 23, 2002, he was recaptured by Moroccan authorities, who had acted on a tip from Swiss investigators. The Swiss requested extradition but were denied.

With the numerous changes occurring within the Federal Air Marshal Service, including the transition to TSA, another change in March 2003, moved the program away from the Department of Transportation for the first time in almost forty-decades. On March 25, 2003, the TSA was placed under the umbrella of the Department of Homeland Security (DHS); this came immediately after President Bush signed the Homeland Security Act (HSA). The Federal Air Marshal Service, with over 40 years of experience in civil aviation security, was now in a new security administration and folded into another new government department. The break away from the old traditions of the Office of Civil Aviation Security, and the decades of knowledge gleaned from that experience, was slowly fading under the new guard. The new leadership forming within the ranks of the FAMS came with a lot of valuable experience, lacking only in the very valuable expertise of aviation security. [305]

The Department of Homeland Security was formed in November 2002, and was responsible for protecting U.S. citizens at home, including protection up to and away from the borders of the contiguous states. Its creation, in part to help prevent further terrorist attacks, fit the mission of the FAMS well, and the transition from DOT to DHS seemed fitting. This move would help *"align better the ability of the DHS to respond to terrorist events or emergencies, as stated in their mission."* [306]

For the following year, the air marshals would carry out their missions in anonymity. The battle to change the dress code policy continued and other issues became news. The many negative stories all pointed to an agency trying to establish itself after its rapid stand up following the 9/11 attacks. The combination of the speed in which air marshals were hired, along with the explosive nature under which the FAA's Office of Civil Aviation Security under DOT be-

---

[305] (Wikipedia, Federal Air Marshal Service)
[306] (Wikipedia, Department of Homeland Security)

came the TSA under DOT, and the change from the DOT to DHS, caused many of these initial issues. The new FAMS organization was weathering some storms; however, as the case is with most storms, once weathered, the future can be better prepared for.

Chapter XII

Federal Air Marshal Service under ICE

U.S. Immigration Customs and Enforcement
(November 2, 2003 – October 16, 2005)

On November 2, 2003, the Federal Air Marshal Service became part of Immigration Customs and Enforcement (ICE), also housed within the Department of Homeland Security. It was reported that budgeting issues within TSA caused the move to ICE. A statement issued on this new change reported the following: [307]

"[A] new agreement with their respective Homeland Security agencies that will bolster U.S. aviation security by providing a 'force multiplier' to ICE's Federal Air Marshal Service (FAMS)."

The news release, dated February 24, 2004, discussed Director Quinn's involvement in helping garner support from other law enforcement agencies to help with enhanced coordination and emergency surge capabilities if required.

---

[307] (Enforcement)

During the move to ICE the air marshals were told they would be re-designated as Criminal Investigators/ Special Agents. Along with criminal investigative training, they were told they would be given supplemental training in emergency response.

With the November 2003 transition to ICE, new capabilities were at the disposal of the immigration department, and they used the FAMs ability to gain rapid access to flights to their advantage. The repatriation of a fugitive was made possible by using a FAM team while also providing security for the flight.

Only a few months after the FAMS moved over to ICE, a memorandum was issued stating that air marshals would *not* become ICE special agents. This caused some tension within the ranks of the air marshals and the program was once again in a transition phase: Like the Cubans of the 1960s', the air marshals felt they were *"undesirables."*

With the transition to ICE, all was not gloom in the Federal Air Marshal Service and much *was* getting done under Director Thomas Quinn. On February 24, 2004, the new FAMS Mission Operation Center (MOC) was first unveiled to the general public. Boasting state of the art communications, the new MOC was said to have the ability to *"disseminate critical operational intelligence to individual air FAMs worldwide on a 24/7 basis."* The MOC would also generate scheduling for air marshals, booking mission flights based on a threat matrix, which accounts for aircraft fuel load, and a number of other factors. [308]

Also in Herndon, VA, the Systems Operations Control Division (SOCD) and Investigations Division would serve as advantageous *"to the staffing, coordination, and incident management of those flights that are initiated due to investigative and/ or intelligence information."*

The MOC was an important milestone in joining various law enforcement and intelligence agencies in the common goal of thwarting terrorist attacks against the homeland and civil aviation. The SOCD and MOC would begin to serve as a filtering point for all aviation security threats.

On March, 11, 2004, three-days before the general elections in Spain, a coordinated attack on Madrid's train system killed 191 people. The investigation into the attack determined that a Basque separatist group was responsible, in their attempt to sway election results in the country. The *Madrid train bomb-*

---

[308] (Strohm, 2004)
* Referred to in Spain as 11-M.

ings*were just the beginning of terrorist threats towards countries allied with the United States, and this would not be the last time Spain was attacked during the new *"War on Terror."*

On June 29, 2004, a flight from Detroit to Los Angeles, Northwest Airlines Flight 327, alarmed some passengers onboard, when 13 members of a Syrian band created concerns for what was later referred to as a *'terrorist dry run'*. A report later released by the inspector general shed light on the incident, and a 2007 Washington Times article and investigation, delved deeper into the incident.

Twelve Syrian band members and their Lebanese promoter became the focus of passenger, crew, and air marshal attention on Flight 327. The band members were observed during the flight moving rapidly up to the first class cabin and then going into the bathroom for an extended period. They were also observed giving signals to each other during the flight in the cabin while in the boarding area. Prior to boarding Flight 327, the 12 men had acted as if they did not know each other. Members of the band were detained after the flight and questioned at Los Angeles International Airport by the FBI. [309]

The men were later found to have eight *"positive hits,"* in the National Crime Information Center (NCIC) * database; all were traveling on expired visas. In addition, the promoter, of Lebanese descent, had been previously investigated for acting suspicious on a separate flight; he was later detained a third time in September 2004, on a return trip to the U.S. from Istanbul. Other information on the Lebanese individual was redacted from the inspector general's report.

The behavior of thousands of passengers was being observed by FAMs daily. Some of this information was reported through intelligence channels, and would sometimes cause persons to become *"selectees,"* requiring additional screening prior to boarding. The immense amount of information FAMs were collecting was being gathered and analyzed, and similarities were being identified to try and paint a picture of possible terrorist planning or action. By August 2004, that information was continuing to point at plots involving commercial aviation as a possible target. The picture was not all together clear, but the overall end result was the same in most cases: Terrorists continued to be attracted to the aviation sector and aircraft when planning their attacks.

---

[309] (FAM A.)
* The NCIC database has been maintained by the FBI since 1967, and holds records on numerous known criminals other pertinent information.

Although for the U.S., al-Qaeda had come to represent the major threat to the homeland and interests abroad, other terrorist organizations, along with lone individuals, had been the *real threat* to U.S. flagged aircraft. This was also the case for allied countries, and signatories of the many conventions on aviation security that the U.S. shared relations; each country had their own internal and external threats, and al-Qaeda was a small factor among the numerous entities operating around the world. The terrorist groups that targeted these countries utilized the same planning process, and were most vulnerable while in the surveillance phase. Sometimes, however, plots are not uncovered in time, and terrorists move beyond the operational planning stage, to the last stage of the cycle: Attack.

On August 24, 2004, the nearly simultaneous crash of two aircraft that had both departed Mocow's Domodedovo International Airport immediately raised speculation of terrorism. By the 29th of August, investigators in Russia had found traces of explosives in the wreckage. Security services acknowledged this fact, identifying it as Hexogen. Hexogen was also known as RDX*, and was a powerful high explosive. Among others, this was an explosive that was preferred by terrorists for its highly destructive properties.

The bombing of both, Volga Avia Express Airlines Flight 1353 and Siberia Airlines Flight 1047, was claimed to have been carried out by a little known Chechen terrorist group. This bombing and the realization that the threat to aviation had not subsided was not lost on air marshals. Like the July 29, 2004 *"dry run,"* air marshals continued to see suspect activity onboard U.S. flagged aircraft. These men and women continued flying missions, and remained ever more vigilant in detecting suspicious activity.

These occurrences, such as the *"terrorist dry run"* of July 2004, were becoming routine for air marshals, however FAMs were beginning to feel concerned that management was not interested in hearing about the incidents. In a Washington Times article, air marshals voiced concerns over this and other issues taking place within the Federal Air Marshal Service under ICE. Air marshals were still furious over the memo stating that air marshals would not be allowed to transfer to an 1811 position, or that of criminal investigator, as had been promised early on in the transition from TSA to ICE. Air marshals continued searching for comfort and consistency in their new careers. [310]

---

[310] (McLaughlin, 2011 - 2012)
*RDX stand for Research Department Explosive, and was developed to be an alternative to the standard for all explosives: TNT.

The year of 2005 was unsettling for many FAMs, leaving them feeling let down and abused by management and in a constant state of uncertainty with the various changes taking place. The constant stress had negative effects on the quality of life the typical FAM felt. This did not change the fact that they had to always strive to perform at their highest level: It was what the nation demanded of them.

In fact, the typical FAM, having been through the changes of firearms standards from the TPC to the PPC, was still a much higher than average shooter, amongst other law enforcement entities. FAMs were trained at a much higher level than other law enforcement officers, and required to train for more hours in any given year or quarter. Air marshals were required to qualify every quarter for the physical fitness standard and their firearms to remain active.

By 2005, the training for these dedicated men and women was beginning to come more in line with that of other law enforcement agencies and would serve to add credibility to the secretive FAMS. It would also give those FAMs that had no prior law enforcement experience the required training of all sworn federal law enforcement officers. Since there were specific skills to be learned that were unique to the aircraft, students were brought back from the law enforcement academy in Artesia, NM, to the FAA Technical Center in Atlantic City for aircraft specialized training.

After this training, in such subjects as behavioral recognition, aircraft tactics, terrorist tactics, constitutional law, and other related topics, air marshals were released into the aviation realm, to blend in with the traveling public. Their job was to observe, and attempt to detect and deter, terrorist activity. As history had already shown, for nearly eight-decades, aviation had been a tempting target to criminals and terrorists. Having men and women in the aviation domain, with the ability to board flights at will, and with training in detecting potential threats to an aircraft, coupled with knowledge of the entire aviation system, made sense in light of these threats. Come what may and regardless of the challenges they faced, these FAMs were out there, day in and day out, selflessly serving the general public to ensure their safety.

On June 7, 2005, explosions rocked the London Underground train system and a double decker bus during commute hours. In the chaos, fifty-two people were killed, in what would be determined as an attack by *"homegrown Islamist extremists."* The attacks were coordinated, and the explosives detonated almost simultaneously.

The "homegrown" revelation of extremism, not unlike the Unabomber Ted Kaczynski, was not a new one. However, as news media coverage for terrorist attacks continue to flourish, and disheartened or disillusioned people still exist, the number of lone wolves, or homegrown extremists, whether Islamists or not, are bound to remain and possibly increase in the future.

While the FAMs worked to remain positive and keep the skies safe, and after a *"second-stage review"* of the DHS organization, the Federal Air Marshal Service was moved back under TSA; this became effective after being officially approved by DHS Homeland Security Secretary Michael Chertoff on October 16, 2005.

Chapter XIII

Federal Air Marshal Service under TSA

U.S. Transportation Security Administration
(October 16, 2005 – 2012)

With the move back to TSA, after nearly two years with ICE, the air marshals began feeling that their bouncing from one government entity to the next was going to be a trend. Air marshals looked at themselves as *unwanted* by other law enforcement agencies. The constant changes that took place were interpreted as if the government was sending a message: That not even they could decide where the air marshals belonged.[311]

Within two-months of the transition back to TSA, arguably one of the most remembered air marshal incidents to date took place within the Federal Air Marshal Service. On December 7, 2005, as the pre-flight boarding of American Airlines Flight 924 (AA 924) was finishing, a man named Rigoberto Alpizar, a 44-

---

[311] (FAM A. f.)

year-old U.S citizen, came running up the aisle. When challenged by a flight attendant Mr. Alpizar told her *"I have a bomb."* [312]

Earlier that day, Alpizar and a woman had gotten off of an aircraft in Miami, arriving from Quito, Ecuador, on their way to Orlando, FL; the aircraft they boarded was Flight 924. The two had been heard arguing onboard the aircraft just prior to Alpizar's bolting from his seat and rushing towards the front of the aircraft, saying *"I have a bomb,"* or *"There's a bomb on board,"* as reported by witnesses.

After hearing this, two air marshals onboard the aircraft gave up their under-cover status and announced that they were Federal Air Marshals. They followed Mr. Alpizar up the jet bridge, which led back into a crowded Miami airport ter-minal. When Alpizar ignored the air marshals commands to stop, they told him *"If you don't take your hands out of the bag, we're going to have to shoot you."* After Alpizar ignored this, the FAMs fired their weapons in an attempt to stop, what was believed to be, a suicide attack. At the time of the shooting Alpizar had turned and started moving towards the aircraft, as witnessed by one of the pilots.

One of the air marshals fired three shots, and the other six, exhibiting major restraint given the capacity of their firearms. All projectiles were from front to back, and *"non-grazing,"* as reported by the autopsy; out of the nine-rounds fired, only four remained lodged in Alpizar's body, suggesting major over-penetration by the Sig .357 bullets. The autopsy supported the finding that the backpack had been worn across the front of Alpizar's body. The image of a sui-cide bomber with a bomb strapped across their chest is one that has been por-trayed by Hollywood movies on numerous occasions.

Unfortunately, Alpizar turned out to be bipolar and in need of medication. He most likely made the statement of having a bomb because he was attempting to get out of a situation which caused him severe anxiety; the woman with Alpizar was his wife of twenty-years and she had tried to intervene before the shooting, saying *"He's sick."*

The Bush administration commented on the shooting stating that the air mar-shals acted accordingly. Bush spokesman Scott McClellan said, *"...the air mar-shals that were on this flight appear to have acted consistent with the extensive training that they have received, and that's important to note. And so we are*

---

[312] (CNN, Man killed after bomb claim at airport, December 7, 2005)

appreciative of all that our air marshals do day in and day out in terms of trying to protect the American people. " [313]

The realism of terrorism was so beyond the thoughts of the average U.S. citizen, that the men and women working in the national security arena and the vital work they performed on a daily basis would rarely cross their minds. The TSA and DHS and a staggering amount of resources, are brought to bear on trying to remain one step ahead of terrorist plots and surveillance of new targets by terrorist organizations. A casual conversation with a man or woman during travel in the aviation sector may be fed back into the intelligence system by a person assumed to be a regular business traveler, and these are the same men and women that are attempting to protect the general public from another 9/11: The Federal Air Marshal.

By March 2006, another former secret service agent took over as director of the FAMS: Dana Brown replaced Thomas Quinn, and came in at a time when the air marshals were ready for a strong leader to see the Federal Air Marshal Service into a brighter future. Another USSS agent seems business as usual for most FAMs, however Dana Brown was a leader with plenty of experience in management and he intended to see that positive change came from his tenure. [314]

The TSA website reported Mr. Brown's background as *"a senior executive with more than 30 years [of] experience in law enforcement and security management."* [315]

Dana Brown started out his law enforcement career as a police officer in Fairfax County, VA. He then joined the USSS, where he held numerous positions in support of security operations, investigations, intelligence, audits and inspections, and other key domains; he spent 25-years in these positions with the secret service.

Mr. Brown also had military service that many of the air marshals could respect. He was a former enlisted marine and Vietnam veteran and had received several decorations, including a Purple Heart.

Prior to coming on as the Director of the Federal Air Marshal Service at TSA, Dana Brown had been instrumental in *"facilitating the transfer and func-*

---

[313] (Room, December 8, 2005)

[314] (Wikipedia, Federal Air Marshals)

[315] (TSA, Dana Brown: Assistant Administrator for Law Enforcment and Director of Federal Air Marshal Service)

tional realignment of the Federal Air Marshal Service back to the TSA, a move that emanated from Secretary Michael Chertoff's Second Stage Review of the Department of Homeland Security. "[316]

On May 25, 2006, the Service House Judiciary committee released a report called *"In Plane Sight: Lack of Anonymity at the Federal Air Marshal Service Compromises Aviation and National Security."*

Some of the justifications for the bad moral throughout the air marshal rank and file could very well have come from the top down view of management towards the typical flying FAM: As Director Thomas Quinn stated during a May 14, 2004, briefing to committee staff for *"In Plane Sight,"* only the vocal *"two percent"* were complaining about policies and procedures, and he described these air marshals as *"disgruntled amateurs."* [317]

The report went on to expand on the experience of upper management in civil aviation security matters, or lack thereof. It was understood that, with the separation from the Office of Civil Aviation Security, an entity with nearly four-decades of aviation security experience prior to 9/11, there would be a large gap in knowledge and contacts in an area so center to what was necessary within the FAMS organization *after* 9/11. The report expanded on this, stating *"most upper level policy makers at FAMS have little to no direct aviation security experience."* It went on, saying that *"many in FAMS headquarters have never actually served as a Federal Air Marshal, which is understandable given the rapid build-up of FAMs. FAMS management however should be receptive to input from rank-and-file Federal Air Marshals who fly on a daily basis and can make recommendations based upon their actual experience and practical knowledge."*

The report was scathing and pointed towards a need to improve relationships with the air marshals and management. It also pointed at possible retaliatory methods having been used toward FAM Frank Terreri* for a violation of policy. The aforementioned policy was later determined to be unenforceable, and *"was found to be over inclusive and excessively restrictive of free speech."*

Media interactions were also of concern to the committee, in regards to the *"[Federal Air Marshal Service's] over eagerness to disclose sensitive security information to national media outlets."* They referred to three occasions in

---

[316] (TSA, Dana Brown: Assistant Administrator for Law Enforcment and Director of Federal Air Marshal Service)
[317] (Judiciary, May 2006)
*This is the name given in the 2006 Judiciary report.

which the FAMS had participated in *"televised news segments that reveal tactics, positioning, attire, and other sensitive information about the FAMS."*

There was a certain deterrent benefit to be found from news releases on the air marshals, however, the committee found the Federal Air Marshal Service under ICE and Thomas Quinn had went too far in revealing sensitive tactical movements, or *"positioning,"* along with the dress code issue of *"attire,"* taking the stance that the dress code was unrealistic for blending in with the general public.

Soon after the May 25, 2006 report was made public, the dress code policy was relaxed. Air marshals were free to dress in a manner which enabled them to blend in according to their environment, whether on the aircraft or other settings.

Air marshals continued to feed information into the intelligence system about possible probing activity onboard commercial flights. The threat to civil aviation had not subsided since 9/11, and intelligence agencies continued tracking these threats. Fusion centers had been incorporated into the intelligence gathering capability and all reports of suspicious activity were fed into a central system. The fusion centers and the Joint Terrorism Task Force (JTTF) of the FBI, worked closely to disseminate information to other law enforcement agencies, in working partnerships with organizations such as the FAMS. The Federal Air Marshal Service has numerous positions filled with the JTTF and they serve as a special tool in combatting terrorism. [318]

On August 9, 2006, during what was a cold and foggy night in London, England, twenty-four suspects were arrested on suspicion of a plot to blow up aircraft over the Atlantic Ocean with liquid explosives. The plot they were attempting to carry out, was almost an exact copy of the Bojinka plot that targeted aircraft in the Pacific in the early 1990s'. [319]

The aircraft targeted for what would later be called the *2006 transatlantic aircraft plot*, were:

- United Airlines Flight 931 to San Francisco
- Air Canada Flight 849 to Toronto-Pearson
- Air Canada Flight 865 to Montreal-Trudeau
- United Airlines Flight 959 to Chicago-O'Hare
- United Airlines Flight 925 to Washington –Dulles
- American Airlines Flight 131 to New York-JFK

---

[318] (Wikipedia, Federal Air Marshal Service)
[319] (Wikipedia, 2006 transatlantic aircraft plot)

- American Airlines Flight 91 to Chicago-O'Hare

All of the U.S. flagged aircraft targeted were Boeing 777 aircraft; the foreign aircraft were Airbus A330s.* This plot would have major repercussions for civil aviation security. New rules would go into effect at TSA prohibiting any liquid in carry-on luggage of over three U.S. fluid ounces. Any liquids carried onboard had to be separated by passengers prior to passing through security; this policy continues to this day.

The 2006 transatlantic aircraft plot, along with new TSA security rules, caused more delays at airports, particularly at security checkpoints, as the flying public got used to the new procedures. The farther the events of the attacks on September 11, 2001 became, the less they were part of the human conscious- ness. People began getting perturbed at checkpoints and pointed their frustra- tions at TSA security screeners. The general public is one that usually pays little regard to their personal security and understands little of the tasks involved in safeguarding civil aviation against the aviation security pandemic of the last eight-decades. Unfortunately, as people became more confident the further away these events become, with a false sense of security, their frustrations were taken out on those who's duty it was to prevent further attacks from occurring: Terror- ists have taken advantage of this American mindset in the past, and have a ten- dency to wait for long periods before attacking their targets.**

The FAMS under TSA and Director Dana Brown would attempt to learn more about aviation security. They also branched out to perform liaison work with local law enforcement at joint mass transit operations, which would even- tually morph into VIPR (Visual intermodal Prevention and Response) teams. Mr. Brown would also attempt to patch up the services moral and began reach- ing out to air marshals in new ways. *"Lunch with the Director"* became one of Mr. Brown's programs, in which he would pick an air marshal from a random office and meet with them for lunch. He did this to talk with the average FAM to see what his or her concerns were and how they might be fixed. Dana Brown was taking the Federal Air Marshal Service in a new and positive direction un- der TSA.[320]

On August 23, 2006, an incident took place on a flight from Amsterdam to Mumbai, India. Eleven Indian passengers were observed by air marshals

---

[320] (Wikipedia, Federal Air Marshal Service)
*Both aircraft were wide bodied, and carried a considerable amount of fuel.
**The planning of the attacks on 9/11 were said to have stemmed from the Bojinka plot in 1994, and was finally approved by Osama bin-Laden in 1998 or 1999.

onboard to be acting suspiciously, passing cell phones back and forth on the aircraft. The men were detained for questioning, but determined not to be a threat and later released.

On December 30, 2006, Spain was again attacked by Basque separatists, this time targeting the Madrid Airport. On that date a van exploded in a terminal parking area; the blast killed two and injured some fifty-two others. With the event occurring within hours of the execution of Saddam Hussein in Iraq, it was initially thought that the attack may have been Islamic militant retribution for the dictator's death sentence. This was not the case, however it did serve to show that airports remained tempting and vulnerable targets for terrorists. The vulnerability of airports, as shown by the Madrid airport bombing, and the attacks success, was proof for the need of the various security measures being implemented by U.S. airports in response to the 9/11 attacks. [321]

On February 5, 2008, class number 801 graduated air marshal training. The TSA website commented on their graduation and included quotes from some of the new FAMs: [322]

- *""I like having that feeling of accomplishment, every time the plane lands safe that will be a big thing for me."*
  FAMS Class 801 graduate
  Los Angeles Field Office"
- *""My wife worked with the American Red Cross in Alexandria, Va., on 9/11 ... She has been very supportive of my career with FAMS."*
  FAMS graduate
  New York Field Office"

In June 2008, Robert S. Bray took over as Director of the FAMS in the Office of Law Enforcement at TSA; this happened shortly after Dana Brown announced his retirement. Robert Bray was another former secret service agent and he came to the position intent on continuing to improve moral in the workforce: He took serious the recommendations made by the 2006 judiciary committee. He would also continue to build the ground based VIPR teams at various offices to support mass transit joint operations. [323]

Director Bray was coming in at a time when aircraft terrorism appeared to be waning. However, as terrorism targeting aviation appeared to be on the decline, this did not mean it was not a tempting target to terrorist organizations, nor did it

---

[321] (Wikipedia, 2006 - Madrid-Barajas Airport Bombing)

[322] (TSA, More than 40 Air Marshals Take To The Skies)

[323] (Wikipedia, Federal Air Marshal Service)

mean that there were no plots currently being planned for attacking more U.S. aircraft.

The *terrorist planning cycle* of terrorist operations requires these individuals to gather intelligence on their targets. This *surveillance phase* is the most vulnerable stage of the planning cycle for the terrorist. Although the majority of information on a target nowadays can be obtained from the internet, as the terrorist nears a certain phase of their planning they must come out and physically observe the target area, even if just for a short period of time. This vulnerability is the weakest link in the terrorist's preparation for an attack and it is at this time that they are most susceptible to detection.[324]

Most terrorists do not wish to be caught; they wish to carry out more attacks in the future. Other than suicide bombers, their goal is to live to fight another day, and this gives way to focusing on attacking targets that have already been surveilled and for which a wealth of knowledge already exists, thus negating the exposure of the terrorist to the target prior to the attack. This was one of the main reasons that aviation continued to be a tempting target to terrorist organizations: They had built up a wealth of information on aviation.

Going back to the early 1990s', intelligence agencies knew that terrorists were infiltrating the aviation system to see how it worked behind the scenes. They were getting positions within the aviation sector, or recruiting those already inside, to get a firsthand look at the inner workings of airports, security, and all things aviation related.

Sun Tzu said *"Know your enemy,"* and the FAMs of the 1990s' trained to be the most knowledgeable of the inner workings of the aviation system as well: They trained like the terrorists did. They understood how the venders operated, how baggage moved through the airports, and how the entire aviation system worked. Given that the air marshals were closely tied to the intelligence community, they also understood the problem of the insider threat, and they did some deterrent related exercises in this regard during the mid-1990s' at JFK airport. The air marshals of the 1990's also used media to their advantage for its deterrent capability, as had the post-9/11 FAMs, later pointed out by the 2006 Judiciary report. However, it was sometimes necessary and justified to show a force's capability in order to deter future attacks.

This in-depth knowledge of the aviation system, gave the terrorists a reason to continue targeting aviation going into 2009. As Director Bray worked to improve the service, and air marshals and management alike strived to learn more

---

[324] (State, 2003)

about aviation security and their roles in the growing Office of Law Enforcement within the TSA, other events would rock the aviation system and show that terrorism and other criminal activity onboard commercial aircraft would continue to be a problem.

On September 9, 2009, a Boeing 737 aircraft, Aero Mexico Flight 576, departed from Cancun en route to Mexico City. Three Bolivian men hijacked the aircraft shortly after take-off and demanded to speak to the president of Mexico, Felipe Calderon. The men claimed to have an explosive device. [325]

Shortly after Flight 576 touched down in Mexico City, Federal Police stormed the aircraft and removed the hijackers without firing their weapons; the hijacking and rescue lasted little over three-hours. The *"explosive device"* they claimed to have was detonated by police, however, no explosives were detected.

Flight 576 served the aviation industry with one more hijacking, and although the incident ended without anyone being hurt it showed that explosives would remain part of the terrorist tactic for trying to gain compliance during a hijacking event, or to simply destroy an aircraft: This would not be the last time such tactics were used.

This event, like many before it, proved that criminals and terrorists could hijack an aircraft with no weapons. This fact negated the need to bring explosives or weapons onboard, and defeated all but the most robust of aviation security programs, and remains the case to this day.*

The trend of terrorists and criminals posing a risk to civil aviation would continue to be a factor, just as it had since the beginning of commercial passenger air travel. The intelligence on these threats *would* continue to come in, however, by late 2009, the intelligence community was still attempting to put all the pieces together in order to understand and disrupt terrorist plots. While law enforcement needed to be right all the time, terrorists only needed to be successful once to fulfill their mission.

On November 19, 2009, a middle-aged man walked into the U.S. embassy in Abuja, Nigeria, with information on his son. He spoke with two CIA officers regarding the extreme views his son was demonstrating, and told them his son

---

[325] (Wikipedia, Aeromexico Flight 576)
*Arguably the most robust aviation security system in the world, Israel uses different methods to detect possible terrorist activity on their airline, El Al. The approach used by Israel would be too cost prohibitive in the U.S., and is easier done in the small country, due to the small size of their national airline.

was likely in Yemen. The man was afraid that his son had become affiliated with a terrorist organization.[326]

On December 25, 2009, the man's son, Umar Farouk Abdulmutallab, boarded Northwest Airlines Flight 253 in Amsterdam, Netherlands. He had been trained by al-Qaeda in the Arabian Peninsula (AQAP) in Yemen to carry out an attack against the U.S. using explosives. He was wearing explosives concealed in his underwear upon boarding Flight 253 bound for Detroit. Having trained in Yemen for this operation under the guidance of Anwar al-Awlaki* and AQAP, Abdulmutallab was ready to carry out a suicide attack against the U.S. and the 249 people onboard Flight 253.

A man in his 50s was seen helping Abdulmutallab in the Amsterdam airport by witnesses. The man was reported as speaking in an American sounding accent, and as being *"smartly dressed."* This gave speculation as to whether the U.S. government was involved in some sort of covert operation to have Abdulmutallab carry an inert explosive device, or if the man was using a cover and was an actual terrorist facilitator aiding Abdulmutallab in the attack and ensuring he did not lose his nerve prior to the attack.***

During the flight, Abdulmutallab was seen getting up to go to the bathroom shortly before the crew prepared for landing. He spent twenty-minutes in the lavatory and then returned to his seat, at which time he draped a blanket over his body. Passengers heard noises and smelled burning, while others witnessed fire on Abdulmutallab's pants. [327]

The man was taken to the front of the aircraft, and when questioned by a flight attendant on what he had in his pants, Abdulmutallab replied *"Explosive device."* He was quickly detained, and upon landing was taken into custody by law enforcement.

Found on Abdulmutallab's body was a pouch in his underwear containing the explosive PETN and TATP**; these were the same explosives used by Richard Reid in his attempt to destroy American Airlines Flight 63, and by a host of oth-

---

[326] (Wikipedia, Northwest Airlines Flight 253)
[327] (Wikipedia, Northwest Airlines Flight 253)
* Anwar Al Awlaki was a radical, American born, Muslim cleric. He was very influential in Yemen, until being killed by a U.S. drone strike in September 2011.
** Pentaerythritol Tetranitrate and Triacetone Triperoxide are explosives.
***This is a role that terrorist facilitators typically perform, along with other logistics.

er terrorists in numerous attacks over the past decade, making them two of the most popular explosives due to the ease in which they could be made. The location of the explosive device on Abdulmutallab's body, led to him being labeled the *"Underwear Bomber."* The failure of the mixture to detonate properly was a bitter win for the U.S. intelligence community and homeland security, unless it *was* an operation set up by U.S or foreign law enforcement, or an intelligence agency, and then it would be considered a success by any measure: This conspiracy theory has never been proven.

This incident brought the realization that there were still terrorists that saw aviation as a target of allure. Intelligence and law enforcement agencies in the U.S. took criticism for not doing more to prevent the possible catastrophe that could have befallen Northwest Airlines Flight 253. The response from the FAMS came in heightened flight coverage on international routes that were seen as possible targets for other attempts. The TSA would also implement new screening procedures because of the attempted bombing of Flight 253.

The air marshals were beginning to feel more at home within TSA, and increasingly better conditions were made within the Office of Law Enforcement at TSA, to ensure the flying FAM was given a nurturing environment in which to work. The VIPR teams working with mass transit, along with the canine team and explosive dog handler program*, gave FAMs an opportunity to take ground assignments, along with increasing the law enforcement coverage in other critical areas of transportation. The ground time and break given to FAMs participating in these programs was essential, due to the long and strenuous hours spent in the air protecting civil aviation from the skies.

It would appear from the outside that the job of a FAM is an easy one. Managers during the ICE period, and the over whelming majority of information available on the FAMS suggests, that managers were of the same opinion: That the job was as easy as the typical flying FAM having to sit in a seat all day and collect a pay check.

The stresses on the body from lack of sleep and continuous changes between time zones, as is the case for the typical FAM flying missions around the world, have long been known. Studies by the FAA in the 1990s' sought to establish an adequate rest period for crew members. This study came to form new policy, requiring crew members to have a certain number of uninterrupted hours of sleep in any given work day. [328]

---

[328] (FAM A. f.)

*This program has since been discontinued within FAMS.

In 2010, a sleep study was started with the FAMS as TSA moved forward to try and improve the quality of life for air marshals on constant flight status. The study, performed by Harvard University researchers, involved looking at air marshal schedules and taking results from volunteer questionnaires in which air marshals had reported sleep patterns for a one-month period. This should be a positive step forward in the move towards a better quality of life for air marshals.

On June 25, 2010, John S. Pistole assumed the role of Administrator for TSA. Mr. Pistole came with a background of prior service with the FBI, where he ultimately served as the Deputy Director from October 2004 to May 2010. He is said to have played important roles in sculpting terrorism policies while serving with the FBI in this top-tier position. His background and understanding of terrorism policy and related issues, married well with the mission of the FAMS.[329]

While air marshals continued their mission to protect the traveling public, terrorists again targeted aviation for attacks, this time in the supply chain against cargo aircraft.

On October, 29, 2010, two explosive devices were found onboard two separate cargo aircraft (an Airbus A320 and a Boeing 777); the bombs were concealed in two Hewitt-Packard (HP) LaserJet printers: The plan to blow up these aircraft would be called the *Cargo Plane Plot*. The explosive content was PETN and determined to be several times more than needed to *"level a house."* [330]

The first package containing explosives left Sana'a, Yemen, on a 144-passenger plane, arriving in Dubai. A UPS aircraft picked up the package and transported it from Dubai to Cologne, Germany. Another UPS aircraft then took the package to East Midlands Airport in Leicestershire, United Kingdom. The package was scheduled to continue on to Philadelphia, PA, and then O'Hare in Chicago, IL, however, British authorities had been tipped off to the explosive device prior to the plane's landing in Leicestershire, and they performed a thorough search for the hidden device.

The search that was performed involved explosive canine teams, explosives experts, and assistance from the infamous Scotland Yard. However, no explosives were found in the printer or onboard the aircraft. After inspection, the Boeing 767 was allowed to depart for Philadelphia with the explosive still intact:

---

[329] (Wikipedia, Federal Air Marshals)
[330] (Wikipedia, Cargo planes bomb plot)

Scotland Yard and explosives experts had inadvertently disrupted the explosive that was due to detonate within three-hours.*

Scotland Yard became aware of the fact that the package they had let leave likely *did* contain a bomb, when another printer was found to be housing explosives; a FedEx aircraft was inspected in Dubai, at which time an explosive was discovered. The Fed Ex aircraft was due to fly on to Newark airport in New Jersey, and then, like the other cargo plane, to O'Hare in Chicago, IL.

This was another lucky break for law enforcement and aviation security professionals. The terrorist's use of PETN had been an issue in the past for aviation security experts, since the explosive had a very low vapor pressure that was hard to detect. It was noted by the Director of the Homeland Security Policy Institute at George Washington University, that *"It is evident that had we not had the intelligence, our security countermeasures would not have identified these improvised explosive devices."* [331]

After the cargo plane plot, the TSA began looking at new ways to screen passengers, as the threat to civil aviation remained high; printer ink cartridges weighing more than one-pound were eventually banned from all luggage onboard aircraft.

In December 2010, in response to the attempt on Flight 253, new technology began being used at airports deemed as *"high-threat."* These *'advanced imaging machines'* used backscatter X-rays and high-frequency radio waves to create 3-D images and detect possible security threats on a person's body, such as explosives or weapons. The TSA announced that if passengers wished to decline this new technology they could instead go through a pat-down search; these measures would raise concerns over privacy, with pat-downs involving screeners using their hands to check around the groin and breast areas of passengers.

By 2011, the Federal Air Marshal Service had been making many changes since it moved back from ICE in 2005. Its many field offices around the country had been outfitted with the latest and best in training equipment, for air marshals to have the best available training, and the organization continued to grow and mature over the years since the troubling times under ICE and Director Thomas Quinn. Although some problems occurred at various offices around the country, the majority of the work force began voicing their approval for the changes.

---

[331] (Bennett, November 3, 2010)

*The actual printer that the bomb was placed in had been searched. It was correctly identified by its serial number, which had been given by an informant; however, traces of explosives could not be found initially by investigators.

The current organization of the Office of Law Enforcement/ Federal Air Marshal Service, as shown by Wikipedia, is as follows: [332]

- Assistant Administrator TSA Office of Law Enforcement (OLE)/Director of FAMS: Robert S. Bray
- Deputy Assistant Administrator TSA OLE/Deputy Director of FAMS
- Assistant Director, Office of Field Operations
  - Deputy Assistant Director, Eastern Region (11 Field Offices)
  - Deputy Assistant Director, Western Region (10 Field Offices)
- Assistant Director, Office of Flight Operations
  - Transportation Security Operations Center
  - Systems Operations Control Division/FAMS Mission Operations Center
  - Investigations Division
  - Liaison Division
  - Flight Programs Division
  - Emergency Preparedness Division
- Assistant Director, Office of Training & Workforce Planning
  - Training Management Division
  - Federal Air Marshal Training Center (New Jersey & New Mexico)
- Assistant Director, Office of Security Services & Assessments
  - Office of Security
  - Office of the National Explosives Detection Canine Team Program
  - Security Assessments Division
  - Explosives Division
- Assistant Director, Office of Administration & Technical Services
  - Management & Organization Division
  - Management Operations Division
  - Policy and Procedures Division
  - Infrastructure Support & Development Division

The Administrator of TSA, John Pistole, has ultimate authority over all of TSA, including the FAMS. His leadership and vision, along with that of Mr. Bray, is essential if the Federal Air Marshal Service is to continue moving in a positive direction.

On May 2, 2011, a raid took place in Abbottabad, Pakistan. During the night time raid, Osama bin-Laden was killed by members of the elite SEAL Team Six.

---

[332] (Wikipedia, Federal Air Marshal Service)

As described in his book, *No Easy Day: The First Hand Account of the Mission that Killed Osama bin-Laden*, the former SEAL Team Six member Mark Owen* said that Osama bin-Laden had been positively identified; the world's most wanted terrorist was officially dead. Almost a decade after the attacks on 9/11, *Operation Neptune's Spear* had brought justice to the innocent victims killed in New York, the Pentagon, and Shanksville, PA. [333]

Most U.S. citizens would see the death of Osama bin-Laden as a major win in the War on Terrorism. Others in the national security field knew better than to think that one terrorist's death would bring an end to the violence and bloodshed that has prevailed against the world's civil aviation interests. It wasn't long before this point was proven, by yet another brazen attack against a major international airport.

On June 24, 2011, a twenty year old Islamic terrorist entered Domodedovo International Airport intent on killing foreigners. At approximately 4:42 p.m. local time, the man had walked into a crowded international airport's baggage claim area and detonated his suicide vest. The result of the blast left 37 dead and injured 173. The Russian civil aviation security governing body quickly placed rules on visitors of the airport, requiring them to be checked before having access to the passenger ticketing area, known as the non-sterile area.

The bombings and attacks on airports, in both the sterile and non-sterile areas, had been prevalent for some time as a threat against civil aviation. Airports in the U.S. continue to represent an alluring target for terrorists. Thankfully, in the last few decades, airports have not been attacked in such a manner in the homeland, however, as terrorists continue to evolve and become more desperate in their attempts to attacks U.S. targets that are continually being hardened**, and with the ease of access and ability of passengers to move unimpeded in the non-sterile area, they may become ever more popular in the future.

On January 29, 2012, an attempted hijacking took place on a Chinese passenger aircraft. Like most hijackings before it, the attempted hijacking of Tianjin Airlines Flight 7554 started shortly after take-off. In an attempt to breach the cockpit door, which was locked, one or more of the men used a crutch***. Two

---

[333] (Owen, 2012)

*The name is an alias.

**A *Hard target* is one with stringent security standards.

***One of the hijackers most likely carried the crutch as a disguise to appear injured, serving a dual purpose: The hijacker would use the crutch in an attempt to breach the cockpit and it also made the individual appear to be injured and a non-threat.

in-flight air marshals stopped the six men, and crew helped to hold the suspects until the flight landed in Hotan, China; one other hijacker may have been found later, which, if true, points to the possibility of a *'sleeper'* waiting to act later during the hijacking; this was a tactic that had been used previously by other hijacker teams, such as Kuwait Airways Flight 422 in 1988. [334]

The fact that hijackings, or attempted hijackings, are still occurring, shows that commercial aircraft remain a target. Bombings and attempted bombings over the last decade have been prevalent, and there is no indication that terrorists have stopped targeting civil aviation or will stop in the near future. Fortunately, as the example of Flight 7554 shows, there are air marshals still deployed worldwide to help prevent the many possible deadly consequences.

Current State of FAMS

Currently, the FAMS are said to keep the highest firearms qualification standard in all Federal Law Enforcement. Due to the close confines of an aircraft cabin, air marshals must have the ability to be able to shoot accurately in the crowded confines among passengers; this is a requirement that the general public demand. The PPC qualification standard is shot quarterly, and each air marshal must attain a score of 255 or higher out of a possible 300 points; this relates to an 85% for the qualification standard in order for an air marshal to carry their weapon. [335]

Beginning in July 2007, the TSA significantly increased the number and frequency of VIPR deployments, from an average of one exercise per month, to one or two exercises per week. Due to some initial safety concerns with using air marshals as uniformed Law Enforcement Officers, potentially compromising their identities, the TSA changed their policies and made the VIPR exercises more *"officer-friendly." [336]*

Also, along with VIPR teams, some air marshals continue to serve within the Joint Terrorism Task Force (JTTF) of the FBI. These men and women help with intelligence operations and attempt to thwart terrorism on U.S. soil. Some canine teams have also been assembled in support of various activities within the TSA. This is all possible to the modern day air marshals authority under 49USC114

---

[334] (NEWS, 2012)

[335] (FAM A. f.)

[336] (Wikipedia, Federal Air Marshal Service)

(p), as opposed to the pre-9/11 air marshals, whom only had 49USC44903 (d), or special aircraft jurisdiction, to rely on for authority*.

A more recent OIG report was released early in 2012, and spoke of troubles among rank and file air marshals and supervisors; much of the commentary came from incidents taking place at the Orlando Field Office in Florida. Blame was placed on both groups in the report, but in light of this, the evidence suggests that reconciliation has already begun within the Federal Air Marshal Service: Director Bray appears to have made great strides in improving conditions within the FAMS. [337]

Regardless of the past differences and growing pains when the program moved from the FAA to TSA, and through its myriad of transitions within different government agencies, the current air marshals that serve the public are proud to provide a selfless sacrifice to their country, as have so many others before them.

Training

Much of the information in regards to the training for current Federal Air Marshals can be found on the internet. All respective candidates go through an intense, two-part training process, which includes seven-weeks of basic Law Enforcement training at the Federal Law Enforcement Training Center (FLETC) in Artesia, New Mexico, and further FAM specific training at the William J. Hughes Technical Center in New Jersey.

All of their training is tailored towards the specialized role of Federal Air Marshals, such as constitutional law, physical fitness, behavioral observation, defensive tactics, emergency medicine, and other law enforcement techniques. The perfection of marksmanship is constantly stressed during training. The candidates who successfully complete training are assigned to one of many field offices across the country.

---

[337] (General D. o., January 2012)
* The changes in jurisdiction between pre-9/11 air marshals and post-9/11 air marshals placed a broader range of law enforcement powers that put the FAMs more in line with other Federal Law Enforcement Officers (FLEOs). Pre-9/11 FAMs were not allowed to take their weapons home, and were not recognized under the 6C coverage for FLEOs.

The Federal Air Marshals that currently work protecting passengers and national security interests day after day, work in the shadows, blending in with the travelling public all around the world. They are a capable force, and the only law enforcement agency that can deploy hundreds, if not thousands, of law enforcement officers within hours. The fact that Federal Air Marshals have been utilized for over five-decades, lends credence to the important position they are imparted with.

In Closing

The Federal Air Marshal Service has come a long way since its humble beginnings: From the early days of the FAA Peace Officers, with the passing of laws and legislation making air piracy a crime, to the studying of hijackings and watching as Islamic extremism threatened the entire aviation system. From the expansion and wane of the 'sky marshal program' in the early 1970s', to the expansion of the Federal Air Marshal Program after the tragic events of TWA 847 and the later counter-terrorism specialization in response to changes in terrorist tactics, air marshals have, for the last five-decades, been an integral part of the layered security approach towards protecting civil aviation.

Beyond all the politics, and out of reach of the airline industries, stands the Federal Air Marshal. The amount of terrorism and other criminal acts targeting commercial aviation that the U.S. and the rest of the civilized world have faced since 1930 is alarming. The actions of the leaders of this great nation have made great strides in affording a last line of defense of aircraft in-flight with the continued use of air marshals on select U.S. air carrier flights.

In the rapid standup of the service after the attacks on 9/11, there were strides to be made and overcome in building up the new FAM service after the end of the FAA FAM Program. The TSA has helped to establish a welcoming home for those men and women serving as air marshals across the nation, since the FAMS came back over from ICE in 2005. The process has taken time and is ongoing, but the current Federal Air Marshal Service is heading in a positive direction, and the men and women of the FAMS, whom represent every background and ethnicity that make up this great country, are proud of how far the service has come.

Thousands of the men and women of the Federal Air Marshal Service wake up every day to blend in with the general public and provide a service that is key, not only as a deterrent, but as a message to would be terrorists and criminals targeting aviation for attack.

The U.S., with its Federal Air Marshals, sends the message that, in the words of retired Vice Admiral Cathal Flynn:

"Anytime a U.S. airliner is flying in the world FAMs can be aboard; that woman up in first class can be a FAM; that student in economy can be a FAM; and every person in between"

Federal Air Marshal Historical Timeline

(May 1930 – May 2012)

1. **May 1930** – First recorded Hijacking. (Occurring outside the U.S.)
2. **1947** – Hijackings start up again. (Occurring outside the U.S.)
3. **1947** – 1st lethal Hijacking. (Occurring outside the U.S.)
4. **1947 to 1958** – 23 Hijackings occur during this period. (Europeans seeking political Asylum)
5. **1955** – 1st act of criminal violence on a U.S. aircraft.
6. **1958** – "No fly" rules in place barring Cuba – U.S. air traffic.
7. **1960** – 1st suspected suicide bomber on U.S. airliner; Investigation still remains open
8. **May 1, 1961** – 1st Hijacking of a U.S. airliner. (to Cuba)
9. **August 3, 1958** – Federal Aviation "Agency" comes into existence from the preceding CAA
10. **1961** – "Homesick Cubans" begin hijacking aircraft at a rapid rate.
11. **1961** – John Marsh , an attorney with the FAA, begins working on a project to establish laws in regards to air piracy; previously there were no laws on the book for air piracy.
12. **May 1961** – FAA committee established for civil aviation security.
13. **May 1961 to August 1961** – three more hijackings occur between Cuba and the United States.
14. **August 3, 1961** - hijacking attempt thwarted by INS Agent Leonard Gilman.
15. **August 9, 1961** – Hijacking from Mexico City to Cuba. The hijacker is a former French Army soldier having fought in Algeria. He is onboard with a Columbian diplomat that had been on tour opposing the dictator Fidel Castro, and this makes for possible tension between the U.S. and Cuba worse. It is determined that the U.S. must do something about the hijackings.
16. **August 10, 1961** – President John F. Kennedy talks about using armed guards on flights.
17. **August 1961 – March 1962** – U.S. Border Patrolmen fly as armed guards on flights.
18. **August – September 1961** – recommendations from FAA committee for regulations on air piracy.

19. **September 8, 1961** – President John F. Kennedy signs Public Law 87-197, air piracy act.
20. **February 19, 1962** – the first FAA Peace Officers training commences.
21. **February 19 to March 2, 1962** - FAA Peace Officers Course dates.
22. **March 1, 1962** – 17 FAA Peace Officers graduate from training as FAA Peace Officers.
23. **March 2, 1962** – 17 FAA Peace Officers are sworn in by Robert F. Kennedy.
24. **March 7, 1962** – Operation Slingshot Memo #1 distributed to 17 FAA Peace Officers.
25. **March 20, 1962** – Operation Slingshot Memo #2 distributed to 17 FAA Peace Officers.
26. **March 22, 1962** – Personally charged equipment purchased for FAA Peace Officer duty purchased by 17 FAA Peace Officers.
27. **March 26, 1962** – FAA Peace Officers travel to Washington DC for meeting regarding Operation Slingshot.
28. **March 27, 1962** – Operation Slingshot meeting.
29. **Fiscal Year 1962** – 1st recalled missions flown by FAA Peace Officer Joseph Pontecorvo.
30. **July 1963** – article is published in FAA Horizons magazine on "Skyjack Unit" of FAA Peace Officers.
31. **July 1963** – FAA Peace Officers begin being referred to as "Sky Marshals" within FAA for shorthand, and to avoid confusion with regular Flight Standards personnel, based mostly off of the July FAA Horizons Article calling them a Skyjack Unit.
32. **September 14, 1963** – "Convention on offenses and certain other acts committed on board aircraft" held in Tokyo; this would later be referred to as the "Tokyo Convention".
33. **December 4, 1963** – Tokyo convention goes into effect.
34. **May 7, 1964** – Pacific Airlines Flight 773 is hijacked from Reno to San Francisco, and crashed near San Ramon, California.
35. **August 6, 1964** – FAA emergency rule put in place requiring the locking of the cockpit door prior to departure.
36. **1965** – Administrator Halaby suggests to President Lyndon Johnson that FAA be folded into Department of Transportation and cabinet post.
37. **March 27, 1966** – attempted hijacking of an aircraft from Santiago de Cuba to Havana in attempt to reach the United States. Captain of flight resists hijacking and is shot and killed along with a crew member. Hijacker is eventually given the death penalty in Cuba.
38. **1967** – Federal Aviation Agency becomes the Federal Aviation Administration when a new Department of Transportation (DOT) combines major federal responsibilities for air and surface transport.

39. **1967** – FAA Administrator no longer reports to the President but would instead report to the Secretary of Transportation. New programs and budget requests would have to be approved by DOT, which would then include these requests in the overall budget and submit it to the President.

40. **April 23 – 25, 1968** – recurring training for FAA Peace Officers held at Port Isabel. This would be the last recurrent training for the FAA Peace Officers before they were relieved of their collateral duties within Flight Standards.

41. **July 19, 1968** – the FAA announces that "sky marshals" will board random flights in Florida due to the high volume of hijackings coming from the region to Cuba.

42. **October 23, 1968** – hijackings reach a "cult" status as on this date the grandson of a former U.S. Vice President hijacks an aircraft to Cuba from Florida.

43. **November 24, 1968** – three men hijack Pan Am Flight 281 out of New York's JFK airport to Puerto Rico. Pilot is forced to fly to Havana, Cuba. The U.S. State Department evacuates the passengers on a government aircraft.

44. **Early 1969** – Military personnel start being trained as sky marshals. Mostly military police are recruited for this duty and trained at Ft. Dix. Some of the remaining FAA Peace Officers as well as other FAA personnel help train the military "sky marshals" at Ft. Dix.

45. **August 29, 1969** – Hijacking of TWA Flight 840. Leila Khaled, whom would gain major publicity for her role, is one of the hijackers. This hijacking represents a shift towards more violent, politically motivated, hijackings and bombings.

46. **September 1969** – increased mission tempo for remaining FAA Peace Officers due to violent extremist hijacking of TWA 840.

47. **October 1969** – U.S. Marshals Service has started their own Sky Marshal security program due to high amount of Cuban hijackings out of Florida.

48. **1969** – Anti Air Piracy Task Force has started to implement a screening program at Eastern Airlines in Washington DC.

49. **1969** – Paper "Task Force on Deterrence of Air Piracy", or FAA-AM-78-35, is released.

50. **Late 1969** – Project ZEKE commences within the air piracy task force. Only the task force is aware of ZEKE.

51. **Late 1969** – The remaining FAA Peace Officers are thanked for their service and they are officially stood down as Special Deputy U.S. Marshals in light of other programs running by this time. FAA takes a back seat on the program and stands down all of their FAA Peace Officers.

52. **March 17, 1970** – Eastern Airlines Flight 1320 is hijacked going from Newark to Boston.
53. **June 4, 1970** – hijacker commandeers an aircraft at Dulles Airport in Virgina demanding $100 million from the government; project ZEKE is attempted, however, hijacker is caught prior to ZEKE being used. Although not the first, this hijacking represented a move towards the use of hijackings for extortion.
54. **September 6, 1970** – Dawson's Field hijackings. This was a major co-ordinated hijacking of four aircraft (a fifth attempt was unsuccessful on an El Al flight), which were eventually blown up in Syria (three aircraft) and Cairo (a 747, too large to land in Syria).
55. **September 11, 1970** – President Nixon gives speech on air piracy and the hijacking problem. It is during this speech that he orders more sky marshals to fly, and also military personnel to be trained, for the "surge".
56. **October 1970** – Military personnel begin being trained in a surge capacity for sky marshal duties at Ft. Dix, New Jersey.
57. **October 28, 1970** – Master Agreement signed between Department of Treasury and Transportation. Calls for two-year crash program for sky marshals due to rash of hijackings.
58. **October 31, 1969** – one of the longest hijackings in history occurs when a U.S. Marine, a veteran of the Vietnam War, hijacks an aircraft bound for SFO, eventually giving himself up in Italy. This hijacking is highly publicized and copycat hijackings follow.
59. **March 17, 1970** – hijacking of Eastern Airlines Flight 1320 from Newark to Boston. The hijacking is foiled by the heroic actions of Captain Robert Wilbur, Jr., who fought the hijacker while wounded and safely landed the aircraft; the co-pilot, First Officer James Hartley was mortally wounded.
60. **November 30, 1970** – 1st Class for the training of Customs Security Officers (CSOs) at the Treasury Air Security Officer School (TASOS). A total of 60 people start training on this date for the position of CSO.
61. **1970** – Benjamin O Davis Jr. heads up Federal Sky Marshal Program for Department of Transportation.
62. **Late 1970** – many different law enforcement agencies working in a surge capacity to help work as armed guards/ sky marshals on civilian aircraft.
63. **1971** – Book titled "Sky Jacker; his flights of fantasy", by Dr. David Hubbard of the FAA, is finished, and speaks of the psychological profile of the skyjacker.
64. **November 24, 1971** – a man who became known as D.B. Cooper hijacked Northwest Orient Airlines Flight 305 and receives ransom, then parachutes from plane.

65. **October 1971** – memorandum from former Associate Director William Hall outlines the achievements of the U.S. Marshals Service Sky Marshals.

66. **January 12, 1972** – Braniff Flight 38 is hijacked as it departs Houston TX for Dallas TX.

67. **January 29, 1972** – TWA Boeing 707 hijacked by Garrett B. Trapnell. This man Trapnell is tied to the FAA Psychologist David Hubbard. Trapnell had been Hubbard's patient, and Hubbard was involved in the trial as an expert witness in Trapnell's trial.

68. **May 30, 1972** - three Japanese Red Army (JRA) terrorists, posing as tourists, flew to Israel on an Air France flight. At baggage claim they picked up their luggage which contained weapons, ammunition, and hand grenades. They opened fire in the terminal killing 24 people and injuring 75 others. Kozo Okamoto was the only terrorist to survive the attack.

69. **June 3, 1972** – Western Airlines Flight 701 from Los Angeles to Seattle was hijacked by Black Panthers. Demanded ransom, let passengers get off in San Francisco then flew to Algeria where the two hijackers were granted political asylum.

70. **June 23, 1972** – 9th copycat, D.B. Cooper style, hijacking attempt.

71. **July 31, 1972** – Delta Airlines Flight 841 hijacked by five members of the Black Liberation Army including the elusive George Wright.

72. **November 10, 1972** – Hijacking of Southern Airways Flight 49. This hijacking and the response by the FBI had an effect on the Sky Marshal/ Air Marshal programs.

73. **November 10, 1972** – this hijacking of flight 49 made congress change the authority for hijackings from the FBI and put it back in the hands of the FAA.

74. **Late 1972** – by this time over 150 aircraft have been hijacked.

75. **1973** – speech by U.S. Marshals Service training instructor Jack Cameron tells of the achievements of those serving as Sky Marshals.

76. **December 12, 1973** – by this time CSOs have racked up an impressive record of arrests.

77. **February 22, 1974** – attempted hijacking of Delta airlines Flight 523 by Samuel Byck. This was an event that foreshadowed the flying of a plane into a building. He wants to kill President Nixon by flying a plane into the White House.

78. **June 25, 1974** – U.S. Customs Sky Marshal Program transferred to the FAA.

79. **June 25, 1974** – end of U.S. Customs Sky Marshal Program.

80. **June 25, 1974** – takeover of the air marshal program by the FAA, which will become known as the FAA's Air Marshal security-program.

The FAA calls it this in order to avoid confusion of the three year Sky Marshal programs of the different agencies of the early 70s' programs.

81. **September 2, 1974** – Time Magazine article "The Last Marshal". DOT announces that the sky-marshal program had come to an end. It states that the last Sky Marshal came out of the air in June of 1974.

82. **1974** - Somewhere in this time period Magnetometers start to be used, however only in certain airports deemed high risk for hijackings or bombings.

83. **Fiscal Year 1975** – No FAM missions flown. (FAA archives)

84. **June 27 - July 4, 1976** – hijacking of Air France Flight 139. Israeli commandos assault the building where hijackers are holding the hostages, killing all Palestinian hijackers and rescuing 105 people, which were almost all Israeli hostages. Three passengers and one commando are killed.

85. **Fiscal Year 1976** – Only 1 FAM mission flown during the entire fiscal year. (FAA archives)

86. **September 10, 1976** – TWA flight 355 hijacked by Croatian separatists. One New York police officer is killed while working on a bomb which the hijackers had planted at grand central station.

87. **Fiscal Year 1977** – No FAM missions flown. (FAA archives)

88. **December 4, 1977** – Member of Japanese Red Army hijacked Malaysia Airlines Flight 653, a Boeing 727, which crashed and killed all onboard, after hijacker kills pilot then himself. 100 people die.

89. **Fiscal Year 1978** – No FAM missions. (FAA archives)

90. **March 13, 1978** – United Flight 696 hijacked by American. Aircraft took off from KSFO (San Francisco) and landed in Oakland. The aircraft then continued on to Denver where the hijacker was apprehended.

91. **December 21, 1978** – 17 year old Robin Oswald hijacks TWA Flight 541 flying from Louisville to Kansas City claiming she had three sticks of dynamite.

92. **Fiscal Year 1979** – No FAM missions. (FAA archives)

93. **April 1980** – "Muriel Harbor Cuban Refugee" crisis operations begins. May 3-October 16, 1980, FAA tasked to provide security for relocation effort between Key West and various DOD facilities throughout the US. This mission was beyond FAM resource capabilities, and thus Federal Air Police from DC airports (Dulles and National) were assigned to assist and assigned as FAMS.

94. **Fiscal Year 1980** – there are a total of 205 FAM missions during the year total. (FAA archives)

95. **December 1980** – Billie Vincent comes to work as Special Assistant of Flight Standards for the FAA. He goes on to do some other work with the air marshals.

96. **1980 – 1982** – Lynn Osmus, of whom will later become the acting Associate Administrator for Civil Aviation Security in 2011, works as air marshal in Los Angeles.
97. **Fiscal Year 1981** – only 1 FAM mission to the Georgetown, Guyana "James Jones" cult murders of 1978. (FAA archives)
98. **1981** – Billie Vincent on executive staff for Air Traffic Control.
99. **Fiscal Year 1982** – No FAM missions. (FAA archives)
100. **May 1982** – Billie Vincent assumes role in FAA as the Director of Civil Aviation Security.
101. **August 11, 1982** – Pan Am 830 is bombed 100 miles outside of Hawaii; flight was coming from Japan and killed one and injured 15. A man named Abu Ibrahim is implicated as the bomb maker.
102. **Late August, 1982** – attempted bombing of Pan Am flight from London to Miami to Rio de Janeiro; the bomb resembled the one used on Pan Am 830.
103. **October 1983** – bombing of the Marine barracks in Lebanon. The "DAWA 17", as they become known, are arrested and held in Kuwait and become a motivation for many terrorists and hijackers in the future that demand their release.
104. **December 12, 1983** – U.S. Embassy in Kuwait is bombed. Seventeen men are held in Kuwait in connection with the bombing, and become known as the DAWA 17. The release of the DAWA 17 in Kuwait would become a major motive of multiple hijackings over the course of the next several years, and would further highlight the Islamic terrorism problem in the Middle East.
105. **December 1983** – attempted bombing of El Al Airlines. Suitcase bomb is picked up in an intelligence operation in Greece before the bomb is carried on to the aircraft by a woman that never realized she had been carrying it; the intelligence operation managed to get her suitcase from her apartment in Athens.
106. **Fiscal Year 1983** – there are a total of 37 FAM missions for unknown reasons. (FAA archives)
107. **Fiscal Year 1984** – there are a total of 10 FAM missions for unknown reasons. (FAA archives)
108. **March 16, 1984** – William Buckley, a CIA paramilitary officer, is abducted in Beirut. This abduction and ultimate murder of Buckley was thought to be carried out because of the incarceration of the DAWA 17.
109. **December 4, 1984** – Kuwait Air – KWI-DXB-KHI; and A-310, after an immediate stop in Dubai is hijacked to Tehran by 4 heavily armed men. Over the next six days the hijackers release 153 passengers and crew in several groups. While in Tehran, the hijackers beat and torture 6 passengers and 2 Americans. Kuwait refuses to release the prisoners (DAWA

17). The incident ends DEC 9, when Iranian security forces board the aircraft and overpower the hijackers, who are subsequently released.

110.**June 14, 1985** – hijacking of TWA 847; the hijackers demand the release of the DAWA 17, and in the process a Navy diver, Robert Stetham, was murdered.

111.**June 18, 1985** – Speech by President Ronald Reagan on hijacking and of ramping up air marshals.

Also, NSDD-180 is issued, and Public Law 99-83, calling, among other things, for a mass hiring of FAMs at this time.

112.**June 18, 1985** – about 150 new air marshals are hired by the FAA, in response to TWA 847 and President Reagans order, over the next two-years.

113.**June 23, 1985** - Air India - Jun 23 1985 - B-747 - YMX-LHR - Bomb in Cargo hold explodes over ocean off coast of Ireland - 329 killed.

114.**September 1985** – Greg McLaughlin, of whom will later become the first Director of the FAA Federal Air Marshal Security Program, becomes a FAM. Training is six weeks in Marana, AZ, located between Tucson and Phoenix.

115.**Fiscal Year 1985** – total of 35 FAM missions flown for unknown reasons. All flights are international. (FAA archives)

116.**April 2, 1986** – bombing of TWA Flight 840 - B-727 - CAI-ATH-FCO - Bomb underneath window seat placed by female passenger on the morning flight from Cairo to Athens to Rome - she departs aircraft in Athens - flight continues to Rome where aircraft is to be searched prior to return trip to Athens - bomb not found- explodes in mid-air on return flight to Athens - 4 killed, 9 injured. FAM Team onboard initial flight from ATH to FCO; they depart and continue on to JFK on B-747 while B-727 returns to ATH and explodes. The bomb is suspected to be that of Abu Ibrahim's making, and the terrorist group May 15.

117.**April 17, 1986** - El Al - Apr 17 1986 - B-747 - LHR-TLV - Bomb discovered by Israeli Air Marshal during profiling and search; Anne Marie Murphy was duped into carrying suitcase given to her by boyfriend - main charge concealed in false bottom of suitcase, sympathetic detonator concealed in calculator along with electronic fuse delay - boyfriend arrested/charged/convicted by British authorities - no casualties.

118.**September 5, 1986** - PAA #73 - BOM-KHI-FRA; B747, while boarding passengers in Kara chi, stormed by 4 men dressed as airport security personnel when exiting an airport security marked van, firing into the air. During the confusion, the flight deck crew escapes through the overhead hatch. Hijackers demand a crew to fly them to Cyprus and a US citizen is killed and dumped on tarmac. Negotiations last 17 hours during which time the passengers and crew are herded into the center of the aircraft. When the Ground Power Unit fails and the lights go out, the hijackers, fearing an assault, begin shooting and lob hand grenades into the mass of people; 22 killed, 125 injured. The 4 hijackers and one co-conspirator are tried and jailed in Pakistan and subsequently released. A number of FAMS quit/left the program after this incident, as this was a "routine" flight for air marshals to cover; at this time "air marshal" was not a voluntary position – it was required as a collateral duty by all FAA Inspectors at this time.

119. **Fiscal Year 1986** – 216 FAM missions. (FAA archives)
120. **Fiscal Year 1987** – 268 FAM missions (FAA archives)
121. **July 24, 1987** - Air Afrique #56 - BZY-CDG; DC-10 after departing Brazzaville en-route to Paris is hijacked by lone gunman (Hussein Hariri) who demands aircraft be flown to Beirut and specific prisoners released. The pilot convinces the hijacker they must land for fuel and the aircraft lands in Geneva. While on the ground in GVA, Hariri shoots and kills a French citizen and seriously wounds a flight attendant. Swiss forces storm aircraft and arrest hijacker. Hariri is tried and sentenced to life by Swiss court. Hariri escaped allegedly with aid of accomplices in September 2002 but was recaptured by Moroccan authorities Dec 23, 2002 who were acting on tip from Swiss investigators. Swiss request for extradition was denied. (reference: GMM)
122. **November 29, 1987** - Korean Air - Nov 29 1987 - B-707 - BGW-AUH-BKK - Bomb brought aboard in Baghdad by two North Korean agents, an elderly man and a young girl - they exit plane in Abu Dhabi leaving handbag containing bomb in overhead compartment - main charge liquid explosive concealed in a bottle, sympathetic detonator and digital watch delay fuse mechanism concealed in clock radio; plane departs for BKK. explodes in flight - 115 killed. Both subjects arrested by UAE authorities - male commits suicide during interrogation by biting down on cyanide capsule concealed in cigarette - female attempts same, but is not successful. She is eventually turned over to South Korean authorities and confesses details of entire incident. The attack had been planned 3 years prior when it was announced that Seoul would host the 1988 Summer Olympics. This led to 100% US Air Carrier coverage into/out of Seoul during 1988 Olympics.
123. **Fiscal Year 1988** – 368 FAM missions. (FAA archives)
124. **April 5, 1988** - Kuwait Air #422 - BKK-KWI: four hours into the B-747 flight from Bangkok to Kuwait, while over the Arabian Sea, two men burst into cockpit, guns drawn, and instruct pilot to NOT touch any instruments. Within minutes, they instruct Captain to disengage the auto pilot, change course to a specific heading, and re-engage the auto pilot. The two men are part of a team of seven to nine hijackers. The aircraft is flown under supervision of one of the hijackers to Mashed, Iran. Again, the demand for the release of the DAWA 17. The hijackers

demonstrate a professional, highly trained, disciplined behavior throughout the event. They exhibit a keen awareness of special operations rescue techniques. During the 16 day incident, the aircraft leaves MHD, stops and refuels in Cyprus where the bodies of two Kuwaiti citizens are removed, departs LCA and continues to Algiers. During the night of April 22, with the international media covering the event at ALG, the hijackers leave the aircraft, and are never heard from again.
  The hijackers taking part in this hijacking were referred to as the "A TEAM", by air marshals and civil aviation security experts within the FAA, and the air marshals tactics and deployment strategies were significantly adjusted/upgraded accordingly due to this hijacking. Congress also approved an additional 300 FAM positions due to this event.

125. **Late 1988** -As terrorist hijackings began to decrease, a new tactic began to emerge – bombings.
126. **December 21, 1988** – Pan Am Flight 103 destroyed by a bomb en route from London Heathrow to John F. Kennedy airport (JFK). This bombing would go on to have major implications on civil aviation security.
127. **Fiscal Year 1989** – there are 241 FAM missions during this time. (FAA archives)
128. **Late December, 1989** – in wake of the Pan Am Flight 103 disaster the Aviation Security Advisory Committee (ASAC) was established by the Secretary of Transportation.
129. **Fiscal Year 1990** – there are 343 FAM missions during this time. (FAA archives)
130. **Fiscal Year 1991** – there are 258 FAM missions during this time. (FAA archives)
131. **Fiscal Year 1992** – there are 251 FAM missions during this time. (FAA archives)
132. **Fiscal Year 1992** – Gregory McLaughlin takes over as director of the FAM service. He is appointed to this position by retired Major General O.K. Steele.
133. **Fiscal Year 1993** – there are 266 FAM missions during this time. (FAA archives)
134. **Fiscal Year 1994** – there are 139 FAM missions during this time. (FAA archives)
135. **Fiscal Year 1995** – there are 130 FAM missions during this time. (FAA archives)
136. **1995** – Bojinka plot is uncovered. The plot involves blowing up multiple airliners over the Atlantic Ocean.
137. **FY 1996** – there are 187 FAM missions during this time. (FAA archives)

138. **1996** – The Federal Aviation Reauthorization Act of 1996 mandated the FAA and FBI regularly conduct joint threat and vulnerability assessments at high risk airports.
139. **1996** – FAA report says that "The FAA develops an extensive training program for FAA personnel and others for responsibilities for civil aviation security. Aviation security training for FAA special agents is generally conducted at as resident training at the FAA academy in Oklahoma City." It goes on to say that "…the FAA trained 286 FAA students in basic and advanced aviation security and internal security programs in 1996."
140. **1996** – the 1996 FAA report to Congress on Civil Aviation Security reported that there was a Computer-Assisted Passenger Screening (CAPS) system in place at this time. CAPS applied automated profiling, which had been started through a joint project of Northwest airlines and the FAA. The report said that the development of CAPS had proceeded to the point that full operational capability for Northwest airlines was anticipated for 1997.
141. **1996** – another improvement the 1996 report summarized was the full passenger-baggage match that ensures no unaccompanied bag enters the system, and that a bag is removed if the passenger is not onboard.
142. **1996** – the report of 1996, or annual report to congress on civil aviation security, reported that the Federal Air Marshal program "…provides an armed force whose mission is to protect the travelling public and flight crews on U.S. carriers by deterring criminal and terrorist acts which target aircraft in flight." "…operational training facility is located at the William J. Hughes Technical Center in Atlantic City, NJ." "..force is capable of rapid deployment worldwide,…during 1996, FAMs provided in-flight security on flights of all major air carriers to and from 74 cities in 43 countries." "Just knowing that FAM's could be on board may deter someone who is planning to interfere with a flight."
143. **1996** – Head of FAA security Admiral Cathal Flynn. He said in a statement during Atlanta Olympics "…we could ban aircraft over the stadium" in response to concerns brought up over someone possibly blowing up an aircraft over the stadium during the events.
144. **Fiscal Year 1997** – there are 184 FAM missions during this time. (FAA archives)
145. **Fiscal Year 1998** – there are 137 FAM missions during this time. (FAA archives)
146. **Fiscal Year 1999** – there are 265 FAM missions during this time. (FAA archives)
147. **Fiscal Year 2000** – there are 254 FAM missions during this time. (FAA archives)

148. **November 21, 2000** – Administrator Jane F. Garvey named U.S. Lt. Gen. Michael A. Canavan as the new Associate Administrator for FAA's Office of Civil Aviation Security.
149. **Fiscal Year 2001** – there are 246 FAM missions during this time. (FAA archives)
150. **June 2001** – Lynne Osmus takes over as the Deputy Associate Administrator of Civil Aviation Security at the FAA; she later sees the transition of security programs to TSA following the creation of that agency.
151. **September 10, 2001** – by this point in time the Director of the Federal Air Marshal security program within the FAA's office of civil aviation security is Greg McLaughlin. The deputy administrator of civil aviation security at this time is Lynne Osmus, and the Associate Administrator for Civil Aviation Security is Michael Canavan. The air marshal service at this time has an annual budget of $4 million and 33 air marshals assigned to full time status as air marshals. The other people on at this time were CASLO personnel, or Civil Aviation Security Liaison Officers which were stationed throughout the world at various airports.
152. **September 11, 2001** – four commercial civil aviation aircraft are hijacked and flown into the world trade center towers in New York city, and the Pentagon – another aircraft is prevented by passengers onboard from flying into the White House and crashed in Pennsylvania.
153. **September 13, 2001** – FAM Director McLaughlin is summoned to Washington DC for a meeting with Michael Canavan and White House personnel. Coming out of this meeting is the order of hiring and training 600 air marshals in one-month.
154. **October 4, 2001** – the FAA announces that Michael Canvan will be stepping down as the Assistant Administrator for Civil Aviation Security; Lynne Osmus assumes the role of ACS1 after Canavan departs.
155. **November 12, 2001** – incident onboard U.S. Airways Flight 969. Air marshals take one man into custody for questioning; flight was diverted from Reagan National to Dulles.
156. **November 19, 2001** – the Transportation Security Administration (TSA) is signed into existence by George W. Bush.
157. **December 22, 2001** – American Airlines Flight 63 – Shoe Bomber attempts to set off an explosive device in his shoe but is stopped by passengers.
158. **January 2002** – Thomas Quinn, former U.S. Secret Service, is hired as the new Director of the Federal Air Marshal *program* (not yet called a *Service*). Gregory McLaughlin stays on as the Deputy Director.
159. **July 4, 2002** – shooting at El Al ticket counter at LAX airport. Air marshal at the airport responds during the shooting, and is later given a citation.

160. **August 31, 2002** – Delta Airlines Flight 475: violation of protocol in effect at the time for passengers to remain seated 30 minutes prior to landing. A man is held for questioning by air marshals onboard flight, and the cabin is held at gunpoint.
161. **March 25, 2003** – TSA comes under the Department of Homeland Security (DHS), and thus breaks away from the Department of Transportation – the first time for the Federal Air Marshals since the early 1960s'.
162. **November 2, 2003** – the Federal Air Marshal Service becomes part of Immigration Customs and Enforcement (ICE).
163. **February 24, 2004** – the new Mission Operations Center (MOC) in Herndon, Virginia, is unveiled to the public.
164. **June 29, 2004** – 12 Syrian nationals are detained for questioning by air marshals on Northwest Airlines Flight 327 after exhibiting very strange behavior during a flight. The incident is later labeled a *"dry-run"*.
165. **August 24, 2004** – Nearly simultaneous bombings of two aircraft in Russia.
166. **October 16, 2005** – DHS Homeland Security Secretary Michael Chertoff approves moving the Federal Air Marshal Service back to TSA.
167. **December 7, 2005** – Rigoberto Alpizar is shot by air marshals in Miami when he is heard saying he has a bomb. It later turns out that Alpizar suffers from bipolar disorder.
168. **March 2006** – Dana Brown replaces Thomas Quinn as the new Director of the Federal Air Marshal Service.
169. **May 25, 2006** – the Service House Judiciary Committee comes out with a report called *In Plane Sight: Lack of Anonymity at the Federal Air Marshal Service* on this date.
170. **May 25, 2006** – dress code for air marshals is relaxed, allowing them to better blend in with passengers.
171. **August 29, 2006** – 24 suspect arrested in London over a plot to blow up multiple aircraft over the Atlantic, much like the Bojinka plot.
172. **August 23, 2006** – eleven Indian passengers taken into custody by air marshals for acting suspiciously; they are later released.
173. **June 2008** – Robert S. Bray takes over as Director for the Federal Air Marshal Service shortly after Dana Brown announces his retirement.
174. **September 9, 2009** – hijacking of Aero Mexico Flight 576. Commando's later storm the plane in Mexico City; hijackers taken into custody and no shots fired or people injured.
175. **November 19, 2009** – man walks into embassy in Nigeria to tell of his son's new Islamic views and changes in behavior.
176. **December 25, 2009** – attempted bombing of Northwest Airlines Flight 253 ; terrorist becomes known as the "underwear bomber".

177. **June 25, 2010** – John S. Pistole assumes the role of Administrator for the TSA.
178. **October 29, 2010** – two separate cargo aircraft are found with explosives onboard after authorities are tipped off.
179. **December 2010** – new technology begins being used at major airports throughout the U.S., causing some passengers to become concerned over privacy issues.
180. **May 2, 2011** – Osama bin-Laden is killed by members of SEAL Team Six in Abbottabad, Pakistan during a night time raid.
181. June 24, 2011 – Suicide bombing inside Domodedovo International Airport; 37 killed, 173 injured.
182. **January 29, 2012** – attempted hijacking of Tianjin Airlines Flight 7554.

Works Cited

(n.d.). Retrieved 2011, from Trigger Time: http://www.trigger-time.com/

(n.d.). Retrieved from Aviation Safety Network: http://aviation-safety.net/database/record.php?id=19640507-0

(Various), U. A. (n.d.). Various de-classified documents on Korean Air Flight 858.

Convention on Offenses and Certain Other Acts Committed On Board Aircraft (Tokyo Convention). (1963). Retrieved from McGill University: www.mcgill.ca/files/iasl/tokyo1963.pdf

"Passenger - 'Beautiful Girl' was serious". (1978). *Lakeland Ledger* .

Reagan on Hijacking of TWA Flight 847. (1985, June 14). Retrieved March 5, 2009, from History.com: http://www.history.com/audio/reagan-on-hijacking-of-twa-flight-847#reagan-on-hijacking-of-twa-flight-847

Multiple news broadcasts on the FAA Federal Air Marshal Program (1996). [Motion Picture].

S. 2268 - Public Law 87-197. (2010). Retrieved from John F. Kennedy Presidential Library and Museum: 14. http://www.jfklibrary.org/Research/Ready-Reference/Legislative-Summary-Main-Page/Legislative-Summary/Aviation.aspx

An Airliner Hijacking with a Different Ending. (2011, September 8). Retrieved 2012, from Crime Flie News: http://www.crimefilenews.com/2011/09/airliner-hijacking-with-different.html

49 USC Chapter 465 - Special Aircraft Jurisdiction of the United States. (n.d.). Retrieved 2009, from uscode.house.gov: http://uscode.house.gov/download/pls/49C465.txt

Administration, D. o. (2012). *"Summary of the background and current status of the Federal Civil Aviation Security program".*

Administration, D. o. (August 1976). Trained and Ready: The Air Marshals Carry On.

Administration, D. o. (January 1, 1988 - June 30, 1988). *Semi Annual Report to Congress on the Effectiveness of the Civil Aviation Security Program.* DOT/ FAA.

Administration, D. o. (January 1, 1997 - December 31, 1997). *Annual Report to Congress on Civil Aviation Security.* DOT/ FAA.

Administration, D. o. (July 1, 1988 - December 30, 1988). *Semi Annual Report to Congress on the Effectiveness of the Civil Aviation Security Program.* DOT/ FAA.

Administration, D. o. (July 31, 1972). *"Summary of background and current status of the Federal Civil Aviation Security Program".*

Administration, F. A. (1972). Sky Marshals Training at Quantico, VA . *Pictorial Archives of the FAA.*

Administration, F. A. (2000, November 21). *Press Release - U.S. Army Lt. General Michael Canavan Named to Head FAA Office of Civil Aviation Security.* Retrieved 2012, from Federal Aviation Administration: http://www.faa.gov/news/press_releases/news_story.cfm?newsId=5285

Administration, F. A. (n.d.). FAA Archival Records - From 2001 Internal Report. *1974 - 2001 FAM Mission Flights .* DOT/ FAA.

Administration, F. A. (n.d.). Obituary for Kenneth Hunt.

Administration, T. S. (n.d.). *TSA: Director of the Federal Air Marshal Service, Dana Brown, Today Announces His Plans to Retire at Year-End.* Retrieved 2010, from Transportation Security Administration: http://www.tsa.gov/press/happenings/dana_brown_retirement.shtm

Administration, U. D. (January 1, 1995 - December 31, 1995). *Annual Report to Congress on Civil Aviation Security .*

Administration, U. D. (January 1, 1996 - December 31, 1996). *Annual Report to Congress on Civil Aviation Security.*

Agency, C. I. (December 22, 1988). *Spot Report: Pan AM 103: Analysis of Claims.*

Agency, F. A. (1962). FAA Peace Officers Course - General Information. U.S. Government.

Agency, F. A. (1962). FAA Peace Officers Course Training Manual. U.S. Government.

Agency, F. A. (1963). Sky Jack Unit Ready to Grapple Emergencies in the Skies. *FAA Horizons*(July).

Agency, F. A. (March 12, 1962). Requisition for Stock/ Special FAA Inspector.

Agency, F. A. (March 20, 1962). Operation Slingshot Memorandum #2.

Agency, F. A. (March 7, 1962). Operation Slingshot Memorandum #1.

Aleman, M. A. (2012). Interviews of Moses A. Aleman; formerly worked in FAA Civil Aviation Security, 1972 - 1995. Phone.

Ali, G. C. (2011, December).

All Avialable Research Material On the Federal Air Marshals. (n.d.).

Appeals, U. S. (n.d.). Docket Nos. 95-7784, 95-7787, 95-7789.

August 1, 1962 Speech. (n.d.). Retrieved January 2010, from John F. Kennedy Presidential Library and Museum: http://www.jfklibrary.org/Research/Ready-Reference/Press-Conferences/News-Conference-40.aspx

Auken, B. V. (December 9, 2005). *Miami airplane shooting: Washington's "war on terrorism" comes home.* Retrieved 2012, from World Socialist Web Site: http://www.wsws.org/articles/2005/dec2005/shot-d09.shtml

Aviation Security Chronology - taken from DOT website. (n.d.). Retrieved 2012, from Scribd.com: http://www.scribd.com/doc/13723746/T7-B16-FAA-AVSEC-Chronology-Fdr-History-of-Aircraft-Regs-and-Incidents-Incl-Hijacking-182

Axelrod, A. (1999). *The Complete Idiot's Guide to 20th Century History.* Alpha Books.

Baker, A. (August 9, 2008). Terrorist's Release Reopens Wound of Unsolved Bombing. *New York Times.*

Benjamin O. Davis, J. (July 28, 1972). Civil Aviation Security.

Blank, J. K. (2010, March 7). Joseph K. Blank Interview; former Branch Manager Flight Standards for FAA (1967 - 1980). Phone.

Board, C. A. (January 9, 1958). *Accident Investigation Report.* U.S. Civil Aeronautics Board.

Board, N. T. (n.d.). *Aircraft Accident Report - Trans World Airlines, Inc., Boeing 707-331B, N8734, in the Ionian Sea, September 8, 1974.*

Breckenridge, K. (August 19, 2003). The Fateful Flight of PAL 773.

Centennial of Flight. (n.d.). Retrieved 2010, from http://www.centennialofflight.gov/essay/government_role/security/PO L18.htm

Clarke, R. A. (2004). *Against All Enemies: Inside Americas War on Terror.* Free Press.

CNN. (August 23, 2006). *12 arrested after Northwest Airlines turned back.* Amsterdam, Netherlands: CNN.

CNN. (December 7, 2005). *Man killed after bomb claim at airport.* Retrieved from CNN.com: http://articles.cnn.com/2005-12-07/us/airplane.gunshot_1_rigoberto-alpizar-air-marshals-orlando-bound-plane?_s=PM:US

CNN-IBN. (n.d.). *How Govt lost the IC-814 hijack deal.* Retrieved from IBNLive: http://ibnlive.in.com/news/govt-fumbled-ic814-taken-away/20846-3.html

Coll, S. (2004). *Ghost Wars: The Secret History of the CIA, Afghanistan, and Bin Laden, from the Soviet Invasion to September 10, 2001.* Penguin Press.

Coll, S. (2008). *The Bin Ladens: An Arabian Family in the American Century.* Penguin Books.

Commission, 9. (July 22, 2004). *Final Report of the National Commission on Terrorist Attacks Upon the United States.*

Company, D. C. (February 1998). Treasure Island. *Inside Out.*

Congress, U. (n.d.). *Anti Hijacking Act.*

Customs, B. o. (1971). Sky Marshals Trainees Study at Ft. Belvoir. *Customs Today*.

Customs, T. D. (January 1971 - August 1972). "Law Enforcement Statistics on the CSO program".

Sky Marshal are led by an Ex-Lifeguard. (December 7, 1970). *Sunday's News*.

Don Phillips, G. L. (May 16, 1990). Laxity by Pan Am, FAA blamed in Jet Bombing . *Washington Post*.

DOT. (n.d.). *History of Aircraft Regs and Incidents*. Retrieved from SCRIBD: http://www.scribd.com/doc/13723746/T7-B16-FAA-AVSEC-Chronology-Fdr-History-of-Aircraft-Regs-and-Incidents-Incl-Hijacking-182

Easter Seals. (n.d.). Retrieved 2011, from Easter Seals: www.easterseals.com/site/PageServer

Edward McCleskey, D. M. (2007). *Underlying Reasons for Success and Failure of Terrorist Attacks: Selected Case Studies*. Homeland Security Institute.

Enforcement, U. I. (n.d.). *News Release*. Retrieved from www.ICE.gov: http://www.ice.gov/graphics/news/newsrel/articels/fams_022404.htm

Examining, U. S. (November 5, 1970). *"Job Description and Duties of Customs Security Officers"*.

Fagan, D. (2011, December 1). Interview of Dennis Fagan; former Sky Marshal/ CSO (1971 - 1974). Phone.

FAM, A. f. (n.d.). Interview of Anonymous former FAM. In Person.

Flight Standards Service. (n.d.). Retrieved 2010, from Federal Aviation Administration: http://www.faa.gov/about/office_org/headquarters_offices/avs/offices/afs/

Flynn, V. A. (2012). Interview of Vice Admiral (USN Ret.) Cathal Flynn; former Assistant Administrator for Civil Aviation Security - FAA (1993 - 2001). Phone.

Fricks, F. A. (2011, September 16). Interview of Sybille Frein Von Fricks. Interviewed in Person.

Geary, M. (2008). *Father Wanted to go Live in Cuba*. Retrieved 2010, from El Paso Times: http://elpasotimes.typepad.com/morgue/2008/05/

General, O. o. (March 2, 1962). Order 261-62. *FAA Peace Officer's Appointment Letter*.

Glenda Ali (nee, T. (2011, April). Interview with Glenda Ali. *in Person*.

Glines, C. (May 1971). Sky Marshalling: A New Occupation. *Air Line Pilot*.

Gordon Rayner, D. G. (April 7, 2008). Airline Terror Plotters Planned Bigger 9/11. *The Daily Telegraph (London)*.

Grado, M. (2009). Retrieved from Tru TV Crime Library: http://www.trutv.com/library/crime/notorius_murders/mass/jack_graham/8.html

Grant, A. (May 6, 2011). *Flying changes in the aftermath of 9/11.* Retrieved from Cleveland.com: http://blog.cleveland.com/metro/2011/05/flying_changes_in_the_after mat.html

H.L. Reighard, M. J. (November 1978). *Task Force on Deterrence of Air Piracy.* U.S. Department of Transportation.

Hall, H. V. (1999). *Lethal Violence: a Sourcebook on Fatal Domestic Aquaintance, and Stranger Aggression.*

Harry F. Norman, J. (2011, November). Interviews of Harry F. Norman, Jr.; former Sky Marshal/ CSO (1971 - 1974). Phone.

Herschaft, A. G. (November 24, 2009). Abu Ibrahim, 'Bomb Man' Terror Suspect: US Offers $5 Million Reward For Palestinian. *Huff Post.*

Holden, R. T. (n.d.). The Contagiousness of Aircraft Hijackings. Indiana University.

Holley, J. (August 10, 2005). Top Female Law Officer Bonni G. Tischler Dies. *The Washington Post.*

Hubbard, D. G. (1971). *The Skyjacker: His Flights of Fantasy.* Collier Books.

ICAO Home Page. (n.d.). Retrieved 2011, from International Civil Aviation Organization: http://www.icao.int/Pages/default.aspx

Investigation Jobs/ GS-1800. (n.d.). Retrieved 2012, from Federal Jobs Network: http://federaljobs.net/Occupations/gs-1800_jobs.htm

Judiciary, C. o. (May 2006). *In Plane Sight: Lack of anonymity at the Federal Air Marshal Service compromises national security.*

Kent, R. J. (1980). *Safe, Separated, and Soaring: A History of Federal Civil Aviation Policy 1961 - 1972.*

Killen, A. (January 16, 2005). The First Hijackers. *New York Times.*

Korean Air 858 Archives. (n.d.). Retrieved from U.S. State Department: http://www.state.gov/documents/organization/190928.pdf

Kristof, N. D. (October 10, 1990). Hijacking Prompts Beijing Shake-Up. *Time Magazine.*

Kuriyama, Y. (n.d.). *Terrorism at Tel Aviv Airport and a "New Left" Group in Japan.* University of California at Berkeley.

Laura Dugan, G. L. (November 25, 2005). *Testing a Rational Choice Model of Airline Hijackings.*

Magazine, T. (August 18, 1961). "Aviation: The Skyjack Habit".

Magazine, T. (January 9, 1989). Diabollically Planned: Pan Am's Flight 103.

Magazine, T. (June 15, 1970). $100 Million Skyjack.

Major General Orlo K. Steele - Retired. (n.d.). Retrieved 2011, from U.S. Marines - Manpower and Reserves Affairs: https://slsp.manpower.usmc.mil/gosa/biographies/rptBiography.asp?PE RSON_ID=326&PERSON_TYPE=General

Marsh, J. E. (2011, November 25). Interviews of John E. Marsh; former Legal Counsel for FAA (1958 - 1981). Phone.

Martin J. McDonnel, J. R. (1974). Historic Sky Marshals "Chapter Closed". *Customs Today.*

McCaslin, J. (November 8, 1985). FAA Quietly Graduates First Sky Marshal Class. *The Washington Times.*

McCullers, M. (August 31, 2002). *Federal Air Marshal Mission Report.* http://s3.amazonaws.com/propublica/assets/air_marshals/flight_report_ red_020831.pdf.

McKinney, L. (September 30, 2009). *One Marshals Badge: A Memoir of Fugitive Hunting, Witness Protection, and the U.S. Marshals Service .* Potomac Books Inc.

McLaughlin, G. M. (2011 - 2012). Interviews of Greg M. McLaughlin; former Director of the Federal Air Marshal program (1992 - 2002). Phone.

Meeks, B. N. (February 24, 2003). Senior Federal Air Marshals Demoted. *MSNBC.*

Most Terrifying Hijackings of all time. (n.d.). Retrieved from Investigative Project: http://www.investigativeproject.org/2798/10-most-terrifying-airplane-hijackings-of-all-time

Mueller, N. (Director). (2004). *The Assassination of Richard Nixon* [Motion Picture].

Murray, Brain. (n.d.). Retrieved 2012, from NYPD Angels: http://www.nypdangels.com/cop/cop.php?id=134

National Security Council. (n.d.). Retrieved 2012, from The White House - Washington DC: http://www.fas.org/irp/offdocs/nsdd/nsdd-180.htm

National Security Decision Directive - 180. (n.d.). Retrieved 2010, from Federation of American Scientists: http://www.fas.org/irp/offdocs/nsdd/nsdd-180.htm

NEWS, A. (2012). Chinese Passengers, Crew Thwart Attempted Hijacking.

News, N. (2006). Explosion rock parking lot at Madrid airport.

News, N. Y. (September 30, 2009). Death Notices - William Francis Chilson. *New York Daily News.*

Nixon, R. (1970, September 11). *291 - Richard Nixon: Statement Announcing a Program to Deal With Airplane Hijacking.* Retrieved 2010, from The American Presidency Project.

Noble, R. (2011). Ancient History of the Sky Marshals. *Letter written by Richard Noble to Bob Commaratto.*

NSDD List. (n.d.). Retrieved from http://www.comw.org/qdr/NSDD_LIST_2.pdf

Office, U. S. (December 1988). *Aviation Security: FAA's Assessments of Foreign Airports.* GAO.

Osmus, L. (2010, 2012). Interviews with Lynne Osmus;(Former Associate, and Deputy Administrator, for Civil Aviation Security). Phone.

Owen, M. (2012). *No Easy Day: A First Hand Account of the Mission that Killed Osama Bin-Laden.*

Perez, M. (November 7, 1975). Hijacker: Cuba Suspected of Spying. *Miami Herald*.

Pontecorvo, J. (1962). FAA Peace Officers with Robert Kennedy. *Pictorial Archives of Joseph A. Pontecorvo*.

Pontecorvo, J. (1962). Information taken from Swearing-in Photograph of Kenneth Hunt signing Oath of Office. *Pictorial Archives of Joseph A. Pontecorvo*.

Pontecorvo, J. (2009). Picture - Original FAA Peace Officers in Class Room (1962).

Pontecorvo, J. A. (1962). Kenneth S. Hunt at Swearing-In Ceremony. *Pictorial Archives of Joseph A. Pontecorvo*.

Pontecorvo, J. A. (2009 - 2010). Interviews of Joseph A. Pontecorvo; former FAA Peace Officer (1962 - 1969). Phone.

Pontecorvo, J. A. (March 23-25, 1968). FAA Peace Officers Course, Sixth-Session. *Pictorial Arichives of Joseph A. Pontecorvo*.

Press, A. (August 4, 1961). One Punch Ends Siege: Pair Awaits Hearing; Kennedy says No Swap. *Capital Times*.

Press, A. (Januray 23, 1969). Plane Hijacker Alben Truitt Said In Canada. *The Evening Independent*.

Press, A. (November 12, 2001). D.C. Man Arrested on Flight.

Programs, U. D.-I. (January 16, 2002). *Ashcroft on a Nine-Count Federal Indictment Against Reid.*

Publica, P. (n.d.). *History of the Federal Air Marshal Service.* Retrieved 2012, from http://www.propublica.org/article/history-of-the-federal-air-marshal-service

Report, T. 9. (May 22, 2003). Statement of Jane Garvey to the National Commission on Terrorsit Attacks Upon the United States .

Rustad, S. (2011 - 2012). Interviews of Steve Rustad; former Sky Marshal, 1970. Phone.

Seattle Marine Hijacks a TWA Airliner to Rome on October 31, 1969. (n.d.). Retrieved from History Link: http://www.historylink.org/index.cfm?DisplayPage=output.cfm&file_id=1316

Security, F. A.-O. (July 4, 1972). "Hijacking Incidents and Passenger Screening Statistics".

The Last Marshal. (September 2, 1974). *Time Magazine*.

Service, T. U. (July 11, 1974). Last U.S. Customs Air Security Officers (Sky Marshals) Complete Duty .

Service, U. F. (2008). A Brief Overview of Federal Air Marshal History. Atlantic City: U.S. Federal Air Marshal Service/ Transportation Security Administration.

Service, U. M. (n.d.). The Marshals Service Pioneered the Air Marshal Program. *The Marshals Monitor*.

Simmunition. (n.d.). Retrieved 2010, from Simmunition - Non-lethal Training Ammunition: www.simunition.com

Spiegel, D. (April 22, 2011). Victims Request Damages from Frozen Gadhafi Assets. *Der Spiegel*.

State, U. D. (2003). *Personal Security Detail Operations: Karzai Protection Detail*.

States, N. C. (2004). *The 9/11 Commission Report: Final Report of the National Commission on Terrorist Attacks Upon the Unites States*. W.W. Norton and Company.

Steele, M. G. (2012). Interviews of Major General (Ret.) Orlo K. Steele; former Associate Administrator for Civil Aviation Security - FAA (1990 - 1993). Phone.

Stefani, A. M. (March 6, 2002). *Information: Audit of Deployment of Advanced Security Technologies, Post-September 11, 2001*. U.S. Department of Transportation.

Sullivan, P. (June 14, 2006). James Murphy, at 81; was head of FAA aviation security. *Boston Globe*.

First Female Sky Marshals Join the Force. (Summer 1971). *Customs Today*.

T. Allen McArtur, A. F. (December 22, 1988). "Letter to President of the Unites States on Air Marshals".

Tan, G. C. (1985). Hijacked! *Kuwait Air in-flight magazine*.

Theresa L. Krause, P. (2008). *The Federal Aviation Administration: A Historical Perspective, 1903 - 2008*. U.S. Department of Transportation.

Thornton, M. (March 1, 1987). U.S. Customs Service's Surprise Weapon: The Woman with a Golden Gun. *The Washington Post*.

Times, T. W. (May 30, 2007). Report Confirms Terror Dry Run. *The Washington Times*.

Treasury, D. o. (1972). B-747 Flight Crew Briefing.

Treasury, D. o. (November 30 - December 23, 1970). Schedule: Treasury Air Security Officer School No. 1. *Consolidated Federal Law Enforcement Training Center*.

Treasury, T. U. (October 14, 1972). Combatting International Terrorism. *The Department of Treasury News*.

Tristani, J. (March 30, 2009). One Heck of an In-Air Gunfight on a Civilian Jet. *Boston Globe*.

TSA. (n.d.). *Dana Brown: Assistant Administrator for Law Enforcment and Director of Federal Air Marshal Service*. Retrieved from Transportation Security Administration: http://www.tsa.gov/who_we_are/people/bios/dana_brown_bio.shtm

TSA. (n.d.). *More than 40 Air Marshals Take To The Skies*. Retrieved from Transportation Security Administration: http://www.tsa.gov/press/happenings/40_fams.shtm

U.S. Department of Homeland Security, U.S. Customs, Timeline. (n.d.).
    Retrieved from nemo.customs.gov:
    http://nemo.customs.gov/opa/timeLine_04212011.swf

U.S. Department of Transportation. (n.d.). Retrieved 2011, from The United
    States Department of Transportation: A Brief History:
    http://ntl.bts.gov/historian/history.htm

United Airlines Flight 696. (n.d.). Retrieved from Aviation Safety Net:
    http://aviation-safety.net/database/record.php?id=19780313-0

United States Court of Appeals, S. C. (March 11, 1996). Loraine Stanford, t al
    vs. Kuwait Airways Corporation.

United States vs. Lopez. (n.d.). Retrieved from Leagle:
    http://www.leagle.com/xmlResult.aspx?xmldoc=19711405328FSupp10
    77_11217.xml&docbase=CSLWAR1-1950-1985

unknown. (December 7, 1970). Sky Marshals are Led by an Ex-Lifeguard.
    Sunday's News.

USA, T. (n.d.). *Michael A. Canavan - Biography*. Retrieved from Talon USA:
    http://www.talonusa.com/SiteCollectionDocuments/Leaders/MCanavan
    .pdf

Various. (Researched from January 2009 - June 2012). All available research
    material on threats to civil aviation security.

Vincent, B. H. (2009 - 2010). Interviews of Billie H. Vincent; former Director of
    Civil Aviation Security for FAA (1982 - 1986). Phone.

Wald, M. L. (October 5, 2001). *The New York Times*.

Wikipedia. (n.d.). *2006 - Madrid-Barajas Airport Bombing*. Retrieved from
    Wikipedia: http://en.wikipedia.org/wiki/2006_Madrid-
    Barajas_Airport_bombing

Wikipedia. (n.d.). *Aeromexico Flight 576*. Retrieved from Wikipedia:
    http://en.wikipedia.org/wiki/Aerom%C3%A9xico_Flight_576

Wikipedia. (n.d.). *Air Afrique*. Retrieved from Wikipedia:
    http://en.wikipedia.org/wiki/Air_Afrique

Wikipedia. (n.d.). *Air France Flight 139*. Retrieved from Wikipedia:
    http://en.wikipedia.org/wiki/Air_France_Flight_139#Hijack

Wikipedia. (n.d.). *Air France Flight 8969*. Retrieved from Wikipedia:
    http://en.wikipedia.org/wiki/Air_France_Flight_8969

Wikipedia. (n.d.). *Air India Flight 182*. Retrieved from Wikipedia:
    http://en.wikipedia.org/wiki/Air_India_Flight_182

Wikipedia. (n.d.). *Al Qaeda in the Arabian Peninsula*. Retrieved from
    Wikipedia: http://en.wikipedia.org/wiki/Al-
    Qaeda_in_the_Arabian_Peninsula

Wikipedia. (n.d.). *Beirut Barracks Bombing*. Retrieved from Wikipedia:
    http://en.wikipedia.org/wiki/1983_Beirut_barracks_bombing

Wikipedia. (n.d.). *Bojinka Plot*. Retrieved from Wikipedia:
    http://en.wikipedia.org/wiki/Bojinka_plot

Wikipedia. (n.d.). *Cargo planes bomb plot.* Retrieved from Wikipedia:
   http://en.wikipedia.org/wiki/Cargo_planes_bomb_plot
Wikipedia. (n.d.). *Dawson's Field Hijackings.* Retrieved 2011, from Wikipedia:
   http://en.wikipedia.org/wiki/Dawson's_Field_hijackings
Wikipedia. (n.d.). *Department of Homeland Security.* Retrieved from Wikipedia:
   http://en.wikipedia.org/wiki/Department_of_homeland_security
Wikipedia. (n.d.). *Federal Air Marshal Service.* Retrieved from Wikipedia:
   http://en.wikipedia.org/wiki/Federal_Air_Marshals
Wikipedia. (n.d.). *Federal Air Marshals.* Retrieved 2009, from Wikipedia:
   http://en.wikipedia.org/wiki/Federal_Air_Marshal
Wikipedia. (n.d.). *Hindawi Affair.* Retrieved from Wikipedia:
   http://en.wikipedia.org/wiki/Hindawi_affair
Wikipedia. (n.d.). *John F. Kennedy International Airport.* Retrieved 2011, from
   Wikipedia:
   http://en.wikipedia.org/wiki/John_F._Kennedy_International_Airport
Wikipedia. (n.d.). *Korean Air Flight 858.* Retrieved from Wikipedia:
   http://en.wikipedia.org/wiki/Korean_Air_Flight_858
Wikipedia. (n.d.). *List of Aircraft Hijackings.* Retrieved from Wikipedia:
   http://en.wikipedia.org/wiki/List_of_aircraft_hijackings
Wikipedia. (n.d.). *List of Cuba - United States Aircraft Hijackings.* Retrieved
   2009, from Wikipedia:
   http://en.wikipedia.org/wiki/List_of_Cuba_%E2%80%93_United_State
   s_aircraft_hijackings
Wikipedia. (n.d.). *Malaysian Airlines Flight 653.* Retrieved from Wikipedia:
   http://en.wikipedia.org/wiki/Malaysia_Airlines_Flight_653
Wikipedia. (n.d.). *Mariel Boat Lift.* Retrieved from Wikipedia:
   http://en.wikipedia.org/wiki/Mariel_boatlift
Wikipedia. (n.d.). *National Airlines Flight 2511.* Retrieved October 2009, from
   Wikipedia:
   http://en.wikipedia.org/wiki/National_Airlines_FLight_2511
Wikipedia. (n.d.). *Northwest Airlines Flight 253.* Retrieved from Wikipedia:
   http://en.wikipedia.org/wiki/Northwest_Airlines_Flight_253
Wikipedia. (n.d.). *Operation El Dorado Canyon.* Retrieved from Wikipedia:
   http://en.wikipedia.org/wiki/Operation_El_Dorado_Canyon
Wikipedia. (n.d.). *Pan Am Flight 73.* Retrieved from Wikipedia:
   http://en.wikipedia.org/wiki/Pan_Am_Flight_73
Wikipedia. (n.d.). *Rome and Vienna Airport Attacks.* Retrieved 2012, from
   Wikipedia:
   http://en.wikipedia.org/wiki/Rome_and_Vienna_airport_attacks
Wikipedia. (n.d.). *Samuel Byck.* Retrieved from Wikipedia:
   http://en.wikipedia.org/wiki/Samuel_Byck
Wikipedia. (n.d.). *Southern Airways Flight 49.* Retrieved from Wikipedia:
   http://en.wikipedia.org/wiki/Southern_Airways_Flight_49

Wikipedia. (n.d.). *TWA Flight 541*. Retrieved from Wikipedia:
    http://en.wikipedia.org/wiki/TWA_Flight_541
Wikipedia. (n.d.). *TWA Flight 840 Hijacking (1969)*. Retrieved 2010, from
    Wikipedia:
    http://en.wikipedia.org/wiki/TWA_Flight_840_hijacking_(1969)
Wikipedia. (n.d.). *USS Cole Bombing*. Retrieved from Wikipedia:
    http://en.wikipedia.org/wiki/USS_Cole_bombing
Wikipedia. (n.d.). *USS The Sullivans (DDG-68)*. Retrieved from Wikipedia:
    http://en.wikipedia.org/wiki/USS_The_Sullivans_(DDG-68)
Wikipedia. (n.d.). *William Francis Buckley*. Retrieved from Wikipedia:
    http://en.wikipedia.org/wiki/William_Francis_Buckley
William E. Smith, e. a. (April 14, 1986). Terrorism Explosion on Flight 840.
    Time Magazine.
Wittkowski, D. (August 29, 2000). Mock-hostage exercises train federal air
    marshals at FAA center in EHT. *The Press of Atlantic City, MM
    No.242*.
Xiamen Airlines Flight 8301. (n.d.). Retrieved from Air Disaster:
    http://www.airdisaster.com/special/special-xi8301.shtml

INDEX

About the Author

Clay W. Biles is currently a U.S. Federal Air Marshal. He graduated training in August 2008, as the Distinguished Honor Graduate of his class. He is a former Navy Corpsman and bodyguard for the President of Afghanistan, Hamid Karzai. He lives in California with his wife and three daughters.

CPSIA information can be obtained at www.ICGtesting.com
Printed in the USA
LVOW06s1929041013

355488LV00001B/184/P